Michael Leapman is an award-winning author and journalist who has contributed to most national newspapers and many magazines. He is the former editor of *The Times* Diary and was also the paper's New York correspondent. A Londoner by birth and inclination, he has lived in the capital nearly all his life and written and edited several books about it, including *London's River* and the *Eyewitness Guide to London*. His most recent book is *The Ingenious Mr Fairchild*, the story of the forgotten Georgian nurseryman who discovered the secrets of plant hybridisation.

Also by Michael Leapman

One Man and his Plot
Barefaced Cheek
Last Days of the Beeb
Treachery?
Kinnock
The Book of London (ed.)
Companion Guide to New York
Yankee Doodles
London's River
Treacherous Estate
Master Race (with Catrine Clay)
Eyewitness Guide to London (main contributor)
Witnesses to War
The Ingenious Mr Fairchild

THE
WORLD FOR A
SHILLING

❧ ❧

THE STORY OF THE
GREAT EXHIBITION OF 1851

MICHAEL LEAPMAN

review

Copyright © 2001 Michael Leapman

The right of Michael Leapman to be identified as the Author of
the Work has been asserted by him in accordance with
the Copyright, Designs and Patents Act 1988.

First published in 2001
by HEADLINE BOOK PUBLISHING

First published in paperback in 2002
by REVIEW

An imprint of Headline Book Publishing

10 9 8 7 6 5 4 3 2 1

All rights reserved. No part of this publication may be
reproduced, stored in a retrieval system, or transmitted,
in any form or by any means without the prior written
permission of the publisher, nor be otherwise circulated
in any form of binding or cover other than that in which
it is published and without a similar condition being
imposed on the subsequent purchaser.

Every effort has been made to trace and contact the
copyright holders of all materials in this book. The author and
publisher will be glad to rectify any omissions at
the earliest opportunity.

ISBN 0 7472 6648 4

Typeset by Avon Dataset Ltd, Bidford-on-Avon, Warks

Printed and bound in Great Britain by
Clays Ltd, St Ives plc

HEADLINE BOOK PUBLISHING
A division of Hodder Headline
338 Euston Road
London NW1 3BH

www.reviewbooks.co.uk
www.hodderheadline.com

For Lara Emily, child of the Millennium

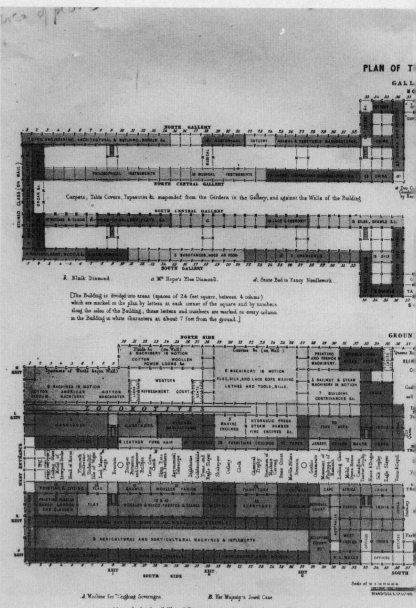

PLAN OF T...

NORTH GALLERY

CIVIL ENGINEERING, ARCHITECTURAL & BUILDING MODELS &c.

CUTLERY   ANIMAL & VEGETABLE MANUFACTURES   CHINA

PHILOSOPHICAL INSTRUMENTS   MUSICAL INSTRUMENTS   CHINA

NORTH CENTRAL GALLERY

Carpets, Table Covers, Tapestries &c. suspended from the Girders in the Gallery, and against the Walls of the Building

SOUTH CENTRAL GALLERY

PLATE &c.   LACE & EMBROIDERY   SILKS, SHAWLS &c.

SUBSTANCES USED AS FOOD   CHEMICALS   SILK

SOUTH GALLERY

A. Black Diamond.   *o.* Mr Hope's Blue Diamond.   *d.* State Bed in Fancy Needlework.

[The Building is divided into areas (spaces of 24 feet square, between 4 colums) which are marked on the plan by letters at each corner of the square and by numbers along the sides of the Building; these letters and numbers are marked on every colum in the Building in white characters at about 7 feet from the ground.]

NORTH SIDE

GROUN...

COTTON POWER LOOMS   WOOLLEN   CANVAS &c. (on Wall)   PRINTING AND FRENCH MACHINERY.   WOOLS AND FLAX &c.

6 MACHINERY IN MOTION   FLAX, SILK, AND LACE ROPE MAKING LATHES AND TOOLS, MILLS.   5 RAILWAY & STEAM MACHINERY IN MOTION

7 BUILDING CONTRIVANCES &c.   INDIA

WESTERN REFRESHMENT COURT

LOCOMOTIVES

CARRIAGES   CARRIAGES   MAKING ENGINES   HYDRAULIC PRESS STEAM HAMMER FIRE ENGINES &c.   FINE ARTS

LEATHER FURS HAIR   FURNITURE CEILINGS   PAPER   JERSEY   CEYLON   MALTA   INDIA

PRINTING & DYEING   FLAX   SHAWLS   WOOLLEN FABRICS   HARDWARE   FURNITURE   HARDWARE   CAPE   AFRICA   INDIA

FLAX   WOOLLEN & MIXED FABRICS & SHAWLS   FURNITURE   CANADA   INDIA

9 AGRICULTURAL AND HORTICULTURAL MACHINES & IMPLEMENTS

WEST INDIES   OFFICES   INDIA

N.S. WALES   OFFICES

SOUTH SIDE   SOUTH

A. Machine for Weighing Sovereigns.   *B.* Her Majesty's Jewel Case

Against the South wall, West of Transept, are several examples of cements (Encaustic and Parian) and of wall decorations together with specimens of woods and ivory, and painted imitations of wood and stone.

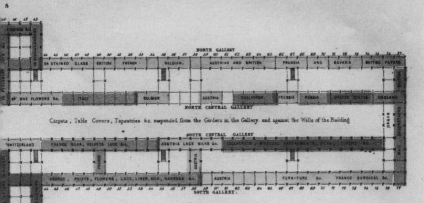

[The Articles are divided into Classes and Nations, and the Names of such Classes and Nations are given on the Plan, and marked upon the iron girders of the Building.]

C Toledo Swords, &c.   D Queen of Spain's Jewels.   E. Mr Hope's Jewels

Against the South wall, East of Transept, are arranged examples of woven and felted articles, sheets of metal, and examples of metal manufactures.

CONTENTS

ACKNOWLEDGMENTS

Researchers coming fresh to the Great Exhibition are, I suspect, invariably surprised and delighted to discover that the Commission, established by Queen Victoria in 1850 to organise the event, is still in being. When it became clear that the Exhibition would make a healthy profit she perpetuated the Commission so that it could spend the money on buying the land south of Hyde Park that now houses the Royal Albert Hall, Imperial College and a clutch of museums. It is still the landlord of the area and uses the income for academic and scientific purposes. It also holds a complete archive on the Commission's activities and has on loan the Windsor Archive of Prince Albert's correspondence on the Exhibition. I spent many fascinating hours with these documents in the Commission's offices and am most grateful to the archivist, Valerie Phillips, for her responsive and good-humoured assistance.

The British Library and London Library have been rich sources of contemporary material. I have also been made welcome at the Institution of Civil Engineers, where a debate took place in 1850 about potential safety hazards in the Crystal Palace, as well as at the records offices of Surrey and West Yorkshire, where I undertook research about local visitors to the Exhibition. The librarian at the Yale Center for British Art in Connecticut kindly sent me copies of material relating to the Liverpool Excursion Club and the archivist at the Duke of

Northumberland's estate at Alnwick Castle copied for me some letters relating to the visit to the Crystal Palace by estate workers. I am grateful, too, to the garden writer Charles Lyte, who alerted me to the charming story about Queen Victoria and the Sussex trugs. As always, my wife Olga has been of immense help with the research, in particular in ferreting out from the Public Record Office the reports by foreign police-men assigned to London for the Exhibition. She also compiled the index. Most of the illustrations have come from the com-prehensive collection at the Victoria and Albert Museum, and from the archives of *Punch* and *The Illustrated London News*.

The idea for this book was brought to me by Heather Holden-Brown and Lindsay Symons at Headline. Lindsay has shepherded it through the production process with skill, understanding and infinite enthusiasm.

LIST OF ILLUSTRATIONS

INTRODUCTION

The Great Exhibition crystallised a particular moment in early Victorian Britain when a series of profound social, political and economic changes converged. Its enormous and largely unexpected success influenced the life of the nation and the image it had of itself for decades, and into the present time. Its impact can be fully understood only in the broad context of the life and attitudes of mid-nineteenth-century Britain, specifically London.

This book is therefore not just about the Crystal Palace and what was in it, but is a snapshot of British life in 1851 with the Exhibition at the centre of the frame. While I hope I have described its contents in enough detail to give the flavour of an actual visit, I have also dwelt on issues such as relations between the classes, the British attitude to foreigners and the social revolution inspired by cheap railway travel – all brought into sharp focus by the events of that amazing year.

The correspondence among the Exhibition's Commissioners about how to deal with factory workers and agricultural labourers from the provinces reveals genuine fears of mob violence. The reports of the foreign policemen who came to London to look for revolutionaries among their visiting countrymen offer a fascinating and sometimes comic insight into low-life and the underworld. The writings of contemporary observers illuminate assumptions about class and society and, on a more prosaic level, describe the many inconveniences of life in Victorian London – among them fear of crime, a chaotic public transport system and deplorable sanitary arrangements. I have quoted freely from correspondence, literature and especially the press, because the language and tone in which these matters were discussed helps us understand attitudes that may seem alien and scarcely explicable 150 years on.

From the vantage point of the twenty-first century it is easy to mock the Victorians for their prejudices, their snobbery, their taste in furniture, their rotund use of English and their fascination with elaborate and ingenious gadgets. Readers may feel that at times I have come close to doing just that. But they were, too, people of resolve, energy and imagination, eager to experiment, impatient for progress but at the same time wary of its ramifications. Those qualities were manifest in the men who organised the Great Exhibition and the many other people – visitors as well as exhibitors – who contributed to its undoubted success in attracting something like a quarter of the country's twenty-two million inhabitants. With hindsight we can criticise it for the indiscriminate nature of its exhibits, with useful innovations like sewing machines and the electric telegraph displayed alongside fantastic contraptions for tipping people out of bed and playing the violin and piano simultaneously. But who was to know then what would catch on and what would fade into oblivion?

In the final chapter I have made comparisons between the Exhibition of 1851, housed in Joseph Paxton's magnificent glasshouse, and the Millennium Dome at Greenwich, the giant marquee designed by Richard Rogers, one of our leading modern architects. Both reveal much about the societies that spawned them but the Dome was much the less successful in tapping the popular mood, attracting roughly the same number of visitors despite being open more than twice as long.

There have been other books about the Great Exhibition, most written by professional historians. This is not an academic work, although it is based on original research using the wealth of contemporary documents, literature and press reports. My aim has been to describe one of the defining events of the Victorian era, to throw light on what drove it and to interpret its lasting significance.

Michael Leapman
April 2001

CHAPTER ONE

❦ ❧

THE PEOPLE MUST
HAVE AMUSEMENTS

The Great Exhibition of the Industry of All Nations is
the first public national expression ever made in this
country as to the dignity and artistic quality of labour . . .
the first attempt to dignify and refine toil.

Henry Mayhew, *1851, or The Adventures of Mr and Mrs Cursty Sandboys*
and Family who Came up to London to Enjoy Themselves
and to See the Great Exhibition (London, 1851)

In the countryside, four a.m. used to be known as the ploughboy's hour. Farm workers are accustomed to getting up before first light; but for 780 residents of four east Surrey villages, Thursday 12 June 1851 was decidedly not to be a day like any other. They were going to London; many for the first time, even though the capital was little more than thirty miles to the north. By five they had to be washed, scrubbed and into their best clothes – the men in smocks, the women in their Sunday dresses – to assemble at their four meeting places. The largest group came from Lingfield because the prime mover behind the excursion was the Reverend T. P. Hutton, rector of the village's rambling Gothic church of St Peter and St Paul – so spacious that it has been called 'the Westminster Abbey of

Surrey'. He had secured the support of the rectors of nearby Limpsfield and Crowhurst and had also recruited people from the hamlet of Felbridge, which would not be blessed with its own church for another fourteen years.

The Lingfield contingent assembled by the village pond beneath the 400-year-old oak alongside the Cage, a small gaol built seventy years earlier for the confinement of minor offenders. After leading the villagers in prayer, Hutton lectured them on how they would be expected to conduct themselves. On every count they would have to be a credit to him and to the village. They murmured assent and piled into horse-drawn wagons, generously laid on by the farmers and gentry who employed them, some of the latter even accompanying the party as guides. It would be pleasing to report that God, in response to their initial act of piety, had arranged a fine, clear day for the unique adventure; but as the sun began to rise over Tunbridge Wells to the east, revealing a deep orange sky and dark, angry clouds, they knew this was not to be. Red sky in the morning, shepherd's warning. The rain, drenching and persistent, set in soon after dawn and scarcely let up all day.

Unkind weather is a hazard that country people learn to live with and it did nothing to dampen their spirits, for this was going to be a day out that they would remember for the rest of their lives. Not only were they to visit the capital, but they were to get there by steam train on the South-Eastern Railway (linking London and Dover), which had been operating for only nine years and on which few of them had travelled before. When they got to town they were going to Hyde Park to visit Joseph Paxton's fabulous Crystal Palace, surely the most famous building in the country, and see the Great Exhibition of the Works of Industry of All Nations, described by everyone who had visited it as the marvel of the age, indeed of any age. They had each paid 1s 6d (equivalent to seven and a half pence today) for the excursion – a bargain, seeing that entrance to the Exhibition itself cost a shilling. The true cost of the day was about double what they paid and the balance had been contributed by the aristocrats and gentlemen who occupied the many grand houses in the district. The farmers had done their bit by giving their workers the day off.

Lingfield is at the heart of the Surrey Weald, the gently undulating landscape of woods and pastures that lies between the North and South Downs. The road to Godstone station leaves the village to the north-west, breasting a slight hill as it passes the common, before reaching the main London to East Grinstead highway at Blindley Heath. Here the wagons turned due north and soon afforded the travellers their first real excitement of the day: the road here is dead straight, and for more than a mile south of the station, during the last several minutes of their journey, they could look ahead and see, gradually looming towards them, the impressive bridge that carried the railway over it. These sturdy brick bridges, so familiar today, were then a novel feature on the landscape, enabling the speedy new trains to soar across the existing roads and their plodding horse traffic as they raced across country.

At the compact little station they were welcomed by the smartly uniformed stationmaster, John McCabe, who had helped Hutton arrange the excursion. The railway companies had informally agreed, before the Exhibition began, not to run excursions to London until July, so that the expected hordes of visitors would not disrupt the capital's social 'season'. It soon became apparent, though, that there was an enormous demand for special trains as soon as the entry fee went down to a shilling in the last week of May, and that self-denying agreement fell by the wayside. The South-Eastern had more experience of the excursion business than most lines, regularly taking Londoners on trips to the Kentish seaside resorts and Canterbury, and occasionally across the Channel to France. It had run its first Exhibition excursion, carrying between 600 and 700 people, the previous week, on Wednesday 4 June.

The Lingfield visitors joined the three other contingents and formed groups along the platform. Soon an insistent, pulsating rhythm reached their ears as the steam engine, smoke billowing from its tall funnel, came clanking and whistling down the line from Edenbridge and drew noisily into the platform. The locomotive was painted dark green, on a reddish-brown frame. The elegant funnel had a copper top shaped like an inverted bell, and behind it was a huge polished brass dome on a pedestal. The South-Eastern had twenty-six of these engines, most of them called after ancient Anglo-Saxon leaders – *Hengist*, *Horsa*, *Egbert* and the like.

The clergymen assigned each group to a specific carriage and they crammed into the wooden seats. Before long, with a jolt and a loud hiss, they felt the unfamiliar sensation of iron wheels grating on an iron track, then of the train swaying ever more markedly as it gathered speed. Some were no doubt alarmed – they were, after all, travelling much faster than they had ever done in their lives – and there must have been near-panic when suddenly, scarcely a mile from Godstone, everything went dark as the train entered a short tunnel.

It was open country as far as Redhill, where the train turned north and passed through another tunnel before chugging through the new, expanding suburbs of Coulsdon, Purley and Croydon. Finally they arrived at London Bridge, the terminus for all lines from the south-east, its shiny glass-roofed engine shed giving them a foretaste of Paxton's giant glasshouse in the park. They walked from the station to a pier on the Thames and gazed in wonder at the scores of ships that crowded the broad river, waiting to unload at the busy quays on the north bank. A steamboat was ready at the pier: they boarded it and headed west in the choppy water, through a span of John Rennie's twenty-year-old London Bridge, passing the great dome of St Paul's Cathedral, and tied up at Westminster Pier, beneath the neo-Gothic grandeur of Charles Barry's just-completed Houses of Parliament.

All the travellers had been issued with rosettes of coloured ribbon, for easy recognition should they become detached from the main group. At the pier they were formed into squads of fifteen and twelve and marched in procession, three abreast, the few hundred yards to the medieval Westminster Hall, now incorporated by Barry into his Parliament complex. Having seen the hall, they resumed their military formation and proceeded in the rain through St James's Park, up Constitution Hill to Hyde Park Corner, where the London home of the great and venerable Duke of Wellington, alongside Decimus Burton's elegant screen, was pointed out to them. From there they walked west along Knightsbridge – already thronged with thousands heading for the big show – until, shortly after noon, they entered Hyde Park at the new Prince of Wales's gate, close to one of the Exhibition's entrances.

After passing between two lodges that served as police headquarters, they were confronted with a truly breathtaking spectacle. They were now directly in front of the main entrance, in the centre of the palace's shimmering southern wall – which, in recognition of the year in question, Paxton had made exactly 1,851 feet long. Even on so dull a day, the light playing on the huge expanse of glass – 956,165 square feet of it – made for intriguing, near-ghostly effects. Once through the turnstiles, the visitors could look upwards to the large semicircular electric clock, confusing at first because it was not of the familiar round shape, but easy to read once they got the hang of it. It had been designed to blend with the curved glass roof of the great transept, 108 feet high, that formed the north–south axis of the building. (The terms of church architecture were commonly used to describe the Crystal Palace: its main body, running east to west, was called the nave.) At the far end they could see how the glass enclosed three of Hyde Park's majestic elm trees. They walked on, through a pair of ornate iron gates, to the very centre of the building, marked by a twenty-seven-foot coloured glass fountain that was to remain for many one of the enduring images of the extraordinary display.

Just what had they imagined the Exhibition would contain, in the days of spring and early summer when they had been looking forward so eagerly to their visit? Some people seem to have assumed it would be a sort of freak show. A music-hall song of the time, speculating on the wonders in store for visitors, listed a seventeen-headed goat, a chorus of twenty-five mermaids, rhubarb as long as your arm and a machine that would make old women young. One of the many ironic tales of fictional family outings to the Crystal Palace, 'Trip to the Great Exhibition of Barnabas Blandydash and Family', dangled the prospect of a telescope so powerful that it could look into houses in New Zealand and watch the occupants having breakfast.

Few in the Surrey group would have been naive enough to expect any of that; but what may have surprised them, as it surprised many first-time visitors, were the efforts that had been made to give the whole experience a cheerful and inviting aspect. This was no solemn trade fair, with aisle after dreary aisle of the worthy products of industry. The emphasis was on display, with the most spectacular and innovative of the 13,937 exhibits given the greatest prominence. There were statues in every direction, many depicting Queen Victoria and her consort Prince Albert, one of the Exhibition's instigators. These were set off by countless potted plants, palms and flowers. The ironwork was painted in pale colours – predominantly blue and yellow – that enhanced the airy feel of the glass enclosure. The displays were on two levels, the ground floor and the gallery that fringed it.

Country visitors to the Exhibition.

As the visitors stood near the fountain, and began to absorb the marvels that surrounded them, they quickly discovered that they were the object of much curiosity themselves. Although the Exhibition had been open since the beginning of May, the higher charge for admission during the first three weeks meant that only fairly recently had the working classes been able to afford to go. Hutton's group was one of the first – and biggest – organised visits of labourers. The London newspapers had all assigned reporters to write long daily reports of the doings in the Crystal Palace, and they fell upon the Surrey farm workers with relish, the *Times* representative declaring with unbridled enthusiasm that 'more

perfect specimens of rustic attire, rustic faces and rustic manners could hardly be produced from any part of England'.

The reporter from the *Morning Chronicle* had spotted these
paragons as soon as they arrived:

> The honest fellows appeared delighted, though some-
> what confounded, by the vastness of the Crystal
> Palace and the strange collection of objects among
> which they found themselves. It was amusing to
> observe how they seemed to stand in awe of the build-
> ing: its greatness paralysed them; they hardly liked to
> penetrate into the huge compartment which opened
> on each side, but stuck close to the crystal fountain,
> or, if they moved forward, kept close together in small
> parties – the young ones held by the hand lest they
> should be lost, and even the adults seemed appre-
> hensive of a similar disaster. To guard against this the
> rosettes had been provided.

Almost immediately, Amos and Elizabeth Saunders of
Lingfield lost track of their young son, but he was quickly
found and, once the general sense of disorientation began to
wear off, Hutton's well-prepared plan of campaign was put
into effect. The visitors were split into groups, each with its
own leader, who held aloft a card with his name on it. The
leaders had been given a map, and they led their groups in
different directions.

To their left, the western end of the nave accommodated
most of the displays from Britain and its colonial possessions.
Near the beginning of this section was the medieval court,
designed by Augustus Pugin (responsible for much of the
internal decoration of the new Houses of Parliament), which
was to do much to establish the Victorian Gothic style. There

were wonders aplenty. A knot of people clustered around the fabulous Koh-i-Noor diamond from India – impressive for its size, although unskilled cutting meant that it did not gleam as brightly as its legend had boasted. Also from the East came a rich collection of exotic silks and ornate furniture and even a howdah and elephant cloth: it would be some weeks before the organisers could acquire a stuffed elephant to display these at their best. One of the largest exhibits was a model of Liverpool Docks, its five miles of river frontage reduced to forty feet, complete with 1,600 meticulously accurate miniature ships.

Yet the displays were not confined to the exotic and bizarre. There were machines designed to perform the everyday tasks with which the villagers were familiar, and examples of ordinary household products, not just luxuries for the well-off. Alfred Tennyson, the new Poet Laureate, in his ode to the opening of the Exhibition, celebrated its practical aspect:

> . . . lo! the giant aisles
> Rich in model and design;
> Harvest-tool and husbandry,
> Loom and wheel and enginery,
> Secrets of the sullen mine,
> Steel and gold, and coal and wine,
> Fabric rough or fairy-fine . . .
> And shapes and hues of Art divine!
> All of beauty, all of use,
> That one fair planet can produce.

Even if that last couplet was an overstatement, here was a comprehensive showcase that honoured the common herd as much as the privileged élite. Of practical interest to this particular group of visitors were the new machines that would take some of the hard labour out of their everyday lives – and quite transform the world of their children and grandchildren. There were sophisticated reapers and threshers, mostly still powered by horses but a few making use of developing steam technology. Though impressed, some of the harder-headed farm workers will have wondered whether these new marvels were robust enough to withstand many hours of working with the heavy soil of the Weald. Some of the huge looms and other machines that were revolutionising the cloth industries of the north were shown in operation, powered by steam engines housed just outside the Crystal Palace itself. In one area, fifteen machines had been set up to show the whole process of cotton spinning.

On the domestic front, the Surrey visitors must have marvelled at devices they could not dream of possessing – gas cookers, electric clocks, primitive washing machines. Like many others, they were intrigued by De La Rue's patent envelope maker, whose intricate moving parts deftly folded and gummed the paper into shape, simulating the most precise and skilled operations of the human hand at the rate of thousands per hour. The *Illustrated London News* described how it 'closely followed several actual movements of the human form divine'. Operated by two children, it produced sixty envelopes a minute, responding to a demand created by the introduction of the penny post eleven years earlier. Another machine could roll up to 100 cigarettes a minute.

Among further curiosities that will have attracted the attention of the villagers, if they came across them in the limited time at their disposal, were some destined to have less of an impact on their lives: a carriage drawn by kites, furniture made from coal – including a garden seat from Osborne House, Queen Victoria's seaside home in the Isle of Wight – a knife with precisely 1,851 blades, a false nose made of silver, a

De La Rue's patent envelope machine.

buttonless shirt for bachelors and a set of artificial teeth fitted with a swivel device that allowed the user to yawn without displacing either the lower or the upper range.

To the right of the entrance, in the eastern part of the building, were the exhibits from overseas – a random collection that depended largely on which governments had responded most enthusiastically to the idea of the Exhibition. The French were dominant, with their sophisticated designs of fabrics and furnishings as well as a few technological wonders, notably a prototype submarine. The Americans had produced an eclectic display – rather smaller than had originally been expected – that ranged from a stuffed squirrel to a giant model eagle and from the highly practical McCormick reaper, through a set of unpickable locks, to some peculiar musical innovations, such as a piano that could be played by four people at once and a violin and piano joined in such a way that a single musician could play them both at the same time on a single keyboard.

Yet the essence of a day at the Great Exhibition did not lie just in the objects on display. People were a vital part of the pageant. It regularly attracted a throng of 50,000 and more, representing an unprecedentedly broad cross-section of British society. It was the first mass spectacle that appealed to almost every social class – and the first time that the wealthy and privileged had found the courage to mingle so freely with their perceived inferiors. The young Queen and her consort, Prince Albert, had set the example, visiting Crystal Palace nearly every day when they were in London and making a point of walking through the crowds as they toured the stands: people made way for the royal party and cheered lustily. Victoria and Albert had been there, as it happened, on the arrival of the Surrey farm workers, greatly adding to their sense of awe.

By four p.m., the pre-arranged time for their departure, the Surrey contingent had in itself become an object of wonder. Native Londoners gathered round them as they prepared to leave, with what the press described as 'looks full of curiosity, not unmingled with a species of half-pitying interest'. Not content with looking, the townies proceeded to quiz the country folk about their reactions to what they had seen. What had they been most struck by? Had they understood it all? Would they like to make another visit if they could? The responses, if any, to this impertinent line of questioning are unrecorded, but the group clearly conducted themselves with sufficient dignity to provoke a lyrical outburst from the *Times* man:

> After some little marshalling they left the Exhibition in close order, moving three abreast – an affecting array of young and old, male and female, in which each observer might read with his own eyes the evidences of a laborious life, little relieved by intelligence or education, but simple, unpretending and not unaccompanied by domestic virtue or happiness . . . The rector, the Rev. Mr Hutton, deserves great praise for this truly benevolent and pastoral act, which ought to be extensively imitated.

When they had all been mustered, they retraced their steps of the morning down Knightsbridge and across the park to Westminster, where they were marched into the large National School Room on Tufton Street, just behind Smith Square. (The National Schools were the precursors of the Church of England schools, now part of the state system.) Here the adults were treated to a glass of beer and showed their appreciation by giving a wholehearted rendering of the National Anthem: on previous occasions when they had sung 'God Save the Queen', they had not imagined that they would ever come face to face with the lady in question. The steamer took them back to London Bridge, where they boarded the train for Godstone. There the wagons were waiting for them, and they arrived at their homes soon after dusk. There was plenty for them to talk about – but most may have gone straight to their beds, to be up early next morning for the milking and to catch up with the chores they had neglected for the sake of their grand day out.

* * *

The local paper, the *Surrey Standard* (at that time incorporated into the *Sussex Express*), was even more enthusiastic about the expedition than the national press had been. Of the participants, it wrote that 'their good conduct throughout the day was admirable and proved they were worthy of the confidence placed in them'. But there was more to it than that. Britain's ruling classes were becoming increasingly worried about the emergence of a militant working class and the consequent possibility of conflict. Only three years earlier, when much of Europe had been rocked by revolution, the Chartists in Britain had provoked riots by workers agitating for better conditions and political reform. There was a growing feeling that more serious clashes could be avoided only by reaching out to the working class in a benign manner – a strategy that would today be seen as hopelessly paternalistic.

Until the nineteenth century, working-class aspirations had been encapsulated in the image of an urchin in a flat cap, pressing his nose against the window of a great house, where his betters were engaged in their social rituals of dining well or dancing in accordance with the current fashion. Now the urchin was to be invited to the party, though strictly on the host's terms. The Crystal Palace was an apt if unconscious symbol of this new state of affairs: the walls were all of glass but the lower orders were now inside, joining in the fun.

Against this background, the *Surrey Standard* went on to comment:

> We cannot conclude this brief summary of so pleasing
> an instance of good feeling and cordial co-operation
> without expressing our deep sense of importance of
> its interesting character, our pleasure at its perfect

success and our hope that, if not too late, the example may be followed. The clergy and gentry of the district will find their best reward not in that approbation extorted from the public but in that 'one self-approving hour' which must have followed a day gladdened by the sunshine of so many merry faces, and unattended by the mixture of any of those debasing accompaniments which too often render the peasant's holiday a debauch rather than a festival.

We hail the excursion of the three parishes as a first movement in a right direction. The people must and will have amusements. Shall the wise and the good provide them, or shall they be left to those who are animated only by the stimulus of gain – gain which, unfortunately, can only be secured by the moral deterioration of those from whom it is to be gathered?

Someone else, too, was impressed by the visitors and their demeanour. Queen Victoria kept a detailed daily journal of her doings. The entry for 14 June 1851 reads, in part:

> Quite forgot to mention that on the morning of the 12th we saw three whole parishes – Crowhurst, Linchfield and Langford, from Kent and Surrey (800 in number), walking in procession two and two, the men in smock frocks, with their wives looking so nice. It seems that they subscribed to come to London, by the advice of the clergyman, to see the Exhibition, it only costing them 2s 6d.

She meant Limpsfield, not Linchfield; and Lingfield, not Langford. Moreover, they were not whole parishes, none is in Kent and the villagers paid 1s 6d, not 2s 6d. The great thing

about being a monarch is that you are not obliged to be a slave
to detail.

CHAPTER TWO

❧ ❧

A PRINCE FINDS A PURPOSE

The Queen, at the risk of not appearing modest (and yet
why should a wife ever be modest about her husband's
merits?), must say that she thinks Lord John Russell will
admit now that the Prince is possessed of very
extraordinary powers of mind and heart. She feels so
proud of being his wife that she cannot refrain from herself
paying tribute to his noble character.

Queen Victoria, in a letter to Lord John Russell, 1851

Early in March 1850, Henry Forbes, Mayor of Bradford – the
fastest-growing woollen town in West Yorkshire – received an
unusually, almost comically large envelope in the mail from
London. In it was the most magnificent invitation card he had
ever set his eyes upon. It was from Prince Albert and the Lord
Mayor of London, Thomas Farncomb, asking him to attend a
banquet at the Mansion House on 21 March, for the purpose
of spreading the word about plans for the following year's
Great Exhibition. So excited was the Mayor that he rushed to
show the card to his friend, the editor of the *Bradford Observer*,
who in turn hastened to share his amazement with his readers:

We have been favoured with a sight of the card of
invitation, which of itself is almost worthy of a place
in the proposed Exhibition. It is enamelled and of a

large quarto size, the letters being printed in gold. The arms of His Royal Highness Prince Albert appear conspicuous, the arms of the City of London and the Lord Mayor being engraved on a smaller scale. The whole is surrounded by a beautiful gold border.

And he added the laconic payoff line: 'We need scarcely add that the Mayor has accepted the invitation.'

Even by the standards of the Mansion House, administrative headquarters of the wealthiest square mile in Britain, it was a uniquely splendid occasion. By 5.30, as dusk was beginning to fall, a large crowd of onlookers had gathered in the street outside to see the first of nearly 200 guests arriving. Mayors of provincial cities had turned out in force, and many of the guests were in official costumes of one kind or another – foreign ambassadors in court dress, military men in uniform, bishops in their vestments and masters of city guilds in livery. Among politicians who had obeyed the royal summons were the Prime Minister, Lord John Russell; Sir Robert Peel, a former Prime Minister; Lord Palmerston, foreign secretary and a future Prime Minister; and William Gladstone, also a Prime Minister in the making. But these were not the celebrities that most of the crowd had turned out to see.

At 6.15, the faint sound of distant cheering grew louder as a royal carriage made its way along Cheapside. In it was Prince Albert, dressed in the resplendent uniform of an Elder Brother of Trinity House, the lighthouse authority. After being greeted by the Lord Mayor, he and his party were led down the long corridor of the Mansion House, which was decorated with scores of shrubs and lined by eighty members of the Honourable Artillery Company, forming a guard of honour as the parade made its way to the pre-dinner reception.

The meal itself was to be held in the Egyptian Hall, the main banqueting room of the house designed by George Dance the Elder in 1739. The massive columns around its four walls had been adorned for the occasion with symbols representing the British counties and regions. Painted shields were attached to them, as well as models and stuffed animals depicting the particular district's characteristic agricultural products and manufactures. The Prince's chair was at the head of the table, and behind it two figures representing peace and plenty. At the opposite end of the hall was a figure of Britannia, holding a plan of the proposed Exhibition. Around her were four angels, delivering to the four corners of the world an invitation to display their wares in London next year.

At seven o'clock, with the rest of the company already seated, the Lord Mayor and the Prince entered the hall and took their places. Turtle soup was served, then there was a choice of six kinds of fish – including eel – and even more main courses, among them lobster, mutton, pigeon and raised ornamental pies. After fruit, cakes and ices, a loving cup was passed around the company, in accordance with a Mansion House tradition. Then grace was performed by a group of vocalists, the loyal toast was drunk and the National Anthem sung before the Prince rose to speak.

He began by expressing gratification that his plan for the Exhibition had met with so much approval, and explained the ambition that lay behind it:

We are living at a period of most wonderful transition, which tends rapidly to accomplish that great end – to which all history points – the realisation of the unity of mankind ... Gentlemen, the Exhibition of 1851 is to give us a true test of the point of development at which the whole of mankind has arrived in this great

> task, and a new starting point from which all nations
> will be able to direct their further exertions.

He believed that the world had reached a stage where all knowledge and innovation were recognised as being the property of the international community as a whole, not something that needed to be protected by secrecy from the gaze of outsiders. The Exhibition would embody this ideal. He was loudly applauded for his insistence that the event should be paid for not by the Government but by donations from the people of the country. He urged those local officials present to begin raising funds in their own localities.

As he sat down, the Prince was cheered to the echo. The next speaker was the Archbishop of Canterbury, followed by the French ambassador, M. Drouyn de Lhuys. In a subtle speech, the ambassador observed that the excellence of British products lay in their cheapness and durability, not their 'fine glossy surface' – a thinly veiled slur based on the reputation that French goods enjoyed for being better designed. The most rousing speech came from Sir Robert Peel, much venerated as an elder statesman. 'Gentlemen, I have no fear of failure,' he declared. 'I am confident that we shall succeed. In spite of the cavils of some . . . such is the spirit of Englishmen that this great undertaking shall not be permitted to fail . . . but shall be borne triumphant over every obstacle by the energy and determination of the British people.'

After that tour de force, the rest of the evening could only be an anticlimax. The mayors of York and Dublin and the Lord Provost of Edinburgh spoke, and finally the Earl of Carlisle, a member of Russell's government. Proposing a toast to 'the working man of the United Kingdom', the Earl urged that the Exhibition should embrace all classes, as well as all nations. 'It is pre-eminently intended to be the festival of the working man and of the working woman.' Scarcely anybody in the room fell into that category, but it did not prevent them from cheering the impeccable sentiment with unbounded enthusiasm, before they emerged into the chilly night and sought the carriages that would take them to their homes or lodgings.

The evening had been an indisputable success. Until then, for Henry Forbes and the other civic dignitaries for whose benefit the extravaganza had been mounted, the Great Exhibition had been an insubstantial idea that they had read about in the newspapers; something that might or might not happen in faraway London, a place they seldom visited despite the rapid new railway services. True, the fact of its royal patronage lifted it out of the ordinary, but even that did not mean that the ambitious scheme would automatically go ahead, for already influential voices had been raised against it. The dinner, with its glittering guest list and impassioned speeches, had convinced the mayors that, far from being a pious aspiration, the Exhibition was more likely than not to become a reality, and that their communities should seize the chance of playing a role. Most went home determined to drum up support and funds from local businesses and to start thinking hard about the products they could display.

During the eighteenth century, the British had grown accustomed to foreign royalty, even if they never exactly warmed to them. The four Hanoverian Georges were by turns incomprehensible, mad, extravagant and licentious, but they seemed to serve their constitutional purpose. When Albert, the second son of the Duke of Saxe-Coburg-Gotha, married Queen Victoria in 1840 – when both were aged twenty-one – her subjects were prepared to tolerate him, but they did not see why they should be required to take him to their hearts. According to his biographer, Robert Rhodes James, fashionable London society viewed him at first as 'an insufferable German Puritan on the make'. He had no polite small talk, and a Teutonic sense of humour that found no outlet in the strictly formal salons of the British aristocracy: as a youth he had once thrown stink bombs from his box in the theatre into the stalls below.

Albert's destiny as Victoria's Consort had been decided at a very early age. His cousin Leopold had been married to Princess Charlotte, George IV's only child and as such the heir to his throne, but she died in childbirth in 1817. Albert and Victoria were both born two years later – also cousins, because Victoria's mother was Leopold's sister. Before long the ambitious Saxe-Coburgs had calculated that they now had a second chance to cement their links with the British crown. Albert was educated in things British from the start, and in 1836, the year before Victoria ascended the throne, he went to London with his father to inspect his cousin. The young pair got along famously and the two families agreed in principle that they should marry. Albert immersed himself yet more deeply in British affairs and perfected his command of the language.

Even though it was an arranged marriage, contracted when the couple had scarcely emerged from childhood, there is little doubt that it was a loving one. Just before the ceremony, the Queen wrote in her journal: 'To feel I was and am loved by such an angel as Albert was too great a delight to describe! He is perfection; perfection in every way.'

Despite this evidence of regard, Albert was realistic enough to recognise that the role of Consort would be a thankless one. 'My future position will have its dark sides,' he wrote to his stepmother, and so it initially proved. The first setback came when the Government's plan to award him an annuity of £50,000 was rejected by the House of Commons and the sum reduced to £30,000. The instigator of the cut was Colonel Charles Sibthorp, a prominent jingoist with an aversion to foreigners, who was later to achieve further renown as one of the most vociferous critics of the Great Exhibition.

This financial blow was not Albert's greatest concern: as he said, it meant simply that he would not be able to patronise the British arts and sciences as generously as he had intended. His chief difficulty was to find himself a role beyond that of accompanying the Queen at official functions. Victoria herself, although devoted to him, initially made the problem worse by refusing to let him take part in government business. Soon, though, he persuaded her to appoint him her secretary, and he began gradually to wield more influence in affairs of state, especially when the Queen was otherwise engaged giving birth to their nine children. He also instigated reforms that led to the more efficient running of the royal household, and in doing so displayed his methodical approach. Concerned about the inefficiency of the palace kitchens, he commissioned a technical report from an up-and-coming scientist, Lyon Playfair, who would later play an important role in his plans for the Exhibition.

None of this, though, amounted to a fulfilling full-time occupation, and the Prince involved himself in good works. In 1844 he became President of the Society to Improve the Condition of the Working Classes. At the same time he pursued ever more energetically his interest in the world of knowledge, making contact with a number of societies with a view to becoming involved in their work. In 1843 he joined the Society of Arts, formed in 1754 'for the encouragement of arts, manufactures and sciences'. Its main purpose was to award prizes for useful, well-designed inventions, and in 1756 it staged its first small exhibition. For the rest of the century it fought a losing battle in trying to persuade manufacturers of the virtues of good design. In those early days of the Industrial Revolution, practicality and cheapness were the most prized

Henry Cole

qualities, with aesthetics some way down the list.

The French had been quicker to recognise the importance of design, and Europe's first major exhibition of manufactures was held in the Temple of Industry in Paris in 1798, followed by others every few years on a fairly regular schedule. By the time Albert joined the Society of Arts, there had been no exhibition in London for many years, although some of its members were starting to urge that it was time to follow the French example.

When the Duke of Sussex, president of the society since 1816, died a few months after Albert joined, the young Prince Consort was the obvious choice to succeed him. The following year, when important exhibitions were held in Paris and

Berlin, the society's secretary, Francis Wishaw, proposed that its own exhibitions should be revived and, if the first met with any success, possibly become an annual event. Prince Albert agreed to the experiment, and in 1845 a small exhibition, offering £300 in prizes, was mounted at the society's head-quarters in John Adam Street, behind the Strand (where it occupies the same premises today).

One of the prizes went to a tea service designed by Felix Summerley, alias Henry Cole, one of that distinctive breed of Victorian polymaths who recognised no limits to the scope of their talents and succeeded in nearly everything they turned their hands to. Leaving school at fifteen, Cole worked as a clerk in what was to become the Public Record Office and studied painting in his spare time. Rising to be Assistant Keeper of Public Records, he was a main force behind the construction of a dedicated records office in Fetter Lane, off Fleet Street. (To prove the need, he appeared before a Parlia-mentary inquiry carrying a mummified rat that had been found among some badly gnawed precious documents.) He also wrote children's books; designed and possibly invented Christmas cards; and helped Rowland Hill create the penny post in 1840. Developing his interest in art, he edited the *Journal of Design*, as well as the *Railway Chronicle*. His prize-winning tea service was fairly basic in the context of the fussy fashion of the day, but it continued to be produced by Minton for some years. In the wake of his success, Cole joined the Society of Arts, became one of its most active members and was elected to its council almost immediately.

The annual shows attracted growing interest and encour-aged members of the council to think in terms of mounting a large national exhibition in 1851, on the French model and on a scale never before attempted in Britain. At the beginning of 1848 Cole put the idea to Prince Albert and at first received a cautious response. The plan involved a far greater commitment of resources and – even more important – of the Prince's personal reputation than the modest shows staged so far. He had already clashed with courtiers, who saw themselves as guardians of royal protocol and dignity and felt that at times the Consort acted too hastily, as young men will do, without weighing up the consequences. So he was now wary of committing his support to any project without first consulting advisers – in particular his private secretary, Colonel Charles Phipps, a man very much wedded to tradition – and canvassing their views on the chances of success.

The Prince therefore told Cole and his colleagues that he would not back the idea until he was sure that the Government would give it a fair wind, although in truth he was already greatly enthused by it. Here at last was a chance to spearhead a project that would raise his national profile in a wholly benevolent way, spanning three areas to which he was especially committed: trade, science and the arts. Here was something that would engage him and stretch his abilities.

Members of the council of the Society of Arts joined him in lobbying for political support, and they received some encouragement from Whitehall, even though the final decision would have to be taken by the House of Commons. In 1849 Cole went to France with the architect Matthew Digby Wyatt, who had been commissioned by the society to report on what lessons could be learned from that year's Paris exhibition. In his memoirs, Cole recalled: 'It was my first visit to Paris and with Mr Digby Wyatt I put up at the Hotel de la Ville de Paris. We were awakened at midnight by the stifling odour of emptying the cesspools, altogether a novel sensation, which the years have not obliterated from my mind.'

It was the accepted practice of the time to regard foreigners with suspicion, not to say derision, and the British routinely believed that the French had deplorably low standards of hygiene – a view periodically reinforced by cartoons in *Punch*, the satirical journal established in 1841. That made it all the more remarkable that Cole and Wyatt's visit should spark an idea that was to have a profound impact on the scope and nature of the Great Exhibition. The Paris event was restricted to French goods, but in talking to its organisers, the British pair learned that there had been some discussion that year about inviting exhibitors from overseas. The notion was scotched by French manufacturers, reluctant to face outside competition. The British Parliament, after acrimonious debate, had in 1846 introduced a measure of free trade with the repeal of the Corn Laws – a move that had the popular effect of reducing food prices, although it was still opposed by a significant body of tradespeople. Wyatt and Cole calculated that the spirit of free trade would be enhanced if the proposed Exhibition was opened up to all nations. It would symbolise Britain's self-confidence and ensure that the world's eyes turned towards London.

Another prominent member of the Society of Arts, Francis Fuller, had also been to Paris, and was equally convinced that the London Exhibition should be international. Shortly after his return, he had a chance meeting on a train with Thomas Cubitt, the master builder, who was on his way back from Osborne House, where he was installing improvements for the royal couple. When Fuller mentioned his idea, Cubitt was enthusiastic and promised to recommend it to Albert on his next visit to Osborne.

In June and July 1849 Cole and Fuller had further meetings with the Prince, at which he agreed that the Exhibition should be international. At the second of these meetings, Sir Robert Peel was present and made the important point that before proceeding too far it was vital to test the opinion of

British manufacturers, whose co-operation in sending their best products to London would be crucial to the Exhibition's success. Cole and Fuller said they would take soundings and report back to the Prince in September. In August, four representatives of the Society of Arts visited the manufacturing towns of Lancashire and Yorkshire to meet leading industrialists, explain the project and gauge their reactions. They were largely favourable, although the manufacturers stressed that good design should not be the only criterion for awarding prizes. Cheapness – the prime quality of British products – had to be taken into account, otherwise the French and other foreigners would win the bulk of the awards. Manchester in particular did not want its mass-produced products to be compared unfavourably with the more expensive luxury goods created by French craftsmanship.

At the September meeting, held in the royal family's Scottish castle at Balmoral, it was agreed that the next stage was to involve the City of London. The decision had already been taken not to ask Parliament to finance the proposed Exhibition but to raise the money by subscription. The City, the nation's financial boiler room, was the obvious place to start looking for funds, and it was felt that stressing the royal connection would improve the chances of a successful appeal. In September Col. Phipps wrote to London's Lord Mayor asking him to consult leading financiers and assess their likely support for the proposal, now being projected as Prince Albert's own idea.

On the morning of 17 October 1849, the Lord Mayor invited some of the most influential London merchants, bankers and traders to the Mansion House to meet a deputation from the Society of Arts, who would flesh out the project. More than 300 turned up to hear Cole setting out the aims of the proposed Exhibition and laying particular stress on the

Prince's role. 'During the last two years His Royal Highness has been watching the symptoms of public feeling on this question with great intentness,' he said, and went on to explain the Prince's reasons for making the Exhibition an international one:

> Whilst it appears an error to fix any limitations to the productions of machinery, science and taste, which are of no country but belong as a whole to the civilised world, particular advantage to British industry might be derived from placing it in fair competition with that of other nations.

He went on to list some of the exotic items that visitors might expect to see:

> In the class of animal substances, we shall probably have enormous elephants' tusks from Africa; leather from Morocco and Russia; beaver from Baffin Bay; the wools of Australia, Yorkshire and Tibet; silk from Asia and from Europe and furs from the Eskimos . . . We shall have spices from the East; the hops of Kent and Sussex; the raisins of Malaya and the olives of the Pyrenees . . . gold from California and the East Indies; silver from Mexico, Russia and Cornwall; iron ore from Wales, Wolverhampton and Tunbridge Wells.

The prizes offered were expected to amount to £20,000. Although government funding would not be sought, the Society of Arts would ask the Government to appoint a Commission to oversee arrangements.

Cole then discussed possible sites. Somerset House in the Strand had been offered, but there was also talk of putting up a temporary building in the southern part of Hyde Park. It was anticipated that around 100,000 foreign visitors would come to Britain for the event: 'London will act the part of host to all the world at an intellectual festival of peaceful industry suggested by the Consort of our beloved Queen and seconded by yourselves – a festival such as the world never before has seen.'

He sat down to prolonged cheering. A number of City figures spoke in favour of the scheme, and the meeting carried a resolution supporting the Exhibition and the concept of funding it by subscription. Most of the press, too, was becoming more enthusiastic by the day. *The Times* observed: 'This peaceful metropolis is the asylum of the outcast and unfortunate. All parties find refuge here . . . What office so proper to London as the reconciliation and improvement of the civilised world?' And it lauded the concept of nations competing through 'the rivalry of civilised art, instead of the old rivalry of brute force'.

The *Morning Chronicle* banged the patriotic drum: 'Englishmen are afraid of no competition. They have nothing to fear and are willing to learn.' Yet there were sceptics, among them the *Standard*: 'There are plenty of products of foreign industry in the shops of Oxford Street, Regent Street, Pall Mall, the Strand, Fleet Street and Cheapside.'

During the autumn, Cole, Fuller and others continued their tour of the provinces. In their discussions with industrialists they encountered the same broad approval as they had in their earlier visits. In rural areas, though, the story was different. Farmers and landowners could not see what was in it for them. One of the investigators, Hepworth Dixon, wrote to Prince Albert from rural north Yorkshire: 'Ignorance, indifference, hostility: these are in brief the characteristics of the agricultural towns which I have visited today.' The same reaction was later reported from Kent, where because of opposition led by the clergy and aristocracy, fewer than forty people turned up at a public meeting.

All in all, though, the prospects of raising funds seemed good; but donations would inevitably take time to come in, and some money was needed quickly if the plans were to be advanced. In November the organisers did a deal with James and George Munday, heads of a firm of building contractors, who would advance them £20,000 in exchange for a share of the profits. In January 1850 the Queen announced the appointment of a twenty-four-man Royal Commission, under Albert's presidency, to turn the plans for the Exhibition into reality. Among its members were the Prime Minister, Lord John Russell; Lord Derby, Leader of the Opposition; Lord Granville, a prominent member of the Government who was the Commission's active vice-president; three more peers of the realm; Sir Robert Peel; William Gladstone; the builder and engineer William Cubitt (Thomas Cubitt's brother); and the architect Charles Barry.

With the increasing likelihood that the Exhibition would go ahead, and the newspapers devoting more and more column inches to discussing the prospects, public interest was beginning to mount. The British have always warmed to public spectacle. Periodic fairs, where farmers and craftsmen sold their products while street entertainers drew the crowds, were an ancient tradition. Since the seventeenth century, pleasure gardens in London and other large cities had tried to simulate a celebratory atmosphere every day during their opening season. The theatre attracted all classes, although the auditorium was still segregated between rich and poor.

The arrival at London Zoo of unusual beasts from distant parts of the Empire was invariably hailed by large crowds and excited press coverage. In June 1850 *The Times* devoted more than a column to a detailed description of a new hippopotamus:

> It now and then uttered a soft, complacent grunt and, lazily opening its thick, smooth eyelids, leered at its keeper with a singular protruding movement of the eyeball from the prominent socket . . . No living specimen has been seen in Europe since the period when they were last exhibited by the third Gordian [AD 238–244] in the amphitheatre of Imperial Rome.

As advances in engineering and technology produced a spate of wondrous inventions, there was a tendency to treat these as spectacles as well. Excited crowds formed to watch the early railway trains get up steam, and even more modest happenings drew an audience: in the 1850s, advertisements in the London newspapers regularly invited the public to watch chickens and other poultry hatch in a newly invented incubator in the West End.

Some were expecting still greater marvels from the Exhibition. At the end of January 1850, a correspondent to a Sheffield newspaper wrote that he had heard of a race of men with tails that had been discovered in the interior of French Africa, 'repulsively ugly, enormous mouth, thick teeth, no beard and body not hairy'. He suggested that the French government should be asked to produce a male and female specimen at the Exhibition. A few days later there was a report of preparations being made in India to send exhibits: 'Many of the rude machines of the natives will be found to be as remarkable for their ingenuity as the more perfect contrivances of European artificers.'

However, the Commission was determined from the start that the Exhibition would not be a collection of curiosities but a display of practical innovation and design. Early on, William Felkin, the Mayor of Nottingham and leader of the committee co-ordinating that city's contribution, clearly spelled out the criteria:

> Articles notable only for their singularity will not be admitted . . . A counterpane composed of a million hexagonal morsels of coloured cloth, and put together by the labour of years, if arranged without elegance or design, would not be admissible . . . It may be very creditable for a ploughman to have constructed a steam engine; or for a shop boy to have devised and put together a threshing machine; yet neither would, of itself, constitute a valid ground for admission here.

The Commission appointed two Special Commissioners to tour the country and drum up support. They were Lyon Playfair, the scientist who had reported for Prince Albert on the royal kitchens, and Colonel John Lloyd, an engineer whose adventurous past had included an early survey of the projected Panama Canal, a daring ascent of an unconquered peak in Mauritius, engineering work for the South American revolutionary Simon Bolivar, and arrest by the Russians in Poland. Playfair and Lloyd's energetic efforts, allied to those of Digby Wyatt, who was responsible for publicity, led to enthusiastic meetings in all parts of the country. By now there was support even in rural areas, after a promise that agricultural products would find a place at the Exhibition.

Scores of committees were formed and subscriptions pledged. The Queen gave £1,000 and Prince Albert, unwilling to upstage her, £500. At the other end of the social scale came contributions of shillings and even pennies from people wanting to be identified with the project, however modestly. Businessmen took collections among their employees and reported the results to the press: builders employed by Thomas

Cubitt gave £40, printers at Waterlow's £21 10s and railway-men with the London and South-Western £29 13s. The Duchess of Sutherland formed a committee of ladies to ensure that women's interests were not overlooked.

One of the first acts of the Commission was to cancel the financing arrangement with the Mundays, after concern had been expressed about the propriety of commercial involvement in this national endeavour. This meant that the Commissioners were now totally at the mercy of subscribers, who were proving less ready to respond to their appeals than might

Prince Albert the fund-raiser, as seen by Punch.

have been suggested by the widespread enthusiasm expressed for the project. There was no shortage of pennies and shillings from the poor, but that was not enough. Many more large cheques from the rich were urgently required. *Punch* commented on the shortfall in a cruel cartoon depicting Prince Albert begging on the street, above this verse:

> This empty hat my awkward case bespeaks,
> These blank subscription lists explain my fear;
> Days follow days, and weeks succeed to weeks,
> But very few contributors appear.

Despite this embarrassment, the Commission had no alternative but to press on. The first critical decision that had to be made was to determine the site. Apart from Somerset House and the south side of Hyde Park, suggestions had included Leicester Square, Regent's Park, Primrose Hill, Victoria Park, Battersea and an alternative spot in Hyde Park, on its northeast corner. Everyone agreed that the original site earmarked in Hyde Park would be most convenient, as being close to the centre of town – everyone, that is, except the well-heeled residents of Belgravia and Kensington, who feared a miserable summer as people of all classes from all over the globe rampaged around their patch. In an attempt to pacify them, the Commissioners gave an assurance that whatever building was erected to house the Exhibition would be temporary, and would be removed as soon as the show was over. As we shall see, the residents refused to be mollified, and for some months after the Commission announced its decision in February it seemed as though the venue might have to be moved, or indeed the whole project cancelled.

Having determined the site, at least to their own satisfaction, the Commissioners had to move urgently to decide what kind of structure should be erected there. If the Exhibition was to have any chance of opening by the target date of 1 May 1851, there was perilously little time to construct a building of the size that would be required. In March 1850 they invited tenders from architects for suitable designs, warning as they did so that they would not necessarily choose any of those submitted in their entirety, but might cherry-pick the best elements from several to produce a master plan of their own. At least they now had enough money pledged to be able to set aside £100,000 for whatever structure they chose, although to achieve that they had been forced to scrap the original plan to offer cash prizes. People would have to be persuaded to compete just for medals, for global honour and acclaim, rather than financial reward.

Perhaps it was the gossip about the Mayor's glamorous dinner invitation in March 1850 that gave Abraham Priestley his big idea. Priestley, aged forty-one, was the landlord of the Hope and Anchor Inn, a large tavern on the corner of Market Street and Bank Street in the centre of Bradford, where he lived with his wife Eliza, their six children and two servants. It is unlikely that he had ever been to London, but from what he had read about the 1851 Exhibition it was going to be a unique event that ought not to be missed – and now, with the Midland Railway having opened its line from Bradford to Leeds in 1846, and Leeds being on a main route to London, it was feasible to make the journey.

Of course it would cost money – there would be the rail fare, almost certainly an admission fee, and the need to spend a night or two in London: going there early in the morning and back late the same night, while possible in theory, would leave precious little time to see all there was to see. The trouble was that his customers, most of them weekly wage-earners in the woollen mills, lived virtually from hand to mouth, and would not be able to stump up the few pounds needed when the time came for the trip to be made.

Priestley calculated that advance planning could solve the problem. What if they formed a club to put aside a shilling or two every week for the next year and more? That would leave them with a useful sum when the time came to visit the Exhibition – and if they travelled in a group they could probably negotiate good deals over travel and lodgings. The principle would be the same as that of the co-operative societies and buyers' clubs that had been springing up all over the northern industrial districts since the first co-op, in Rochdale, six years earlier. A flour club had been formed in Bradford only the previous year. He discussed the plan with some business friends, then put the word out to his customers that there would be a meeting at the Hope and Anchor on 11 March 1850 to discuss forming a travel club.

Since the beginning of the nineteenth century, Bradford, just south of the Aire Valley, below the eastern fringe of the Pennines, had become one of the boom towns of the Industrial Revolution. In 1801 the town and its surrounding districts could muster a population of only 13,264 and one woollen mill. By 1851 there were 103,788 people and 129 mills, and it had a virtual monopoly of worsted manufacture in Britain. Worsted is a yarn made up of long-staple wool fibres, the short ones being removed by combing. The yarn is tightly twisted to make it hard-wearing and give it the smooth finish prized in men's suitings. In the 1830s the quality of worsted was enhanced when alpaca wool and mohair were introduced into the blends, a process developed by Bradford's most famous industrialist, Titus Salt.

Until the nineteenth century, worsted had been manufactured chiefly in East Anglia, the traditional home of the wool trade, but when mechanisation was introduced the industry moved to Yorkshire, close to the coal mines that provided its fuel. The subsequent loss of jobs, as more and more were taken over by machines, made it a fertile breeding ground for the militant working-class movement that was beginning to make an impact on the nation's industrial and social life.

In 1825–6, when Bradford's combers and weavers struck for higher pay, many were injured and some killed in the ensuing riot. The radical Chartists came to the fore a few years later, fomenting more riots in 1840 and 1842, and the depression of 1847 led to a further cut in weavers' pay. The following year, when the Chartists were provoking fear among the ruling and manufacturing classes all across Britain, numerous special constables were sworn in to keep order in Bradford, and soldiers arrived by the newly built railway to quell disturbances in the town centre.

Exponential growth inevitably created other difficulties. Housing had to be provided for the large numbers of people, mostly from rural areas of England and Ireland, who came to Bradford seeking work in the mills. Erected quickly and cheaply, the houses were shoddy and unhygienic. Georg Weerth, a German poet and journalist who lived in Bradford in the mid-1840s, described it as 'an evil smelling town'. Tuberculosis was rife and 480 people died in a cholera epidemic in 1848–9 – providing the stimulus to Titus Salt to plan his new model factory and township of Saltaire, a few miles away from the putrid centre.

Economic conditions improved in 1850, but in June of that year the Bradford Long-Pledged Teetotal Association, in its seventh annual report, noted another social problem:

Since the return of commercial prosperity, drunkenness has prevailed to an alarming extent, which partly may be accounted for by the increase of population, the large influx of persons of migratory and unsettled habits; this class generally is not the most sober part of the community.

If the poor were getting the blame, the rich – and in Bradford that meant the factory owners – were by 1850 confident that the worst of the town's problems were behind them. For them, the Great Exhibition could not have come at a better time. It was a chance for them to display to the world the progress that the cloth-weaving industry had made over the last decade. The people of Bradford subscribed more money to the Exhibition, per head of population, than any other town in Britain. And their exhibits were of such high quality that the 1851 juries awarded Bradford manufacturers twenty-one medals for their cloths and yarns.

Priestley's proposed travel club reflected the desire of the mill workers to see how their products compared with those of the rest of Britain and the world. His 13 March meeting was well attended, and the club duly formed, each member committing himself to buying a £5 share, to be paid for in monthly instalments. Priestley and the other administrators announced that they were seeking more subscribers, adding that extra clubs would be formed if there was a demand:

The promoters of these clubs earnestly entreat all artisans and others who can make it convenient to become members, which will be conducted on the most economical principles, so that they may secure necessary funds to enable them to visit the Great Exhibition to be held in London in May 1851, which is so well calculated to improve the moral and intellectual condition of all classes.

Bradford's example was followed in communities all across the country. It soon became apparent that 1851 would see by far the biggest influx of visitors that the capital had ever been required to endure. And many of its citizens were beginning to view the prospect with trepidation, even outright alarm.

CHAPTER THREE

THE WORKERS ARE COMING

It has been customary for the masses to do homage to
the rich and titled; but England, in 1851, shall introduce
on the stage a new drama, in which princes and nobles
shall do honour to the sons and daughters of
toil, and thus at length pay a debt which has been
accumulating for ages.

John Cassell, in *The Working Man's Friend*, 1851

Ever since the French Revolution in 1789, the British ruling class had feared that the anti-aristocratic contagion would spread across the English Channel and the mob would take over. In 1792 the capital's first formal workers' organisation, the London Corresponding Society, was created, its members inspired by Thomas Paine's *Rights of Man*. The Government, alarmed that the movement could take hold, dispersed the society's rallies, arrested its leaders and then banned it; but other radical working-class groupings took its place. Between 1830 and 1832 there were demonstrations in London and other population centres in favour of parliamentary reform, some leading to injury and property damage. The Reform Act of 1832 made Parliament a little more representative but still left power in the hands of the landed gentry. It dampened the protests only temporarily.

In 1838 several working men's organisations co-operated

to produce a People's Charter demanding further reforms, principally universal male suffrage. Supporters of the movement, known as the Chartists, became increasingly militant. The following year there were riots in Birmingham and in Newport, south Wales, where some demonstrators were killed when troops fired on them. Many of the movement's leaders were arrested, including the charismatic Fergus O'Connor – elected to Parliament in 1847.

The Duke of Wellington in 1845, by Count Alfred d'Orsay.

In the early months of 1848 turmoil broke out all over Europe. There were popular uprisings in Berlin, Budapest, Milan, Naples, Rome, Prague, Venice, Vienna and Warsaw. In France, King Louis Philippe abdicated and Napoleon was elected President of the Second Republic. This continental turbulence caused further deep unease in London, developing into something close to panic when the Chartists announced a mass rally on Kennington Common in south London, followed by a march on Westminster to present a petition signed by five million people. The seventy-eight-year-old Duke of Wellington was brought out of retirement to mastermind the defence of the city, deploying thousands of troops to enforce an emergency ban on the march and enrolling tens of thousands of special constables to guard public buildings. The Bank of England was protected by sandbags at ground level and guns on the roof. Queen Victoria left the capital on the advice of her ministers.

When the day came, heavy rain ensured a lower turnout than expected and the rally proved peaceful. Chartism declined from that point – but for the next few years the ruling class was reluctant to lower its guard. What would happen if the Great Exhibition attracted troublemakers from revolutionary Europe, to foment discontent among the thousands of workers expected to pour into London from the industrial Midlands and the north?

Residents of Belgravia and Kensington were the first to express their fears about the impact the Exhibition might have on their lifestyle and property values. It was only in the last twenty years that Thomas Cubitt had developed the area just south of Hyde Park, turning it into a desirable district of well-proportioned stucco-fronted houses and attracting some of the cream of society to live in them. Now these well-to-do householders faced a summer of disturbance from hordes of people of all classes and nationalities, littering the streets, packing the omnibuses and frightening the horses. The seventy-two-year-old Lord Brougham, a former Lord Chancellor, spearheaded a move to have the Exhibition cancelled, or at least moved away from central London, which he feared would otherwise be at the mercy of 'socialists and men of the red colour'. A petition of protest, signed by nearly every resident of Knightsbridge and Kensington Gore, was presented to Parliament.

The Times, which had initially supported the idea of the Exhibition, urged fresh consideration of the venue: 'The whole of Hyde Park and, we will venture to predict, the whole of Kensington Gardens will be turned into the bivouac of all the vagabonds of London as long as the Exhibition shall continue. The annoyance inflicted on the neighbourhood would be indescribable.' The paper feared that residents would be forced to move out of town for the whole summer. It proposed Regent's Park – not then as fashionable as it would later become – as an alternative venue.

The jingoistic Colonel Sibthorp, the MP who had succeeded in having Albert's allowance cut, was an implacable opponent of the whole idea, describing it as 'an industrial exhibition in the heart of fashionable Belgravia to enable foreigners to rob us of our honour'. Realising that this extreme chauvinist view would not necessarily win the argument, he sought to focus opposition on the issue of preserving the amenities of Hyde Park – in particular its elm trees, some of which would have to be felled to allow a building to be erected on the chosen site. Angrily he told Parliament that the elms were to be cut down 'for one of the greatest humbugs, one of the greatest frauds, one of the greatest absurdities ever known . . . all for the purpose of encouraging foreigners'.

The matter of the elms had been raised in June by a correspondent to *The Times*, who said he had seen ten trees daubed with whitewash, presumably as a sign that they were to be cut down. 'I must ask you, sir, to say a word for the trees,' he pleaded. The paper was quick to respond in a flurry of leading articles on the matter. 'By the stroke of a pen our pleasant park – nearly the only spot where Londoners can get a breath of fresh air – is to be turned into something between

Wolverhampton and Greenwich Fair,' it claimed on 27 June. And two days later: 'Dine where you will, go into what drawing room you will, enter into conversation with the first chance stranger, met on a river steamer or in a Kensington omnibus, and on all sides there rises a groan of indignation at the intended pollution of our beautiful park.'

Greenwich Fair, held every Easter and Whitsun until 1857, was notorious for the raucous behaviour of Londoners who went there in their thousands, by road and river. In *Sketches by Boz*, Charles Dickens described it as 'a three days' fever which cools the blood for six months afterwards'. *The Times*'s reference to it was taken up by one of its correspondents, a professional man with a young wife and family, who wondered how Prince Albert would like it if the next Greenwich Fair were held in the grounds of Buckingham Palace. Others complained about losing the elms, and a few were indignant that the horses and carriages that customarily paraded on Rotten Row, just north of the proposed site, would have to be diverted during the period of construction. *Punch* added its voice:

> Albert! Spare those trees,
> Mind where you fix your show;
> For mercy's sake, don't please
> Go spoiling Rotten Row.

Among those on the other side of the argument were Charles Babbage, inventor of the 'difference machine', which has a sound claim to be the precursor of the modern computer. Babbage, eccentric and opinionated, was at first a keen supporter of the Exhibition and would have liked to serve on the Commission. Not only was he passed over, but later his machine would be turned down as an exhibit. On the matter

of Hyde Park, he was scornful of the arguments of the environmental and conservationist lobby, 'as if a building covering 20
acres out of above 320 could prevent the people from enjoying
air and exercise on the remaining 300'.

His quarrel was over the actual site within the park. He
wanted it to be on the east side, parallel with Park Lane, just
over half a mile away from the position proposed. With characteristic attention to detail, he had calculated how much this
would save in journey times and costs for passengers coming
from central London. If there were four million of them (there
would actually be more than six million), each made to travel
a mile and a quarter further than necessary, it would mean an
extra five million miles to be covered, involving £10,000
worth of lost time. It was Babbage's misfortune that his
obsessive and arrogant manner discouraged people from
giving his ideas the attention they sometimes deserved.

Outside London, supporters of the Exhibition were
becoming exasperated at this metropolitan squabbling. The
people of Manchester, an important manufacturing base, were
looking forward to sending their wares to compete with the
rest of the world, and earnestly wished that the Commissioners would get on with it. Reflecting their impatience, the
Manchester Guardian commented:

> The inhabitants of the metropolis invite their country
> cousins up to London, to celebrate a national jubilee;
> and then, because they fall quarrelling among them-
> selves as to whether they shall put us in the front
> bedroom or on the first floor, or in the three-pair
> back, they threaten to revoke the invitation, and spite
> each other, by sending us off in a huff!

The House of Commons debated the issue on Saturday 29

June, when the controversy was temporarily stilled by a national tragedy. On that day Sir Robert Peel had been to a meeting of the Commission in Buckingham Palace, advising them how to handle protests in Parliament about the plan. He was adamant that Hyde Park had to be the site. Riding home from Buckingham Palace, he was thrown from his horse and received injuries from which he died three days later, aged sixty-two. As the country's most respected politician, his loss was keenly felt, but Albert had a special cause for regret. He had been counting on Peel to sway doubtful MPs in the Commons debate. Fearing that a negative vote would lead to the Exhibition being forced out of London, the Prince wrote gloomily to his brother Ernst: 'Peel, who had undertaken the defence, is no more, so we shall probably be defeated and have to give up the whole Exhibition.'

When the debate resumed in the Commons on the Thursday, Sibthorp was again in scathing mood, remarking: 'I would advise persons residing near the park to keep a sharp lookout after their forks and spoons and serving-maids.' The Attorney General, defending the tree-felling in the face of the Colonel's protests, pointed out that 1,000 trees had recently been cut down in Kensington Gardens without any complaint, and there were still many thousands standing both there and in Hyde Park.

The vote was taken and Albert's forebodings proved unfounded. In fact, Peel's death had the opposite effect from what he had feared. Members of the Government who favoured the project – led by the Prime Minister, Lord John Russell – stressed Peel's enthusiasm for Hyde Park, and implied that as a mark of respect to the statesman the scheme should be allowed to go ahead. Sibthorp's motion, calling for the setting up of a select committee to reconsider the whole idea, was defeated by 166 votes to 46. Thus the good people of Kensington and

Belgravia had to come to terms as best they could with the prospect of locking up the silver and keeping a watchful eye on the housemaid.

The site, then, was settled, but not the building that was to occupy it. In response to their invitation to architects, the Commissioners had received 245 designs. While they found that nearly 100 of these warranted an honourable mention, for their 'elaboration of thought and elegance of execution', they could not agree on one that really fitted the bill – as they had hinted they might not when they put the job out to tender. 'No single one,' they reported, 'so accorded with the peculiar objects in view, either in principle or detail of its arrangements, as to warrant us in recommending it for adoption.' Instead, they produced a design of their own, much of it the work of the celebrated engineer, Isambard Kingdom Brunel. On 22 June a drawing of the proposed building was published in the *Illustrated London News* and provoked instant hostility. To begin with it was to be made largely of bricks – an estimated nineteen million would have been needed – provoking fears that it would, after all, be a permanent building rather than the promised temporary one.

Nobody much cared for its low, flat appearance, like a gigantic railway terminus with only a dome to relieve the monotony. Moreover, many doubted whether a structure of that size and solidity could be built from scratch and be ready to open in less than a year, as it would have to be. In any case, it seemed certain to cost more than the £100,000 that the Commissioners had set as a ceiling. The London papers were filled with leading articles and letters from prominent citizens, denouncing the building.

This was the point at which Joseph Paxton arrived on the scene. Born in 1801, he was another of the great nineteenth-

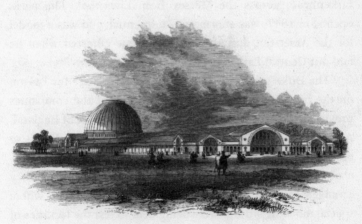

Above: Mons. Hector Horeau's rejected design for the building.

The Building Committee's unpopular design.

century polymaths, beginning his professional life as an under-gardener in the Home Counties before in 1826 he caught the eye of the Duke of Devonshire, then President of the Horticultural Society. Impressed by Paxton's competence and self-confidence, the Duke appointed him superintendent of his extensive gardens at Chatsworth, Derbyshire – where he quickly married Sarah Brown, the housekeeper's niece. The Duke was a collector of exotic tender plants, and Paxton built two innovative conservatories for them using the new technology of the day: large panes of glass within iron frames, instead of the traditional wood. The most magnificent of these, completed only in 1850, was a lily house for the rare *Victoria regis* lily.

By this time Paxton had become a close friend and protégé of the Duke, and spent two years travelling with him in Europe and Asia Minor. During those travels he became interested in the emergence of public parks in large cities, and in the 1840s accepted a commission to design a park for Birkenhead, across the Mersey from Liverpool. The park, opened in 1847, was enormously influential, and was a model for the American designer Frederick Law Olmsted when he laid out Central Park in New York ten years later.

The Duke used his influence to secure a place for Paxton on the board of the Midland Railway, one of the companies providing services between London and the north of England. As the row over the planned Exhibition building began to grow, Paxton went to London for a meeting with John Ellis, chairman of the Midland Railway and MP for Leicester. They arranged to meet at the new Houses of Parliament, where special morning sittings were being held to test the facilities of Barry's building.

Sitting in the Speaker's Gallery, Paxton observed to Ellis that the acoustics of the chamber were very poor, and the conversation turned to the general topic of making elementary mistakes in the design of buildings. Paxton, according to his own account, told Ellis that he feared similar mistakes would be made in the proposed building for the Great Exhibition, and that he had been toying with the idea of submitting a plan of his own, even though entries to the competition had long closed and the Commission appeared to have arrived at a final decision. If he decided to go ahead, he would base his design on the experience he had gained building glasshouses for the Chatsworth garden.

Ellis warmed to the idea and took Paxton along to the Board of Trade in the hope of seeing Lord Granville, a government minister as well as vice-chairman of the Commission. Granville was not there, but the two men did meet Henry Cole, who was often to be found lurking in the corridors of power. He told them that tenders were about to be sought for the proposed building, but that contractors would be free, if they wished, to tender for designs other than that selected by the Commission.

'From this moment,' Paxton was to recall the following year, 'I decided that I would prepare plans for a glass structure, and the first thing I did was to go to Hyde Park and step over the ground.' A few days later he had to go to the Midland Railway headquarters at Derby station to preside at a disciplinary hearing for a pointsman. As Charles Dickens wrote in his account of the matter in *Household Words*: 'As each witness delivered his evidence, Mr Paxton appeared to be taking notes with uncommon assiduity.' In fact he was making his first preliminary sketch for the glass Exhibition building on a pink blotter: it was preserved by his family and has been much reproduced since.

It took him nine days at his Chatsworth office to convert this sketch into detailed plans for a building made principally of glass and iron, which could be prefabricated almost in its entirety, thus reducing the time and cost of erecting it. He rolled up the plans, tucked them under his arm and set out again for London. On the train (it is remarkable how many crucial encounters in the Exhibition story took place on trains) he met one of the Commissioners, the engineer Robert Stephenson, son of the inventor of the steam locomotive and the founder of the London and Birmingham Railway Company; the first to bring long-distance trains from the Midlands into London.

Stephenson was travelling from Newcastle for a meeting of the Commission, and Paxton joined him for dinner in the restaurant car, taking the opportunity to show him his plans. According to Dickens, Stephenson was so absorbed that he continued puffing at his after-dinner cigar for twenty minutes after it had been extinguished. By the time the train reached London, he had agreed to lay the plans before the Commission the following day.

Paxton was an assiduous promoter of his own schemes, and before the meeting he gave Lord Granville an advance look at the plans and also showed them to Lord Brougham, who had been among the most outspoken critics of the brick building proposed by the Commissioners. Many of the Commissioners were stubborn in their determination to stick with the original plan despite the widespread criticism of it. But they could not totally dismiss public opinion, and they agreed to look at Paxton's design if he could get a major contractor to tender for constructing it.

Paxton hurried to the offices of Fox and Henderson at Spring Gardens, close to Trafalgar Square, where he showed his plans to the senior partner, Charles Fox. 'Mr Fox was much pleased with the design,' he wrote later, 'and at once agreed to go heartily into it.' Fox immediately telegraphed Lucas Chance of Birmingham, one of the few glassmakers with sufficient capacity to supply the quantity of glass needed: nearly a million square feet. The tender and estimate were prepared.

Now Paxton set in motion the next phase of his public-relations blitz. He gave a drawing of the proposed building, with a brief description, to the *Illustrated London News*, where it was published on 6 July. It would be 1,848 feet long, 408 feet broad and 66 feet high, with 330 iron columns, 2,300 girders and 24 miles of guttering. (The extra three feet in length would be added later, to make it fit the auspicious year.) The drawing differs little from the building as constructed, except that it does not incorporate the central transept with its curved roof – at 108 feet, tall enough to enclose the prized elms. The transept, which greatly added to the building's popular appeal, was added, according to Paxton, at the suggestion of the builders, although others sought to take the credit later. The clean lines of the design, and the modernity of the materials to be used, were so refreshingly different from the lumpen nature of the building originally selected that public opinion quickly swung behind Paxton's concept.

It would not be the first non-horticultural glass building in Britain. The market for glass expanded greatly after 1845, when Peel lifted the heavy duties on it and repealed the window tax, encouraging British manufacturers to improve their production techniques and lower their prices, which fell by around eighty per cent. Several railway termini already had glass roofs, and two glass and iron designs were among those submitted for the Hyde Park competition – one from Richard Turner, creator with Decimus Burton of the Palm House at Kew, and one from Hector Horeau, designer of glass market buildings in Paris. The Commissioners had indeed praised those two designs for their 'daring and ingenious disposition and construction' but apparently lacked the comparable courage to select one of them. What forced their hand was Paxton's skill at self-promotion and at exploiting the Victorian sense of adventure.

The momentum behind the building became irresistible.

Those critics who had decried the Commissioners' ponderous brick design were greatly relieved to find an attractive alternative, and even people who had originally opposed the whole concept of the Exhibition – notably Lord Brougham – were won round. Doubts were expressed about whether the building would be watertight, and there were questions about it getting overheated on sunny days, but Paxton had ready answers, citing the experience he had gained with the Chatsworth glasshouses. On 15 July the Commission met and decided to give the go-ahead to the scheme, and just two weeks later the foundations of the building would start to be laid.

On his return to Chatsworth after the announcement, Paxton was given a hero's welcome. *Punch* summed up the prevailing opinion:

> We all know the hubbub that you, Mr Paxton, have so magically hushed. Our park was to be desecrated – torn from us . . . and then, Joseph Paxton came. And the Prince clapped his hands and said: 'Paxton, go forth into Hyde Park, take glass and iron and – beauty wedding strength – produce the Industrial Hall of Nations.'

A few weeks later, Douglas Jerrold, *Punch*'s editor, hit on a more fitting name for Paxton's structure. 'The Crystal Palace' seemed to encapsulate the fairy-like qualities of lightness and enchantment that the nation so eagerly wanted the building and its contents to represent.

There were still a few non-believers. Colonel Sibthorp would remain forever inconsolable. The author and artist John Ruskin likened Paxton's building to a cucumber frame. Sir Edward Burne-Jones, the pre-Raphaelite painter, found its design cheerless and monotonous. For Augustus Pugin, the apostle of the Gothic revival, it was all too modern. When Paxton asked him what he thought of it, he replied: 'You had better keep to building greenhouses and I will keep to my churches and cathedrals.'

Even if the environmental objections to the Exhibition had now been largely silenced, there remained the potentially more serious security implications. What was to be done about the threatened incursion not only of all those 'men of the red colour' but also of European Papists, who were always thought to be plotting to overthrow the Church of England? As it happened, the Ranger of the Royal Parks, responsible for their security, was the Duke of Wellington, who had been credited with saving London from the Chartists. He received letters from fearful citizens urging that the Royal Navy be kept afloat in the Irish Sea, so that it could quickly institute a blockade to exclude people in case of emergencies. Others suggested that London should be cordoned off, with troops augmenting the police. Wellington's own recommendation was that a cavalry contingent should be stationed in Hyde Park during the whole summer of 1851; but Albert was against that because it would be out of keeping with the Exhibition's peaceful purpose. All the same, many regiments in the London area were put on alert for the period, ready to deal with troublemakers.

Granville remarked that Wellington viewed the Crystal Palace as 'a large fortress about to be garrisoned by a hostile army'. He was not alone in this view. The Marquis of Normanby, Britain's ambassador in Paris, wrote an alarming note to Lord Palmerston as the planning for the Exhibition proceeded:

I continue to receive numerous communications,

> some anonymous and some from secret sources of
> information, as to the projects of the Revolutionary
> Party . . . giving warnings of various characters as to
> the use which is intended to be made of the prom-
> iscuous assemblage of foreigners to be collected
> within the next few months.

Efforts would be made by socialist agents to 'pervert the spirit
of the population' by travelling with them on the trains and
omnibuses bound for the Exhibition, feeding them poisonous
views. Most would be Germans, because they spoke better
English than the French. Although the ambassador expressed
confidence that most British workers would resist 'the seduc-
tion of socialist eloquence', he warned that 'desperate men, in
perfectly organised bands, will be collected in numbers from
all parts of Europe for purposes of mischief'.

Four days later the ambassador had fresh disconcerting
news. Some French refugees, thought to have connections
with revolutionary movements, were about to be expelled
from Switzerland, and six of them had already received passports to allow them to travel to Britain. Normanby urged that
no further passports be issued to people of this kind. 'The
British Government would wish that there should be no exception made to the general unwillingness to receive anywhere
such persons.'

London's Metropolitan Police were getting worried too. In
a memorandum to the Home Office, the Police Commissioner
declared:

> Amongst the number of foreigners as well as strangers
> from all parts of our own country, there will no doubt
> be many who come for the purpose of committing
> crime . . . There are at present in this town many

refugees from other countries on account of extreme democratic revolutionary principles, they are in common with the political agitators of our own country... The burglar and the thief will have additional opportunities to commit crime, the vagrant and the profligate to cause offence and annoyance.

For all those reasons he calculated that he needed 1,000 extra men and £50,000 to pay for them.

Russell, the Prime Minister, suggested enlisting policemen from Paris and the main cities of Europe, who would be able to recognise any desperadoes from their own countries. Wellington, recalling his glory days at Waterloo, was incensed. 'I feel no want of confidence in my own powers to preserve the public peace and to provide for the general safety without requiring the assistance of French officers,' he declared scornfully. But Russell's less chauvinistic view prevailed, and several European policemen came to London for the duration.

Even if these fears of foreign infiltration were exaggerated, there were those who believed that British workers could spark trouble without external prompting. Prince Albert held the firm view that the best way to head off any threat of trouble from the sons of toil was to embrace them gladly and make provision for their participation in the Exhibition. That was why he had agreed to involve himself in the Society to Improve the Condition of the Working Classes. One of his allies in this benevolent crusade for benign inclusion was Samuel Wilberforce, Bishop of Oxford and son of William Wilberforce, the anti-slavery campaigner. The Bishop had been invited to address the first meeting in February 1850 of the influential committee formed to raise money for the Exhibition in the Westminster area, and he chose as his subject 'The Dignity of Labour', which he believed the Exhibition would celebrate. Colonel Phipps wrote on Albert's behalf congratulating the Bishop on the speech and inviting him to head a committee that was being formed, at the Prince's instigation, to ensure that the interests of the working class were taken into account in the planning for the Great Exhibition, and in particular that suitable accommodation and other arrangements were made for them.

The Central Working Classes Committee, as it was named, included the well-known writers Charles Dickens and William Makepeace Thackeray; Henry Cole (without whom no committee would have been complete); the philanthropist Lord Shaftesbury; two preachers, four publishers, an industrialist, an editor and a few liberal politicians. Crucially, as it turned out, three of its members were former Chartists.

At its first meeting in May, the committee members decided that they could operate effectively only if they were recognised as an official committee of the Commission – such as the Executive Committee, formed to carry out the practical arrangements, and the Building Committee, which had chosen the design. When this request was put to the Commissioners, several expressed their fervent opposition and some reacted with outright alarm at the committee's composition: inclusiveness was all very well, but 1848 was only two years in the past, and they did not want to provide a platform for people who might rekindle the agitation of that nerve-racking time. The Prince's advisers were adamant that it would be improper and damaging for him to associate himself formally with a body that included populists and even potential socialists.

So Dickens, Cole, Wilberforce and the rest were told no, they could not have that formal recognition, although Albert, who was personally keen that the committee should be effective, told Cole that they could say that they had the Commission's blessing and sanction. This was not enough for those members – Dickens prominent among them – who had always doubted the Commission's real commitment to working-class interests. When the committee met in early June, Dickens proposed that it should dissolve itself, on the grounds that without formal recognition 'it can neither efficiently render the services it seeks to perform, nor command the confidence of the working classes'. The resolution was carried and the committee disbanded. The question of how to meet the needs of working-class visitors remained, for the time being, unanswered.

Soon afterwards Colonel Lloyd, who was continuing his nationwide promotional tour, sent a dispatch to Lord Granville from Stockport, in the cotton manufacturing district, that shows how uneasy he and members of his class still felt about wooing the workers:

> I see or think I see a strong and selfish feeling among these classes which it is very important to be guarded in meddling with, that they may not be betrayed into an undue opinion of their own importance and power. So long as the co-operation of the working classes is under perfectly manageable control and thoroughly and entirely subordinate to the mayors and local committees, much kindly feeling will only result and nothing but good will come of it: but a very little oversight and a very little mismanagement may cause great mischief and erect into sudden importance a vast power which may not be reducible again to its proper limits after the Exhibition shall have passed away.

So far, he went on, he had managed to contain the threat by channelling all the demands of the working class through the local committees, but he was not confident that this would always be effective. 'I should therefore feel much relieved in having your opinions and personal instructions to sanction my future conduct in matters bearing upon this subject.' He concluded by expressing a fear that popular lecturers who had been engaged by the Commission to arouse the interest of the masses were 'a dangerous material' and could not necessarily be relied upon.

The point was taken. Granville forwarded Lloyd's letter to Colonel Charles Grey, who had succeeded Phipps as Prince Albert's secretary, adding that he had himself warned Lloyd of the dangers of communicating too freely with the working classes. He also agreed with him about the lecturers, and said no more would be assigned until they had been properly approved. The following month, back in Stockport again, Lloyd reported that, instead of lecturers, he had proposed that 'one or two of the most intelligent and trustworthy of the better class of operatives and manufacturers shall read up some of the great speeches and address the meeting on the objects and advantages of the Exhibition'. A much safer option.

Some thoughtful citizens were less fearful of political uprisings during the following summer than of widespread moral and physical degeneration caused by such a potent mixture of people coming together in one place. The magazine *John Bull* warned:

> The influx of large masses of visitors, whose moral standard in their own homes is considerably below our own, whose passions will, moreover, be set loose and their temptations multiplied in a foreign land, cannot fail to produce . . . an amount of demoralisation which it is frightful to contemplate . . . We

have invited the pestilence into our dwellings, and we shall have to submit to its ravages.

The magazine went on to stress that the threat of pestilence was not merely metaphorical: 'The want of personal cleanliness and the less salubrious habits of life which are known to be prevalent among foreigners will aggravate the evil; dissipation and immorality will add to its virulence.'

An anonymous pamphlet called 'The Philosopher's Mite', addressed to the Commissioners, went into still more alarming detail about the dangers:

> Great, sudden human gatherings, domiciliated in a confined space, are liable to be followed by pestilence . . . The overcrowded vessels which convey your visitors are equally well calculated to be the prologue to the tragedy . . . No history, no poetry, no national code, no religion exists without some allusion to the danger of vast multitudes. . . Since the time of Edward III we know of no invitation to foreigners so unlimited as that of your committee.

The Times, which had swung back to support the Exhibition almost as soon as the Crystal Palace was chosen to house it, poked fun at such health scares, asking in an editorial:

> Is it to be the plague of 1666, the sweating sickness of Henry VII's reign, or the yellow fever, or the cholera of last year, or the camp diarrhoea, or the gaol fever or the influenza? . . . Are we to expect that from 1851 such disorders as leprosy, elephantiasis, goitre and the various complaints hitherto ascribed to particular diets will be naturalised amongst us? Again, how is

the disease or the diseases to come? By personal contact with diseased foreigners, by the poisoning of the
atmosphere, by a stroke of divine displeasure, or
how?

Yet even if such fears were laughable, there remained the
practical issue of how to deal with the influx of horny-handed
visitors. One of several letters to the newspapers on the matter
speculated that they would be accommodated in crowded,
unwholesome lodgings, endangering their health and morals,
or even 'compelled to sleep in the open air or to seek shelter in
the established haunts of begging and profligacy'.

Several suggestions were put to the Commission. Two
businessmen wrote a long letter proposing to establish a
Visitors' Aid, Accommodation and Protection Society to look
after 'provincialists and foreigners' coming to London for
possibly the first time. They wrote that, without such an
organisation, 'it is evident that much confusion will arise'. The
strangers, if they had not made previous arrangements, would
be prey to robbers and fraudsters. The proposed society would
provide guides at railway stations who would take them to
approved accommodation and sell them food at fair prices.
Their scheme appears to have been abandoned, however, and
at the end of the month the Commission appointed Alexander
Redgrave, a civil servant at the Factory Office (part of the
Home Office), to look into ways of ensuring that working-
class visitors were properly accommodated and kept away
from trouble.

After some three weeks in the job, Redgrave came up with
a plan of action. The central principle, he maintained, was to
make arrangements for keeping order 'without the appearance
of any ostensible precautions'. He proposed to seek discussions with the railway companies on means of controlling

the numbers of people carried each day on cheap excursions. The Commission should establish its own register of lodgings with fixed rates, and have its own guides at railway stations. The principal aim was to keep 'the attention of visitors well and truly occupied' lest their thoughts should turn to anti-social acts.

In November, Colonel Lloyd, encouraged by his success in curbing the workers' perilous passions in Stockport, wrote to Granville offering to work in tandem with Redgrave to head off any impending threats of disorder. With so many 'operatives and other classes' congregated together, he wrote, there were sure to be disputes, dissatisfaction and quarrels over real or imagined slights. He proposed himself as a kind of people's ombudsman who could be looked to for redress and protection: 'I have thought from my knowledge of their character, and how far a kind word in time goes with them and disarms them, that I might be useful in this way.' And he added a postscript: 'I am accustomed to speak both Spanish and French.'

Granville was dubious. He wrote to Grey: 'I doubt Col. Lloyd being the best person to appoint as the representative of the Commission for the protection of the lower classes. He is very intelligent and zealous, but a little over-anxious *de faire parler de lui.*' He pointed out that, in any case, Redgrave had not asked for help, but was actively engaged in putting flesh on his plan to recruit official guides.

When Redgrave reported to the Commissioners on the matter in December, he felt he should begin by explaining the caring philosophy behind his proposals:

It is now admitted that the duties of a government include a solicitude, and the exercise of an active yet cautious influence on fostering and expressing an

> interest for the social well-being of the people, in
> promoting their intellectual amusements or in
> elevating the public taste.

Therefore the guides – he suggested they should be retired policemen or ex-servicemen – should be ready not just to take visitors to lodging houses, but also to advise them on what they should do and see during their stay, in addition to visiting the Exhibition. This would prevent them becoming 'stragglers, wandering about the street, making repeated inquiries', and thus 'the annoyance which they might cause, if left to their own resources, would be entirely prevented'. To further assist them, attractions such as the Tower of London should extend their opening hours and reduce the price of admission. The people must and will have amusements.

Granville broadly agreed, but identified a pitfall. In a letter to Grey, he wrote: 'It would place extra responsibility on the Commissioners if any of the guides appointed by them play tricks and are discovered cheating the country visitors.'

Ideally, the Commissioners would have liked to locate a large building where cheap beds could be provided, where they could direct out-of-town visitors with limited means. As they were pondering this, Owen Jones, the architect who had been appointed superintendent of the Exhibition, was approached by Thomas Harrisson, owner of a furniture depository in Ranelagh Road, close to the Thames in Pimlico and a little over a mile from Hyde Park. Harrisson wondered whether he could make a little money by storing the cases in which the exhibits arrived, so they could be used again when the show was over. Jones put it to him that it would be a lot more useful if he could convert his premises to a large dormitory for short-stay visitors. Harrisson said he would look into it if the Executive Committee gave him official backing.

When the proposal was put to the committee, they replied that they could not make any financial commitment, but they undertook to list the hostel in their proposed accommodation register and to brief their guides to direct visitors there. With those assurances, Harrisson felt justified in getting to work on converting the warehouse to dormitories for a thousand people. It included a dining room and kitchen, a bar, a smoking room and a reading room with newspapers. There were good washing facilities and a doctor would attend every morning – all for 1s 3d per person per night.

Redgrave went to inspect the premises on behalf of the Commission, and declared himself satisfied. But he found other landlords reluctant to place their accommodation on any official register because it would mean setting prices in advance. As he noted in a memo in March: 'People think there will be plenty of demand and they will be able to set their own terms when the time comes.' Some agreed to be listed in a periodical publication called *The Circulator*, put out by John Cassell, a former carpenter and reformed alcoholic (his father was a publican), who published magazines and journals for a working-class readership, principally the *Working Man's Friend and Popular Instructor*. In *The Circulator* he gave details of accommodation at a range of prices from £6 a week to 1s 3d a night. Several hundred rooms in private homes were listed at this lowest price – the same as Harrisson was charging – plus 9d for breakfast (bacon or eggs 3d extra).

Rather than being herded together like soldiers in a barracks, most working-class visitors preferred to stay with families, even though private homes offered fewer facilities. Only one other hostel apart from Harrisson's appears to have been established, close to Millbank Prison where the Tate Britain art gallery now stands. It offered 200 beds, for men only, and advertised that 'the sleeping apartments are fitted up in the same style as emigrants' ships' and that 'a night watchman is engaged to assist the men and prevent disputes'. Reading that, potential customers could be forgiven for thinking that they would be more comfortable staying privately.

The magazine *The Builder* pointed out that the 'Mechanics' Home', as Harrisson called his hostel, was not especially attractive, and wished a brighter spot had been chosen: 'The men from the coal districts will not discover that they have left them; and to find their way home alone after dark will be quite out of the question.' The place was scarcely ever more than a quarter full, and by the end of 1851 Harrisson was all but ruined. After making several petitions to the Commissioners for compensation, he was finally awarded £1,000 – about a quarter of the sum he claimed to have lost.

In September 1850 Redgrave met representatives of the railway companies to try to regulate the flow of excursionists. He was keen that the very lowest fares should be offered only to members of organised groups – mechanics' institutes, working men's associations and travelling clubs, such as had been organised in Bradford and by now in some other towns. The railway executives balked at that, pointing out that they were planning to introduce excursion return fares for the same price as a normal single ticket – about a penny a mile, with reductions for longer distances. With such rock-bottom fares they would need to fill nearly every seat on the train, so they could not turn away customers who happened not to belong to the clubs, which in any case were not yet as numerous as Redgrave and the Commissioners had hoped. The operators promised only to provide special trains for clubs if at least 250 members travelled at the same time, and they agreed that the excursion fares would not come into effect until 1 July.

That final concession – which in the event they did not

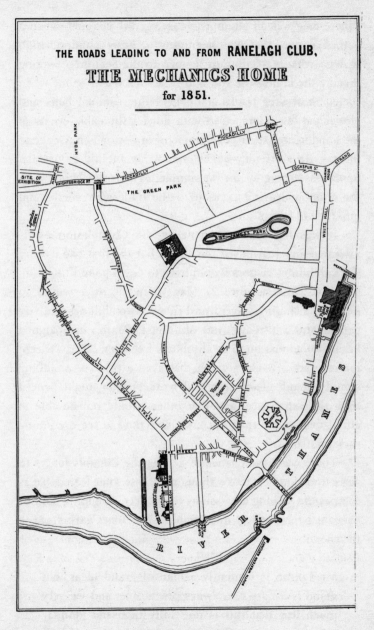

The Mechanics' Home.

adhere to – was an attempt to ease a grave concern, albeit a parochial one, that was beginning to beset London's high society: what was going to happen to the Season? Covering broadly the months of May and June, this was the time when society hostesses traditionally held their annual balls and dinner parties, interspersed with other fashionable events in the London area such as horse-racing at Epsom and Ascot and the regatta at Henley-on-Thames. Only in July would the upper classes migrate for the summer to their stately homes in the country, leaving London to the tradesmen, clerks and other lower orders.

It was the announcement by the Commission of its pricing policy that raised the alarm. For the first two days of the Exhibition, visitors would have to pay a pound to get in, then five shillings until 22 May, when the price would go down to a shilling, except on Fridays (two shillings and six-pence) and Saturdays (five shillings). Paxton campaigned briefly for admission to be absolutely free after 22 May, except for one day a week, arguing that even a price of a shilling would exclude many low-paid workers who might benefit from the experience, and that others would not be able to afford to go more than once; scarcely time to see everything they wanted.

There was little chance of getting the Commissioners to agree to that radical move, though, because some feared that as soon as the shilling admissions took effect, London would be overrun by swarms of undesirables. *The Times* gave voice to their fears:

> Mr Paxton is evidently a man of grand ideas; but grand ideas are not always practicable, and we very much fear that this is not. Fifty thousand Monday idlers from the manufactures of London, mixed with

a few thousand who admit of no description, would
be very awkward customers . . . The place would be at
their mercy.

In a letter to a friend, Lord Granville wrote: 'Paxton's head has
been turned by the events of the last six months, and it is not
surprising that they should have had that effect upon a self-
educated man.'

With the idea of free admission safely scotched, a campaign began for the price to be kept to five shillings until 1
July, giving the aristocracy time to enjoy the Season to the full
before making good their escape. Three months before the
Exhibition was scheduled to open, the Westminster committee
for promoting it, worried about the potential loss of business
for shopkeepers if their wealthiest customers fled the capital
in May or June, sent a memorandum to the Commissioners.
While insisting that they welcomed the decision to make the
Exhibition accessible to as wide a range of people as possible,
they could not 'shut their eyes to the very great influx of the
operative classes . . . and the consequent likelihood of the
higher orders quitting'.

Some, they maintained, had already made arrangements to
do just that. 'Any step which tends to shorten the so-called
London Season will prove greatly injurious to many and ruinous to other tradesmen.' However, the committee in neighbouring Marylebone sent a counter-memorandum, saying that
to delay cheap admissions would be unpopular with the lower
classes and prejudice the Exhibition's success. That view prevailed. The Commissioners refused to change the date; so the
Season would have to take its chance.

The shopkeepers' fears proved unfounded. So great was
the influx of visitors that they all enjoyed a bumper summer
for trade. Indeed, at least one of London's most famous

shopkeepers built his success to a large extent on profits made in the summer of 1851. He was Charles Harrod, who in 1849 had taken over Burden's grocery store in Knightsbridge, then a village a few hundred yards south-west of Hyde Park. It was a modest shop, built some ten years earlier over the front garden of a terraced house and barely breaking even. But the influx of visitors to the Crystal Palace put the business in a strong financial position. A few years later Harrod was able to acquire surrounding properties and increase the range of goods sold, laying the foundations of one of the most famous department stores in the world, which still bears his name.

As well as trying to head off ruffians and troublemakers, the Commissioners had another social scourge to consider: the so-called 'gentlemen' of the press. Like other ruling classes before and since, the powers-that-be regarded a free press as a tre-mendous nuisance – unscrupulous, irresponsible, mis-chievous and cavalier with the facts. Already the newspapers had managed to stir up endless controversies about the plans for the Exhibition, and would doubtless continue in that vein as the opening drew near, and probably for the entire run. In late December the *Morning Chronicle* had published an article abusing Lord Seymour, the Commissioner of Works and a government colleague of Lord Granville, who wrote to Colonel Grey expressing his distaste for reporters. They were only too glad to pick up information from contacts that was either incorrect or 'if correct not of a nature to be made public'.

As a result of this, Granville proposed excluding journal-ists from the Crystal Palace while it was under construction, and making them pay for admission like everyone else after the Exhibition opened. Henry Cole was horrified, and wrote in his memoirs:

I urged that this would be an unprecedented step. The interest of the Exhibition was to attract the press to come and report on everything that was going on as much as possible. Instead of making the Press pay for admittance, the very reverse [sic] would be the safer policy in my opinion, and I entreated the Commissioners not to make so fatal and suicidal a rule. A member of the Commission exclaimed: 'Alas! We are a press-ridden people!' and then the Commissioners present gave up the proposal.

On 11 February, Cole reported triumphantly, Granville agreed to admit an artist from the *Illustrated London News* – and the highly favourable press coverage was an important factor in the Exhibition's success.

The trepidation of the London élite concerning revolution, disaster, disease, the excesses of the yellow press and general inconvenience continued right up to the Exhibition's opening day. It was making potential foreign visitors nervous too. King Ernest Augustus of Hanover wrote a dire warning to his cousin, Frederick William IV of Prussia, advising him not to let his son go through with a planned visit to the Exhibition:

I hear that the ministers as well as Prince Albert are beginning to jibber with anxiety over this rubbishy Exhibition . . . I am not easily given to panicking, but I confess to you that I would not like anyone belonging to me exposed to the imminent perils of these times. Letters from London tell me that the ministers will not allow the Queen and the great originator of this folly, Prince Albert, to be in London while the Exhibition is on.

When Frederick William passed on these concerns to Albert, he received a witheringly ironic reply from the Prince Consort:

> Mathematicians have calculated that the Crystal Palace will blow down in the first strong gale; engineers that the galleries would crash in and destroy the visitors; political economists have prophesied a scarcity of food in London owing to the vast concourse of people; doctors that owing to so many races coming into contact with each other the Black Death of the Middle Ages would make its appearance as it did after the Crusades; moralists that England would be infected by all the scourges of the civilised and uncivilised world; theologians that the second Tower of Babel would draw upon it the vengeance of the offended God.
>
> I can give no guarantee against these perils, nor am I in a position to assume responsibility for the possibly menaced lives of your royal relatives.

And on 15 April, two weeks before the opening, he wrote to his grandmother:

> I am more dead than alive from overwork. The opponents of the Exhibition work with might and main to throw all the old women into panic and drive myself crazy. The strangers, they give out, are certain to commence a thorough revolution here, to murder Victoria and myself and to proclaim the Red Republic in England; the plague is certain to ensue from the confluence of such vast multitudes, and to swallow up those whom the increased price of everything has not already swept away. For all this I am

responsible, and against all this I have to make efficient provision.

He was not exaggerating. Some members of the aristocracy remained implacable to the end. Lady Lyttelton, whose husband had been Under-Secretary of State for the Colonies, wrote of the Exhibition: 'I believe it is quite universally sneered at and abominated by the *beau monde*, and will only increase the contempt for the Prince among all fine folk. But so would anything he does.'

❧ ❧

CHAPTER FOUR

MIRACLE IN HYDE PARK

Great Britain offers a hospitable invitation to all the
nations of the world, to collect and display the
choicest fruits of their industry in her capital;
and the invitation is freely accepted by every
civilised people, because the interest of both the guest
and the host is felt to be reciprocal.

Henry Cole, *Fifty Years of Public Work* (1884)

The first batch of iron columns that would support the Crystal Palace were delivered to Hyde Park on Saturday 7 September 1850, from the iron works at Dudley in the Midlands. Before the end of the month a large wooden hoarding (later incorporated into the floor of the building) had been placed around the Exhibition site, the first of the iron pillars had been put in place and some three hundred men were hard at work – a figure that would rise within weeks to more than two thousand. Every day a large crowd of unemployed labourers gathered near the entrance, hoping to be given work.

Numerous dignitaries visited the site and had their names duly recorded in the *Morning Chronicle*. Eventually there were so many that they hindered the work, and Fox and Henderson, the contractors, levied a five-shilling admission charge to keep the numbers down, the money going to a compensation fund for injured workers. Still an average of eighty people a day dipped into their pockets for the privilege of visiting the world's most intriguing construction site. The contractors were adamant that the building would be sufficiently advanced to hand over to the Commissioners on New Year's Day. *The Times* was awestruck. 'It took three hundred years to build St Peter's in Rome and thirty years to build St Paul's. This is taking three months.'

With the building under way, the Commissioners had to turn their attention towards what was to fill it. Since this was to be the first international exhibition on such a scale any-where, there was no precedent for soliciting overseas contri-butions. The initial plan to lure exhibitors with the offer of substantial cash prizes had been dropped because of the ex-pense, so all that could now be offered was the prestige of winning medals – but weighing against that was the possibility of embarrassment if your most prized products failed to catch the eye of the award juries. The need to interest foreign gov-ernments as well as British manufacturers had been the prime motive for inviting so many overseas diplomats to the Mansion House banquet in March. Most had responded with enthusiasm, and this was being followed up by pressure from British envoys abroad.

As early as May 1850 the signs had been good. Sir Benjamin Hall, the MP for Marylebone and a keen supporter of the project, told a meeting in his constituency that most European countries had responded favourably. The Russians were forming two commissions to choose what to send over, the Spanish and United States governments had already offered free transit for shipping their countries' goods to London, and the Governor of New York was among several US dignitaries who had expressed their intention of crossing the Atlantic for the occasion. At the same meeting, another MP, William Mackinnon, dismissed suggestions that British goods would suffer by comparison with those from overseas: 'It is the foreigner's peculiar genius to invent, while the British do not so much invent as bring things to perfection.' In not a single category, he believed, would Britain be outclassed.

A letter in *The Times* a few days later, from an anonymous London manufacturer, confirmed that there was no evidence of an inferiority complex afflicting British industry: 'It is by no means certain, except in a few manufactures of taste and luxury, that there will be any superiority on the part of foreigners; while in all that appertains to supplying the wants of the million and the middle classes, British manufacturers are unrivalled.' While he conceded that British fabric designers lagged behind their overseas rivals, he thought they would benefit from being able to assess the competition without the expense of travelling abroad. And he warned potential customers for foreign goods, especially furniture, that the quality of workmanship of the samples on display would almost certainly not be sustained in the products as supplied to buyers.

Opponents of the Exhibition were worried not only by the threat of outside competition, but also by the prospect of unscrupulous foreigners taking the chance to steal British ideas. A satirical ditty called 'Song of the Pirates Preparing for the Exhibition of 1851' put it baldly:

> The country clowns think their inventions
> Will make them rich when once but known.
> They little dream of our intentions
> To make their secret mines our own.

Despite the eagerness of many overseas governments to put on a good show, the reaction of foreign manufacturers was mixed. Some saw it as a chance to establish themselves in the lucrative

British market – a view expressed particularly powerfully in the *New York Herald*:

> Although England has her own private motives for getting up this Exhibition, we are convinced that this Republic will profit by it more than she will. She wants peace, so do we. But can it be possible that a nation, overburdened as she is with a national debt of a magnitude almost beyond computation – with a government of the most expensive description; with a nest of non-producers, in the shape of aristocrats, eating away at its vitality; with corruption pervading every fibre and muscle of the body politic – can compete with a young, vigorous, athletic, powerful Republic like the United States of America? We should think not.

Despite such chauvinism, the United States failed to fill all its allotted space, partly because of difficulties in transporting goods across the huge country. Other overseas exhibitors fell short due to a simple lack of enthusiasm. A Chinese official responded to the invitation with a refusal couched in philosophical terms. Since the excellence of a product depended upon the individual talent and genius of its creator, he wrote, it would be inappropriate for any government to attempt to persuade people to enter such a competition. However, anyone in China who wished to submit goods would not be deterred from doing so.

Faced with this inscrutable response, the Commissioners drummed up some Chinese exhibits from British travellers and merchants who had visited the country and brought goods back with them. Several of the items from India and other eastern countries were similarly drawn from British collections. Some countries declined to have anything to do with the Exhibition at all: Venezuela, Persia, Hong Kong and Prince Edward's Island were among those that rejected the invitation.

International exhibitors raised problems that had not been foreseen but that had to be dealt with somehow. The Swiss, for instance, were keen to exhibit their famous cheeses, but were worried about keeping them in good condition. George Prevost, the Agent-General for Switzerland, wrote a plaintive note to John Scott Russell, secretary to the Commission, enquiring about storage facilities for cheeses in the Crystal Palace. Would there be cellars on the site? (Plainly not, given the nature of the building.) Would the exhibitors be allowed to withdraw cheeses should they become over-ripe, and replace them with fresh examples? And could the juries judge cheeses during the early part of the Exhibition, when they would be in their prime?

Russell passed the query to Sir John Bowring, a renowned traveller and linguist, who had been recruited by the Commission to smooth relations with foreign exhibitors. He in turn sought expert advice from a Commissioner, Philip Pusey, who had founded the Royal Agricultural Society in 1840 and was chairman of the juries in two classes – machinery, and products from the vegetable kingdom. Pusey replied that cheese, clearly a product of the animal kingdom, did not qualify for inclusion in the two juries he was heading. There was a class for 'substances used as food' but the guiding principle was that there would have to be something unusual about their ingredients or manufacturing technique to qualify for admission. British farmers had not been told that cheese was admissible, and might justly complain if foreign producers were allowed to show theirs.

He did not want to be dogmatic, though, and proposed a

formula whereby cheeses could be admitted if the Commissioners were keen. 'These cheeses proceed probably from
unusual sources as from sheep and goats, so that under that
head they might be admitted.' The Swiss could be assured
that judging would take place before the opening of the
Exhibition to the public, so the juries would confront their
cheeses at their freshest. As for withdrawing them when they
became over-ripe, that should be left to the discretion of the
exhibitors: there was no need to make a universal ruling on
withdrawal when some cheeses, such as Parmesan, would
last for the duration. And just to make sure nobody would be
put out, he added this postscript: 'If it be decided to admit
cheeses generally, it would be easy to let the circumstance be
known to the English farmers even now, so as to prevent
complaint.'

In the end the Commissioners declared cheese inadmiss-
ible, along with butter (although according to the catalogue,
the French seem to have slipped some of that in) and ex-
plosives. The 273 Swiss exhibits included chocolate by
Suchard, preserved meats, hundreds of watches and clocks,
yards of silk ribbon and a paper model of Strasbourg Cathedral
made with a penknife. Outside the refreshment rooms, the
Crystal Palace would be a cheese-free zone – probably to the
great relief of visitors on the hottest summer days.

The national agents for the foreign exhibitors raised all
kinds of difficulties in their attempts to gain the maximum
benefit from their participation. Arguments about the extent
and positioning of the space allotted them became frequent,
with the French especially hard to assuage. Luckily Lord
Granville, who had the task of smoothing things over, was a
suave, practised diplomat, having served at the Foreign Office
and in the Paris embassy. In March, six weeks before the
scheduled opening, he had a meeting with a number of the

agents to discuss their concerns, and reported on it wryly to Colonel Grey:

> I received a deputation of foreign agents this morning – the Austrian shrewd and businesslike, the Saxon silent, the Prussian intelligent and obsequious, the Frenchman volubility itself, exciting the indignation of his colleagues by his superior speed in talking his own language, and the American, with supreme contempt for the others, not caring for or understanding one word they said.

The first of the 6,556 overseas exhibits, from St Petersburg in Russia, arrived in London on 12 October 1850, nearly three weeks before the closing date for applications for space. In November the first consignment arrived from Prussia – exhibiting with other German states under the name of the Zollverein, their nineteenth-century customs union. Most foreign countries were allotted as many square feet as they thought they could fill – with the exception of the French, who asked for three times their original allotment. Even though they did not get all of it, they were still by far the biggest overseas exhibitors.

The British section, despite filling half the total area of the Crystal Palace, was also oversubscribed. In all, 8,200 exhibitors had requested 420,000 square feet of floor space – about twenty-five per cent more than was available – and 200,000 feet of hanging space. Only 7,381 British exhibitors could be accommodated, and most of the local committees had to settle for less floor space than they wanted, so some aspiring exhibitors were disappointed.

At that early stage the local committees did not have to specify exactly what their area's representatives would be showing. In September the Commissioners issued an appeal for exhibits – including minerals and produce – that were characteristic of particular regions. For the 'substances used as food' category they cited hops from southern England, dried medicinal herbs from Surrey, canary seed from the Isle of Thanet and mustard from Durham. They also sought jets and agates from coastal areas and rock crystals from the mountains.

Some categories of manufacture initially fell short of expectations. A week before entries closed, the press was reporting that, while there had been a huge response from the makers of machinery of all kinds, there was a shortage of items including army caps, rocking horses, walking sticks, mackintoshes and iron bedsteads. A call for more examples of cotton goods, hosiery, gloves and cutlery went out at another big dinner for mayors in late October, this time hosted by the Mayor of York as a return fixture for the Mansion House extravaganza in the spring. Prince Albert and the other Commissioners were guests of honour, and the food was prepared by Alexis Soyer, who had become London's most renowned French chef in his twelve years at the Reform Club. Among his delicacies was a concoction of turtles and ortolans (small birds eaten whole) reputed to have cost a hundred guineas: York was unwilling to be outshone by London in the matter of sophisticated gastronomy.

Although the opening was still six months away, public excitement was growing. The papers were giving more and more space to the forthcoming event, and music-hall artists were writing songs about it. Advertisements were already appearing for the sheet music of pieces celebrating the occasion, including the Great Exhibition Polka, the Great Exhibition Waltz and the Great Exhibition Quadrille. Dozens more would follow. The nation was working itself up into a party mood.

* * *

At the end of November came a hiccup in the construction of the Crystal Palace. It began on the evening of Friday 22 November, when one of the glaziers, William St Clair, called a meeting of all the men working on the site. St Clair was an archetypal *agent provocateur* who appeared to have secured himself a job there specifically to rally the workers. He had brought himself to the attention of Charles Fox, the principal partner in the contracting firm, by writing him a job application that included a loyal verse praising the Exhibition. Safely on the payroll, he began immediately to stir up trouble. He told his co-workers that the money being offered for placing the 293,655 sheets of glass between the glazing bars was unacceptably low. The rate was four shillings a day, provided that the worker affixed fifty-eight panes of glass in that time: if he managed fewer, he would be paid proportionately less; if more, he would get more.

St Clair maintained that the men could not fulfil the fifty-eight-pane norm without skimping the work, with the result that the Crystal Palace would not be watertight. He thought a more realistic figure would be about forty-four a day which, at the going rate, would have meant a daily rate of three shillings. He wanted that to be increased to five shillings, or sixpence an hour, regardless of how many panes were put in; and for good measure he sought a longer lunch break than the allotted half-hour. When he suggested these changes the site manager rejected them out of hand, and the persuasive St Clair managed to get thirty of his fellow workers to strike the following day.

The men were customarily paid on Saturdays, at the end of the working day. Fox and Henderson had devised an elaborate system to ensure that the method of payment was smooth and comparatively quick. When each workman was engaged he was given a number, and at the end of every working day he was handed three brass tokens bearing that number. The following day he would hand in one token every time he reported for work – in the morning, after the breakfast break and after lunch. On Saturday each man's tokens would be counted (and, in the case of the glaziers, his productivity assessed) and he would be paid accordingly. In other words, if he had missed a session of work, he would not be paid for it.

When all these calculations had been made on Saturday evening, a bell would be rung and the men would gather around a booth which served as the pay office, waiting for their number to be called. On 23 November, though, when the bell rang, the men, instead of gathering round the booth, demonstrated their support for the strikers by singing the National Anthem, followed by 'Rule, Britannia!', laying special emphasis on the line: 'Britons never will be slaves'.

St Clair called a meeting of the workers at the Ennismore Arms, a public house that had been built a few years earlier as part of the new residential development at Ennismore Gardens, immediately south of the park entrance nearest to the Crystal Palace. (The pub was destroyed by bombing in 1940.) About 150 of them turned up. As a result of the meeting a letter was drafted to the Commissioners, pleading the cause of 'these loyal men, the bone, sinew and glory of Old England', and another, more outspoken, to Charles Fox: 'Sir, this is to inform you that unless you consult me as to the proposal of your manager Mr Cochrane [on rates of pay], the following advertisement shall appear in the public papers tomorrow.' The advertisement, addressed to Prince Albert and the Commissioners, stated that the work at the Crystal Palace was being botched, that the structure would be unsafe, and that the nation would be disgraced. After quoting the text, St Clair went on to assure Fox that this did not amount to an attempt at intimidation but 'the candid advice of one of your workmen and one who has the honour to be a gentleman as well as a glazier . . . I tell you Mr Cochrane's grasping will destroy your character and our building'. Fox's reply was succinct: 'If you like to work for us according to the terms of [our] proposal, well: if not, you can leave the work.'

The local police superintendent, hearing of the gathering at the Ennismore Arms, sent two constables round there in case of trouble. They reported that, although the men appeared to be in an excitable state, there was no sign of any disturbance. At five a.m. on Monday, before the workers were due to arrive, police went to Hyde Park, fearing that the strikers would form picket lines; but most of the men arrived at work unmolested by the thirty hard-core activists. Later that day St Clair was arrested and charged with sending Fox a threatening letter. The striking glaziers were dismissed and replaced by others, some of them French.

There is no record of any other labour dispute interrupting the construction. Indeed, only two weeks after the strike, when the Commission met for the first time in the shell of the emerging building, the 2,000 workers all left their posts as Prince Albert was departing and, to demonstrate their loyalty to him and to the project, gave him a hearty cheer. As he left, a brewer's dray drew up carrying 250 gallons of beer. 'As if by instinct,' *The Times* reported, 'they [the labourers] recognised that the grateful supply was for them.' The relationship between masters and servants was back to normal.

Since this was the first event of its kind that any of the organisers had been involved with, everything had to be thought through from first principles, from the provision of refreshments to toilet facilities. As regards food and drink, the Commissioners had received some unsolicited but valuable advice in July in a letter from Dr John Lindley, a botanist and former assistant secretary of the Horticultural Society. He disclosed that when he had first organised the society's annual shows at its garden in Chiswick, west London (the precursors of today's Chelsea Flower Show), he decided that cold meat, poultry and wine should be on sale, 'but we found that many of our visitors thought more of eating and drinking than of the objects in the exhibition, and that the garden was converted into an eating-house, with just such consequences as might have been anticipated from the presence of wine, etc.'.

The Horticultural Society's answer had been to limit refreshments to ices, cakes, lemonade, orangeade and iced water.

> We do not now suffer any meat or wine or spirituous liquors to pass our gates, and the consequence has been that the serious inconveniences formerly felt have disappeared. It is true that our visitors were a much mixed class, yet certainly not more mixed than those to be expected in 1851 must of necessity be . . . It is no doubt desirable that something should be provided, but the articles usually to be found in a confectioner's shop – liqueurs, etc., excepted – are all that can be required. To those who want more substantial enjoyment there will, no doubt, be abundant accommodation on the outside of the park.

The Commissioners took all this to heart when they sought tenders for the supply of refreshments in three sections of the Crystal Palace. One, in the very centre of the building, would be in the nature of a tea room, serving ices, pastries, sandwiches, patties, fruit, tea, coffee, chocolate, cocoa, lemonade, seltzer and soda water. The other two would have a more limited range of foods – principally bread, butter and cheese –

with the same drinks plus ginger beer and spruce beer. Prices would have to be moderate. There would be no cooked food, the only heating mechanism being for the drinks.

The chosen caterer would be expected to provide free drinking water to visitors but no alcoholic drinks would be served: 'It would be inconsistent with the nature of the Exhibition to allow the building to assume the character of an hotel, tavern or dining rooms.' This stipulation was criticised by *Punch*, which asserted that it discriminated against foreigners who, being more accustomed to wines and strong drink than the British, were more moderate in its consumption and became intoxicated less often. In any case, the ban did not prevent visitors from bringing their own beer and spirits in with them.

The Commission further ruled that strict standards of behaviour would be imposed on the catering staff, and waiters found guilty of overcharging or incivility would be dismissed instantly. The contract was won, with a bid of £5,500, by Schweppes, the carbonated drinks company founded half a century earlier by Jacob Schweppe, a Swiss jeweller. While nobody complained about the beverages, the quality of the food and service was, perhaps inevitably, the butt of criticism from visitors.

The provision of public lavatories, both inside the Crystal Palace and elsewhere in London, was altogether more difficult. The capital was a chronically unhygienic place. Cholera and typhus were regular summer visitors, the Thames stank and no modern sewer system had yet been constructed. The Metropolitan Sewers Act of 1848 had authorised the Commissioners of Sewers to install lavatories in public places, but scarcely any had yet been opened. The public, if in dire need, had to continue their former habit of using facilities in hotels, public houses and cake shops, where they were expected to buy something in return. Those who could not afford to do that were forced to improvise, to the annoyance of themselves and their fellow citizens.

A leading advocate of public lavatories was Joseph Bazalgette, a young civil engineer who would later find fame as the creator of the sewer system that London needed so badly. In March 1849 he wrote to the Sewers Commissioners with a heartfelt plea to bring to those who traversed the city's streets 'relief from frequent personal inconvenience and occasional pain, if not physical injury'. He enclosed a map marking suitable positions for buildings that would combine four urinals and three water closets, one of the water closets to be 'private' and accessible only to those willing to pay a fee for greater comfort. Only the private cubicle would include a washbasin.

He envisaged that the management of these establishments would be franchised to attendants who would make their money from the hire of the private WC and the sale of toilet paper. They would be manned during opening hours and locked at other times. The boldest part of Bazalgette's plan was that the urine deposited should be stored and sold to farmers and market gardeners to be used as a fertiliser. This operation would be in the hands of the Sewers Commission and the proceeds used to defray construction costs. Nothing if not thorough, he had loitered around the few public urinals in London to note their rate of use. Based on an average deposit of half a pint per person, and taking the best advice on its market value, he thought that each urinal could produce £48 worth a year. Even taking into account the cost of water carts and horses to take the stuff away, sixty urinals could turn an annual profit of £1,280, or about ten per cent of the estimated construction cost of £11,770. 'There can be no doubt that the result must eventually prove a decidedly profitable speculation.'

But the Sewers Commission failed to respond even to such an enticing and carefully costed prospect, and by the end of 1850 little progress had been made towards ending the pain and inconvenience of London's pedestrians. That November the Commissioners received a letter signed by eighty-four eminent figures, including Henry Cole, urging that steps be taken to provide proper public amenities before the expected influx the following May of 'numerous foreigners, who are accustomed to the use of such conveniences in their own capitals'.

The Commissioners replied that they had been trying to find suitable sites for 154 urinals, but so far had identified only four or five, and wondered whether the petitioners had any suggestions. Naturally enough, residents and shopkeepers were reluctant to have them near their premises. The petitioners replied in a second letter signed by still more worthies, including Charles Dickens and Thomas Carlyle. It proposed that urinals could be installed in men's tailors and cigar shops, and in the entrances or courtyards of public buildings. Water closets for women, who of course were unable to use urinals, should also be established, perhaps within the kind of shops that they frequented, such as staymakers and bonnet makers. The amenities should be of 'a decidedly superior character' to the handful of public urinals that then existed – at least as comfortable as those being provided in the new railway stations.

In March a letter to the press from 'A Stout Gentleman' made the same point:

> London is the worst provided city in Europe with such temporary conveniences. If something is not done at once, before the crowds of foreign visitors arrive . . . scenes of a gross character will be incessantly occurring. Our wives and daughters will

be unable to venture out of doors, and the police will be fully occupied with the most absurd, though disgusting office of keeping foreigners in order, while the doors, porticos and railings of our squares will become receptacles of impurity.

And how could he be sure of this? 'I have resided too many years in various parts of the Continent to believe otherwise.'

As it turned out, the Exhibition proved a catalyst for the provision of public lavatories. George Jennings, a sanitary engineer based in Southwark, had made several ingenious experiments in the emerging technology of flush toilets, including one with a built-in bidet, and was an advocate of public provision. In commending his ideas to the Commissioners, he wrote:

I know the subject is a peculiar one, and very difficult to handle, but no false delicacy ought to prevent immediate attention being given to matters affecting the health and comfort of the thousands who daily throng the thoroughfares of your city... I am convinced the day will come when Halting Stations complete with every convenience will be constructed in all localities where numbers assemble.

For the Crystal Palace, Jennings designed both urinals and what he called 'monkey closets' for the use of visitors at a penny a time. (Some say that the euphemism 'to spend a penny' originated at this time, but this need not necessarily be the case, since the price remained at that level for many years.) He is also credited with the idea of placing urinals in a circle round a central pillar, to save space, and of siting them underground in city centres. The drawings in his catalogue of these tasteful and decorative items of street furniture sometimes include a man coming out adjusting his trousers, so as to leave no doubt about their purpose.

Over 827,000 people paid their penny to use the retiring rooms at the Exhibition, and many more men took advantage of the urinals: these being free, there was no record of the precise number. The Commissioners said that their popularity impressed everyone 'with the sufferings which must be endured by all, but more especially by females, on account of the want of them'. Jennings' design, both mechanical and decorative, was soon copied not just in the streets of London but in other cities across the world – a giant step for personal comfort and hygiene. Jennings also had an exhibit of rubber pipes and valves in the general hardware section of the Exhibition, and won a gold medal.

The press, despite the Commissioners' distaste for its inky trade, took a close and increasingly enthusiastic interest in what was going on behind the Hyde Park fence. The London daily papers printed regular reports of progress, still observing in awe that no major project had ever been constructed so rapidly. New machinery was helping to speed the construction. A device for cutting the wooden gutters on the roof turned out 2,000 feet of guttering in one day. Some twenty miles of guttering was required, and it would have taken 300 men to do the job at the same speed. Another machine was devised for cutting the 200 miles of sash bars, each of them forty-nine inches long. No glass sheets of that width had been made in Britain before. Fox himself designed an ingenious device for fitting the roof glass speedily – a glazing wagon with wheels that ran along the gutters. There were seventy-six of these, covered so that glazing could be done in all weathers. The men sat in the back and pushed the wagons backwards as they completed fitting each pane of glass. A similar machine was used to replace broken panes of glass; although once the roof's protective canvas was in place, covering everything except the transept, there were comparatively few of these.

It all made for a remarkable scene, attracting thousands of

Charles Fox's glazing wagon.

spectators. Hammers rang out as scores of workmen put together the wrought-iron roof beams, while nearby, carpenters were cutting up miles of timber strips. Three portable steam engines, driving the machinery for fashioning the hand rails and guttering, added to the noise and excitement. The most spectacular operation was hoisting the curved ribs of the transept roof into place. Because it was winter, the work often had to continue after dark, by the light of lanterns and huge bonfires of scrap timber, treating the evening traffic along Knightsbridge to a magical view.

By January, after the unfinished structure had been formally handed over to the Commissioners, the enthusiasm of the press was barely containable. *The Times* described the emerging Crystal Palace as

> a monument of the extent to which lightness of structure can be combined with permanence and strength, a building remarkable not less for size than for the beauty of mathematical proportions and rectangular outlines . . . Everything is done by the rule and yet everything is graceful, and it might almost be said grand.

But it was still a little worried about the tone of the Exhibition, whether it would 'degenerate into a huge vulgarity', quite out of keeping with the 'sober, sedate and steadfast people' (that is the British) who had initiated it.

In spite of such fears, or maybe because of them, the excitement of the press was at last being reflected among the populace all over the country. The travel clubs, which in some parts had been slow in getting off the ground, were beginning to proliferate. The thriving port city of Liverpool was a good example. At first its residents and merchants had been indifferent to the Exhibition. Theirs was not, after all, a manufacturing town, so what was in it for them? But the *Liverpool Mercury* ran a campaign in support, arguing that what was good for commerce was good for any port. And the interest of the workers was aroused by reports that a scale model of its docks was being made, complete with 1,600 lifelike ships.

In January the local Exhibition committee issued a notice that a club was being formed, with members being required to pay a shilling a week for at least three months, with no more than four weeks' arrears allowed. Both men and women would be eligible, but the committee reserved the right to exclude 'improper characters'. Interest was high and the target figure of

Raising the ribs of the transept roof.

250 – the minimum required for securing a special train – was quickly met.

By March, those newspapers that had so praised the speed and efficiency of the construction only weeks earlier began to express serious concerns over whether the Crystal Palace would be finished on schedule. It was now a race against time, with many thousands of workmen toiling day and night to meet the deadline and avoid the national disgrace of having to postpone the opening, after the months of chivvying overseas exhibitors to get their goods to Hyde Park before the deadline. Responding to the concerns of the press, the Commissioners said they were determined that the Exhibition would open on 1 May as announced, 'and if exhibitors are not ready their spaces will be enclosed with hoardings'.

The man charged with instilling a sense of urgency into the overseas exhibitors was Lieutenant Colonel Henry Owen, the Exhibition's general superintendent. *The Times* sympathised with him:

> He finds himself compelled to tell the 'go-ahead' Yankee that he is not following his national instincts fast enough . . . He must hint to the sensitive, irritable Frenchman that too much fastidiousness will prevent his opening on 1 May. The phlegm of the German must be overcome by him, the sublime composure and fatalism of the Turk disturbed and the cold and sluggish nature of the Russian warmed into action.

As the Crystal Palace neared completion, it was predictable that doubts would be raised over whether it was safe and watertight. The materials and techniques used were so novel, the building so flimsy compared with the solid brick structures favoured by the Victorians, that many feared it would not be robust enough to withstand the tens of thousands of visitors expected to pour in every day. There were particular fears about the strength of the galleries built above the main floor on all four sides of the building, where some of the exhibits were going to be displayed. Worries deepened when high winds broke several panes of glass, and a few weeks later the roof began to leak quite badly in heavy rain.

In January Digby Wyatt, Cole's companion on the 1849 Paris trip who had now been appointed secretary to the Executive Committee for the Exhibition, addressed a stormy meeting of technical experts at the Institution of Civil Engineers. After he had gone into great detail about the materials and methods of construction, several eminent figures in the audience raised points that, on the face of it, seemed quite alarming. Richard Turner, one of the architects whose glass-based design for the Exhibition building had been rejected, said that the glass Paxton was using, at a weight of sixteen ounces to the square foot, was too insubstantial, and that several London conservatories built from glass of the same strength had been destroyed in a hailstorm in 1846. Wyatt and others had argued that the public would be protected by the canvas sheets covering the roof, but Turner pointed out that they did not stretch over the whole building.

Paxton, who was also present, replied that his Chatsworth glasshouses were made of glass of only fifteen ounces to the square foot, and they had survived undamaged for ten years. Then came a scholarly intervention from the eminent Sir George Airy who, as Astronomer Royal since 1835, could be expected to know a thing or two about extreme weather. He was worried that the Crystal Palace would not stand up to the strong gales that usually hit London once or twice a year, packing a punch amounting to between twenty and twenty-five pounds per square foot of vertical surface. He thought the

weakest parts of the structure were not the glass panels themselves but the 'snugs' that joined the vertical columns to the
horizontal girders, and the concrete slabs into which the columns were sunk, which could easily be uprooted in a strong
wind. After a dazzling display of mathematical gymnastics, he
concluded that a strong wind, combined with the tramping
feet of tens of thousands of visitors, would cause the building
to vibrate with increasing violence, until the snugs gave way.
All in all, he had no confidence that the building would
remain intact for the duration of the Exhibition.

Turner now re-entered the fray, declaring his conviction
that a dreadful accident was almost certain to occur unless the
design was modified. Charles Fox, the contractor, did his best
to reassure the gathering about the strength of the joins
between the columns and girders, and added that he had built
around forty acres of glasshouses with sixteen-ounce glass –
and indeed as flimsy as thirteen ounces in the days when glass
carried a punitive duty – with few accidents. He added that
during a powerful gale a few weeks earlier he had gone up to
the roof level of the Crystal Palace and detected no significant
vibration. Apsley Pellatt, a Southwark glass manufacturer,
challenged Fox with a tale of sixteen-ounce glasshouses being
destroyed by winds in Staines, Middlesex. Wyatt, summing
up, assured his listeners that everything had been and would
be properly tested.

The main test involved a joint civilian and military
operation to subject the building to the most severe ordeal. A
complete bay of the gallery was built and, before it was lifted
to its final position, raised slightly from the ground, at which
point 300 workmen crammed on to it. They walked, ran and
jumped, with no harmful effect. Then soldiers of the Royal
Sappers and Miners (today's Royal Engineers) replaced the
workmen, running on the spot and marking time in unison.

Testing the strength of the galleries.

The gallery bay was inspected carefully but no damage was detected.

Anxious to reassure the public beyond a shadow of a doubt, the Commissioners insisted that there should be a test on the actual galleries as built. For this they needed to borrow 300 boxes of shot from the Royal Arsenal at Woolwich, carried through the streets of London on ten ammunition wagons. Carpenters built eight wooden frames on castors, each divided into thirty-six compartments large enough to hold a sixty-eight-pound shot so that it could roll about as the frames were pushed and pulled manually across the gallery floor. Again there were no mishaps.

Diehard local residents were still complaining, though, chiefly about the condition of the section of Hyde Park immediately surrounding the Crystal Palace. Tunisians who had come to London to look after their national exhibits had set up an Arab camp in the park, enclosed by palings. *The Examiner* painted a lurid picture of the 'Saturnalia' in the park at weekends: 'Hyde Park is in the complete, undisturbed, undisputed possession of the young blackguards of London', especially on Sundays, when the boisterous young folk harassed and hustled passers-by 'and have their way of them in any way most diverting to them, at discretion'. Park-keepers and police, fearful for their own safety, made themselves scarce at these times, and the paper warned that if such scenes were allowed to continue, the result would be to 'show foreigners the immense superiority of the British blackguard over the blackguards of any other nation in the world'.

A more delicate difficulty concerned Ann Hicks, an elderly woman who for some years had run a cake and fruit stall by the Serpentine in Hyde Park, living in an adjacent shack. She would have to be moved to make way for the Crystal Palace, but stubbornly refused to go. The first thought was to eject her by force, but this did not appeal to the Duke of Wellington, who, as Ranger of the Royal Parks, had the ultimate responsibility. The Duke went to see her in person and arranged that she would go quietly in exchange for compensation of £92 11s 4d. In October 1851, as the Exhibition was drawing to a close, she contacted the Commissioners to inform them that the money was used up and she was now penniless. She asked either for more money or for permission to reopen her stall, but received neither.

The most frequently told story about Wellington and the Exhibition is sadly untrue, although it has appeared as fact in a number of books and articles. It goes like this: the organisers were worried by a flock of sparrows that had taken residence in the three elm trees enclosed beneath the high curved roof of the transept, and they expressed their concern to the Queen and Prince Albert. The royal pair summoned the Prime Minister, Lord John Russell, who recommended shooting the birds; but Albert pointed out that this would smash the glass.

So they called in the redoubtable Lord Palmerston, who recommended bird lime. Still unconvinced, they went to the very highest authority on deadly combat, the Duke of Wellington. After initially sending the message: 'The Duke of Wellington is not a bird catcher', he relented and went to Buckingham Palace to see the Queen. 'Sparrowhawks, ma'am,' was his terse recommendation.

Most versions of the story end there, without recording the outcome. (Had sparrowhawks actually been used, they would almost certainly have created more mayhem than the sparrows.) The original tale, set down in the memoirs of Sir Lyon Playfair, has a payoff line that shows it clearly to be an intricate political joke:

> In the meantime the sparrows had sent out scouts. When they heard that Lord John Russell had been summoned they twittered, and seemed to be amused. When Lord Palmerston went they showed signs of anxiety but, ultimately, flew about as usual. When their scouts informed them that the Duke of Wellington had gone to the Palace all the sparrows congregated in the tree nearest to the door, and as soon as the advice of sparrowhawks was communicated they flew in a body out of the door, and the Exhibition was never again troubled with their presence.

Public anticipation was ratcheted throughout the winter by news of sensational exhibits being planned and manufactured, and then by the increasing flow of material arriving in London from overseas. A clockmaker in Dudley, Worcestershire, was bringing a clock that would run for 426 days without being wound. An eight-ton lump of zinc ore from New Jersey was passing through New York on its way to Brooklyn Navy Yard for shipping. A block of anthracite measuring seven feet, by four foot six, by three feet was being brought from Swansea: it had taken colliers three days to raise it from the pit bottom to the surface. Ships carrying overseas goods and delegates caused local sensations as they docked in ports outside London. When the steamer *Teizi Baari* arrived in Southampton from Turkey, the local mayor sent three civic officials on board to convey the town's greetings. They were presented with long-stemmed calumets, or pipes of peace, made of amber and precious stones and filled with lighted Turkish tobacco.

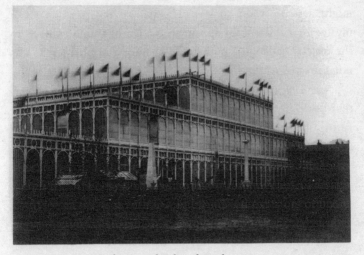

The Crystal Palace from the west.

The Crystal Palace, though by no means complete, was ready to receive exhibits at the end of January and all unauthorised visitors were then barred, however much they were willing to pay. On the Saturday before the ban was imposed, 5,000 of them paid their five shillings for one last look, and on the Monday Members of Parliament were allowed in free for a private view. The very first exhibit delivered that day was presented at the door by a lady milliner, possibly either Emily or Eliza Gwatkin of 37 Westminster Bridge Road, whose entry comprised two bonnets of a new design, one in satin and one crocheted in cotton.

In February came the first exhibits from Portugal, Tunisia and the United States. The steamship *City of Paris* arrived from Boulogne laden with twelve cases of French silks and sixty-two cases of manufactured goods. From Holland came an immense pie, four feet long by two and a half feet wide – presumably for strictly promotional purposes, for it was accompanied by several pies of a more realistic size that people might actually want to buy. The fate of the pie is a small mystery, for it does not appear in the list of Dutch exhibits in the official catalogue: perhaps, like the Swiss cheeses, it was not admitted to the show.

The Times was especially impressed by the Indian objects that were being amassed in the Crystal Palace during the spring, believing that they reflected well on the benevolent manner in which Britain ran its Indian empire:

> We have ransacked that territory not after the fashion
> of ordinary conquerors but with a just appreciation of
> those hidden sources of labour and springs of com-
> merce which, in the end, are more remunerative than
> mines of silver or gold.

By now the streets around Hyde Park were busy with noisy traffic bringing goods to the Crystal Palace. The most vivid description of the scene in the capital comes from that percep-tive observer Henry Mayhew, one of the founders of *Punch* ten years earlier, and later to write the classic *London Labour and the London Poor*, which did so much to provoke the Victorian conscience on the plight of Britain's lowest classes. In 1851 he wrote a satirical account of the adventures of a Mr and Mrs Sandboys, who came to London from the north of England with their family to see the Exhibition and encountered a series of disasters triggered by their gullibility.

To illustrate the impact of the event on the day-to-day lives of Londoners, Mayhew described the roads to Hyde Park, especially from the main railway termini and the docks, filled with heavy vans piled high with packing cases or creak-ing under the weight of heavy machinery, pulled by long teams of horses. They kept to the verges to minimise congestion where they could, but had to venture into the main stream of traffic quite often because many pavements were being re-paired and shop fronts newly painted. The horse-drawn omni-buses – which had already put up their fares to exploit the increase in demand – usually contained at least two or three foreigners, 'light-haired Germans, or high-cheeked Americans, or sallow Turks with their "fez caps" of scarlet cloth'. Many public buildings and museums increased their hours of open-ing but were still finding it hard to cope with the rush. News-papers produced large placards to announce that they were publishing supplements in several languages. 'From the num-ber of gentlemen in beards, felt hats and full pantaloons, visible at the West End, Regent Street had much the Anglo-Frenchified character of Boulogne-sur-Mer.'

Outside the Crystal Palace itself, long queues of wagons formed, waiting to unload, while people pressed their noses to the railings for a better view of the activity. Behind the build-ing, streams of horses and their elegant riders trotted noise-lessly through the park, while at the front passengers crammed the top decks of omnibuses so that they could see what was going on. The nearby taverns were all crowded and some flew flags from their roofs to attract passers-by. Roadside hawkers sold souvenirs and snacks – nuts, oranges and ginger beer. 'All was bustle, life, confusion and amazement,' Mayhew wrote.

Other little touches had been added to make foreigners feel at home. A group of philanthropists, funded by the seventh Earl of Shaftesbury (after whom Shaftesbury Avenue would be named later in the century), got together to create a team of thirty-six shoe-blacks, made up of twelve- to fifteen-year-old boys from the charitable Ragged Schools for destitute children, some coming from criminal families. Shoe-cleaning on the streets was a popular amenity in European cities and in the United States but had not hitherto caught on in London. The lads were given red shirts and black aprons and formed a colourful addition to the capital's street life, as well as causing a stir when a party of them were taken to visit the Crystal Palace itself. By the time the Exhibition closed, they had polished 51,000 pairs of boots and shoes, earning on average 2s 2½d each per day. The shoe-black brigades continued to be a feature of London's streets for many years afterwards.

All this activity was reflected in the spate of Exhibition-related advertisements that were now appearing in the London papers. A Covent Garden tailor offered to run up court dress or military uniforms for the opening ceremony. For out-of-town visitors, a central registration office had at last been set up for providing details of suitable lodgings, offering to provide a list of accommodation on receipt of six postage stamps 'so that visitors can make arrangements before leaving home' – although in the event comparatively few appeared to take advantage of the facility. A centre for visiting clergymen had been established. One advertiser sought to exchange a gentleman's season ticket for a lady's – what domestic or romantic entanglement lay behind that?

Organisers of popular entertainments were keen to find

ways of cashing in. Vauxhall Gardens, on the south bank of the Thames, was nearing the end of its life as London's prime centre of recreation after nearly two centuries, but it could still rise to the big occasion. A masked ball was advertised for the opening night of the Exhibition, a night of 'unparalleled brilliancy, gorgeous illuminations, famous bands', including 'M. Arban and his corps of eminent instrumentalists, the largest quadrille band in England'.

As the opening day drew near, the Queen and Prince Albert made increasingly frequent visits to the site – to the irritation of the contractors, for with each visit the workers would down tools to give vent to their expressions of loyalty, interrupting work that was already behind schedule. The Queen's journal discloses that she was becoming more and more convinced that the Exhibition would mark the defining moment of her reign and, despite the Lady Lytteltons of this world, the acceptance of her husband into the people's affections. On her last visit before the opening, she wrote:

> I came back quite dead beat and my head really bewildered by the myriads of beautiful and wonderful things, which now quite dazzle one's eyes . . . It shows of what immense use to this country this Exhibition is, as it goes to prove we are capable of doing almost anything.

Meanwhile, in contrast to her optimism, the organisers were being confronted with numerous last-minute problems and complaints raised by exhibitors. Many British manufacturers were angry that they would not be allowed to show the price of their goods, arguing that cheapness was one advantage they had over foreign competition. The powerful Leeds committee urged the Commissioners to allow prices to be displayed as a 'test of comparative value and excellence'.

Some of the foreign exhibitors agreed. The Hamburg commission said the ban on pricing was an incurable deficiency in the Exhibition, and the Danes said that because Danish goods were chiefly remarkable for their cheapness, they would not be bringing many over if they were not allowed to show their prices, and consequently would need no more than 450 square feet of space. (Only forty-seven exhibitors came from Denmark, although the Royal Porcelain Factory in Copenhagen put on an impressive display.) The Commissioners refused to change their minds, but said that manufacturers could stipulate which products were exhibited primarily for their cheapness, and this would be taken into account when deciding on award-winners.

There was a smaller furore over a wigmaker (possibly H. P. Truefitt of Burlington Arcade, whose successors Truefitt and Hill are still in business in St James's Street), who complained that his wigs had been placed in the class for manufactures from animal and vegetable substances, rather than in the fine arts section where he thought they deserved to be. According to Cole, when Queen Victoria learned of this dispute she was greatly amused.

Amid this onrush of minor crises, at least fears about the safety and stability of the building were diminishing. On 29 April, two days before the opening, London was hit by a violent hailstorm – no doubt a final stiff examination imposed by the Supreme Buildings Inspector in the sky. Not a pane of glass in the Crystal Palace was damaged.

❧ ❧

CHAPTER FIVE

A DAY TO LIVE FOR EVER

*Dearest Albert's name is for ever immortalised, and the absurd
reports of dangers of every kind and sort, put out by a set of people – the
'soi-disant' fashionables and the most violent Protectionists – are
silenced. It is therefore doubly satisfactory that all should have gone
off so well, and without the slightest incident or mischief.*

Queen Victoria's journal, 1 May 1851

The fears of insurrection and disorder that Prince Albert had dismissed in so cavalier a manner in letters to his relatives had been taken rather more seriously by officials at Buckingham Palace. On their advice it was announced on 16 April that the Queen would perform the Exhibition's opening ceremony on 1 May in private, before only diplomats and invited guests. The press was uniformly outraged. Was this not supposed to be a festival for the whole world, celebrating a new spirit of co-operation between people of all ranks, where working men and women would come from all over and rub shoulders with their betters to inspect the fruits of their labour? What sort of message would it send if the Queen was not confident enough to show herself to her own people?

There were numerous other protests, especially from the 8,000 people wealthy enough to have bought season tickets at £3 3s for men and £2 2s for women, believing that they would be admitted throughout the Exhibition, including on the opening morning. For some of them, the prime motive had been to be sure of being there for the official ceremony. *The Times* was furious: 'Queen Victoria receives every day suffici-ent evidence of the loyalty and affection of her subjects with-out attempting to banish them from her presence upon so interesting and solemn an occasion.'

It was preposterous, the paper fumed, to assume that she would be in any more danger from a French or German social-ist in the Crystal Palace than she was every day when she drove in her carriage through the streets of London. To put her 'in a furniture warehouse with only a few officials present' was to treat her like Lady Godiva – quite a saucy image for the period. 'Where most Englishmen are gathered together then the Queen of England is most secure,' the paper declared confidently, concluding that it would be better to cancel the ceremony altogether than to hold it in a manner so offensive to the people's feelings. But it also suggested a compromise: anybody with a season ticket should be admitted to the open-ing. 'The price of the ticket offers something like a guarantee that the mob would be of a select character.'

Faced with such unanimous indignation, the Government felt obliged to intervene. On 17 April Lord John Russell advised Prince Albert to admit season-ticket holders to the opening ceremony, as *The Times* had suggested. 'The fashion-able society in London might be disregarded,' he said, 'but it would be a pity to alienate the manufacturers and the middle classes.' So keen were the middle classes to witness the cere-mony that thousands of extra season tickets were sold before the Exhibition opened. This surge in demand encouraged the Commissioners to seek to raise the price of season tickets by a guinea, provoking more complaints.

Some angry exhibitors protested that the proposed in-crease gave the impression that the Queen's presence was being exploited in the same manner as that of a famous singer or actor, who could command a higher ticket price than a comparative unknown. Prince Albert quickly vetoed any such rapacious opportunism, and after another 15,000 season tickets were sold at the original price they were withdrawn from sale until after the opening.

Excitement was mounting in the capital, made all the more acute by being mingled with a strong element of trepidation. It was an unprecedented event and nobody could foresee whether its impact would be adverse or beneficial. Would it lead to months of unrest and disorder, or would it be a long summer of celebration? The answer, for better or worse, would not be long in coming.

Thursday 1 May had been declared a public holiday, and soon after dawn broke the sun was shining from a near-cloudless sky. But it was one of those treacherous days of late spring, when early sunshine can herald showers to come. As early as six a.m., the streets of London were crowded with a mass of humanity making its way to Hyde Park, or taking up positions on the roads where the Queen and Prince Albert would ride in state for the opening ceremony at noon. Some were in cabs or crammed on the tops and sides of omnibuses, a few were in grand private carriages or more modest chaises, and tradesmen were making good use of the four-wheeled phaetons and two-wheeled gigs in which they normally made deliveries; but most were taking advantage of the weather to walk, keeping a wary eye out for the capital's notorious pickpockets, for whom any big public occasion represented a superb business opportunity.

Although the majority in the crowd were Londoners, it was swelled by between 50,000 and 100,000 foreigners and out-of-towners who had arrived in the capital by train and steamer in the previous few days. The main-line rail termini had been packed for a week and more, as the rail companies had attached extra carriages – and in some cases extra engines – to their trains to cope with the increased passenger loads. Hotels and guest houses close to the termini were full and turning away guests.

One of the most vivid accounts of the excitement of that May Day morning again comes from Henry Mayhew in 1851, or *The Adventures of Mr and Mrs Cursty Sandboys* . . . His description of the mood of the capital was certainly based on observation rather than imagination. He wrote of bells ringing from every church steeple and boys perched in trees for a view of the proceedings, 'like their independent counterparts, the London sparrows'. He continued:

> For miles round all wore a holiday aspect; the work-people with clean and smiling faces, and decked out all in the bright colours of their Sunday attire, were up and about shortly after daybreak and, with their bundle of provisions on their arms, were soon seen streaming along the road, like so many living rays, converging towards the crystal focus of the world . . . Never was labour – whether mental or manual, whether the craft of the hand or the brain – so much honoured, the first great recognition, perhaps, of the artistic qualities of the artisan.

As they approached the park, the crowd thickened and the hubbub increased. The historian Thomas Babington Macaulay described the scene in his diary:

> I was struck by the number of foreigners in the streets. All, however, were respectable and decent

> people. I saw none of the men of action with whom
> the Socialists were threatening us. I went to the Park
> and along the Serpentine. There were immense
> crowds on both sides of the water. I should think
> there must have been near three hundred thousand
> people in Hyde Park at once. The sight among the
> green boughs was delightful. The boats, and little
> frigates, darting across the lake; the flags; the music;
> the guns – everything was exhilarating, and the
> temper of the multitude the best possible.

Although they knew they were going to have to wait several
hours for Victoria and Albert's arrival, the onlookers in
the park were determined not to miss any of the earlier
comings and goings of the grandees, some recognisable from
drawings in the illustrated papers. The grandees themselves,
sporting their best new summer outfits, were just as excited,
bent on relishing the day to the full. The sudden change of
policy over admitting season-ticket holders had unnerved
some of them and persuaded them that the best way of
ensuring that they were admitted was to arrive early. By
seven a.m. the first visitors had begun to appear at the entrance gates in the iron railings that surrounded the Crystal
Palace.

Exhibitors and their helpers, with proper accreditation,
were allowed in at eight, but for others the gates were not due
to open until nine. By half past eight such a crowd had built
up that people were getting jammed against the railings, their
immaculate clothing in grave danger of dishevelment. At this
point the authorities relented and let women through the gate
to wait on the other side of the rail, the men standing back to
clear a path for them. At nine a.m. precisely, the gates were
opened, then the doors to the Crystal Palace itself, and some

30,000 season-ticket holders passed inside, few of them pausing to buy the shilling catalogues on sale in the aisles but instead hurrying to find the best possible vantage point. Only when they had found it did they cast their eyes upwards and around, taking in the splendid scene that they were now part of.

Rows of seats, covered in crimson cloth, had been placed on the edges of the long east–west aisles, carpeted in red, where the Queen and Prince Albert were due to walk during their opening tour. Most of the seats were filled by female spectators, their menfolk gallantly volunteering to stand behind them. In the middle of the building was the magnificent twenty-seven-foot crystal fountain, which had been kept under wraps until the opening day. Made by Follett Osler, it was a unique piece of glasswork involving large blocks of faultless pink glass, exquisitely cut and polished. A few feet to its north was a raised platform, also covered in crimson, and on it a carpet of Berlin wool woven for the occasion in a variegated pattern by 150 Englishwomen on the initiative of Miss Farncomb, who had been Lady Mayoress to Thomas Farncomb (probably his sister, for he was a bachelor), the Mayor who hosted the Mansion House banquet in March 1850. The early arrivals were amused to see the eminent Lord Granville sweeping the carpet clear of wood shavings, evidence of the last-minute preparations that had kept hundreds of workers and exhibitors in the building for the whole of the previous night.

Standing on the carpet was a magnificent chair, borrowed from the Indian exhibit and covered with crimson velvet. About thirty feet above this extemporised throne hung a blue silk canopy, its corners decorated with ostrich feathers in the shape of the Prince of Wales's symbol. Just behind were Matthew Cotes Wyatt's equestrian statues of the royal couple, alongside two of the enclosed elms. Dozens of palm trees had been placed in the aisles, with banks of colourful azaleas below them. In every direction fine carpets and draperies, part of the Exhibition itself, hung down from the girders. Large sheets of canvas had been placed over the glass roof to avoid glare and overheating, but not over the curved roof of the tall transept, stretching between the north and south entrances and enclosing the three elms. The effect was to create a broad rectangle of sunlight through the middle of the building, the rays reflecting off the crystal fountain and other shiny surfaces.

The first celebrity to arrive, soon after ten a.m., was the Duke of Wellington, celebrating his eighty-second birthday that very day, in full military regalia and accompanied by his daughter, the Marchioness of Douro. After finding his seat he went up to one of the galleries where he had spotted the eighty-three-year-old Marquis of Anglesey, with whom he once had a very public feud. The two went back a long way. Both fought at Waterloo, where Anglesey had a leg blown off. Galloping with difficulty alongside Wellington, he told his commander: 'By God, I've lost a leg.' 'Have you, by God?' Wellington replied insouciantly. The main cause of their enmity, though, was not this apparent callousness: it was political. During Wellington's brief period as Prime Minister from 1828 to 1830, Anglesey had been Lord-Lieutenant of Ireland, but was recalled by Wellington for being, in his view, too conciliatory towards the Catholics.

In the spirit of peace that pervaded the Exhibition opening, Wellington took the Marquis's arm and paraded in front of the crowd to show that all was forgiven. There were more loud cheers for another military hero, Sir Charles Napier, and a rather more muted welcome for the Prime Minister, Lord John Russell, in full court dress. Conforming with the day's mood of reconciliation, Russell chatted cordially with his political rival, Lord Stanley.

Not all the official guests were such pillars of respectability. The net had been cast wide, especially among the foreign invitees. The French socialist Louis Blanc, champion of workers' control, was there, talking to his compatriot and fellow radical Alexandre-Auguste Ledru-Rollin, who had been exiled from France two years earlier because of his opposition to Louis Napoleon's attempt to set himself up as a national leader. Had the pair felt moved to try to start a workers' insurrection here this morning, they would have found little backing among the thousands of season-ticket holders who continued to pour into the Crystal Palace until 11.30. In any case, there was a strong and visible manifestation of law and order, with Sappers and Miners (today known as the Royal Engineers) boosting the police presence. Later, more exotically uniformed functionaries, including Yeomen of the Guard (Beefeaters) and court officials, added extra colour to an already festive scene.

Excitement was mounting, too, in the streets outside, where larger crowds had gathered than for any other public event that anyone could remember – estimates ranged between half a million and a million. The route between Buckingham Palace and the Crystal Palace was up Constitution Hill, then into the park and west along Rotten Row, which led to the north entrance. Every square inch of pavement and grass along the route was jammed to capacity, with a line of policemen, interspersed with Life Guards at regular intervals, keeping the way clear for the procession. People clambered on to the tops of coaches, cabs and omnibuses to seek a vantage point, and a bold few even scaled trees and lamp-posts. Rooms and offices above ground level at Hyde Park Corner were crammed with people pressing their faces against the windows, and balconies were crowded to a degree that looked perilous. The Duke of Wellington had allowed schoolchildren to watch from the roof and high windows of Apsley House, his London home overlooking the royal route. Souvenir stalls, refreshment booths and fairground games appeared at every feasible location within striking distance. Military bands were playing in the park as families picnicked there – if they could manage to find enough vacant grass. Restaurants and public houses were doing exceptionally brisk trade, with people spilling from the doors.

For the Queen, the day had a double significance, for it was also the first birthday of her youngest son, Prince Arthur. His nannies had dressed him in a frock decorated with a blue ribbon and taken him in to see his proud mother and father at breakfast. Later in the day Wellington, Arthur's godfather, would come and present him with a gold cup and some birthday toys.

There had been a short but quite heavy shower soon after eleven o'clock, about half an hour before the royal party were due to set off for the Crystal Palace, and this may have influenced their decision not to ride in the formal state carriage but in a smaller one, drawn by only two horses, that gave better protection. While this disappointed some spectators, they were compensated by the reappearance of the sun just as the procession of nine carriages left the gates to Buckingham Palace, so that the gilt uniforms and swords of the outriders, and the trappings of their horses, glinted in the bright light. Cheers rang out as soon as the trotting hooves of the horses and the jingle of their harnesses came within earshot, while the warmth of the sun on the wet grass of the parks caused a romantic haze to rise along parts of the route.

A few minutes before noon, the expectant crowd of celebrities, Commissioners and season-ticket holders inside the

Crystal Palace saw, through the long southern glass wall, the plumes of the Horse Guards, jogging up and down at a stately trot. Trumpeters in the north gallery played a fanfare as the Queen and her entourage stepped down from their carriages into the small retiring room that had been created for them close to the entrance. Outside, a Sapper hoisted the royal standard on a flagpole that had been placed on the transept roof, and a royal salute was fired from cannons on the other side of the Serpentine lake – defying the predictions of those who believed that the explosions would shatter the glass.

After a few moments the royal party emerged from the retiring room to walk slowly towards the central platform, as a Beefeater, with a theatrical flourish, opened the ornate Coalbrookdale iron gates at the north end of the transept. The Queen wore a pink silk dress embroidered with silver and studded with diamonds, the riband of the Order of the Garter, and a crown-shaped head-dress of diamonds and feathers. The three most significant women in her party – the ten-year-old Princess Royal, the Duchess of Kent and the Princess of Prussia – were all in white. Prince Albert wore a field marshal's uniform decorated with the Order of the Garter, while their eldest son Edward, the nine-year-old Prince of Wales, was in a tartan kilt.

After such a long wait the spectators were relieved at the chance to give vent to their feelings, and loud cheers echoed all through the extraordinary structure. The Queen acknowledged the tribute by bowing repeatedly towards all sections of the building. When the noise subsided, the National Anthem was played on the massive organ in the south transept. Everyone – including the Queen – stood up, and most joined in. Out of deference to the foreign diplomats the second verse of the anthem was omitted, with its references to scattering the Queen's enemies, confounding their politics and frustrating their knavish tricks. As the reporter from the *Bradford Observer* explained: 'Victoria had no enemies there, and her conquests there were the conquests of industry, brotherhood and peace.' At the end of the anthem the cheering began again.

Prince Albert, meanwhile, had moved away from the Queen's side and joined the Commissioners for the Exhibition in front of the dais. He then read a formal address setting out the purposes of the Exhibition and the vital statistics of the Crystal Palace. The address ended on an unashamed self-congratulatory note:

> It affords us much gratification that, notwithstanding the magnitude of this undertaking, and the great distances from which many of the articles now exhibited have had to be collected, the day on which your Majesty has been graciously pleased to be present at the inauguration of the Exhibition is the same day that was originally named for its opening.

In a brief reply to her husband, the Queen praised the 'splendid spectacle by which I am this day surrounded' and hoped it would promote friendly and honourable rivalry between nations. The Archbishop of Canterbury, in a curled wig and surplice with white lawn sleeves, offered a special prayer for the occasion, delivered with particular passion, after which the massed choirs of St Paul's Cathedral, the Chapel Royal, Westminster Abbey and St George's, Windsor, sang Handel's Hallelujah Chorus, while the Queen and the rest of the royal party remained standing. At this point a Chinese mandarin emerged from the ruck of foreign representatives, walked towards the dais and bowed obsequiously in front of the Queen. It later transpired that he was the captain of a Chinese junk moored on the Thames and open to visitors, and he appeared to have attended the ceremony uninvited. So much for the tight security.

Now the procession began. At its head were Paxton and the contractor Charles Fox, whose partner Henderson was absent due to illness. They were followed by the people directly involved in running the Exhibition, then those responsible for co-ordinating the overseas exhibits. Next came the Commissioners, overseas ambassadors, members of the Government, the Bishop of Winchester, the Archbishop of Canterbury and members of the royal household. Behind them were the royal party, led by the Queen leaning on her husband's arm and holding Prince Edward's hand. Prince Albert in turn was holding the hand of their daughter, the Princess Royal.

They made their way to the west end of the nave, inspecting the objects on the north side, then went back to the east end, looking at the southerly stands, before returning to the centre. Thus they covered two lengths of the building, amounting to about three quarters of a mile. It did not take them much more than half an hour – a remarkable pace given the tradition of the period that two court officials, the Lord Steward and the Lord Chamberlain, had to walk ahead of the Queen, facing her: in other words they had to cover the entire route backwards. For all this time the Queen was only a few feet from many of her subjects but, despite the earlier fears, never in a moment's danger. The cheers came in waves as she and her party progressed from one section of the Exhibition to the next.

The circuit completed, the Queen went back to her dais and declared: 'The Exhibition opened.' Earl Breadalbane, a member of her entourage, was instructed to shout the message to all corners of the building, at which there was another flourish of trumpets. After more cheering and waving of handkerchiefs, and another rendering of the sanitised 'God Save the Queen', the royal party left the platform, and as soon as they had done so there was a surge from the aisles as people sought to tread the ground that Victoria had just vacated. Several women climbed up to the Indian chair, to sit for a few seconds on a spot still warm from the royal posterior, before beginning to inspect the exhibits in detail.

Just after one o'clock the royal party drove back to Buckingham Palace through streets now even more crowded than on the outward drive. The sheer volume of humanity caused some jostling at Hyde Park Corner, with carriages damaged and people injured. The throng outside Buckingham Palace had also grown since morning and, in response to loud appeals, the Queen appeared on the balcony with her children. The crowd loved it.

That evening, when Victoria sat down to write her journal, she recreated that joyous morning in her mind:

> The glimpse through the iron gates of the transept, the waving palms and flowers, the myriads of people filling the galleries and seats around, together with the flourish of trumpets as we entered the building, gave a sensation I shall never forget, and I felt much moved . . . The tremendous cheering, the joy expressed in every face, the vastness of the building, with all its decoration and exhibits, the sound of the organ (with 200 instruments and 600 voices, which seemed nothing), and my beloved husband, the creator of this peace festival 'uniting the industry of all nations of the earth', all this was moving indeed, and a day to live for ever. God bless my dearest Albert, and my dear country, which has shown itself so great today. One felt so grateful to the great God,

whose blessing seemed to pervade the whole undertaking.

She was still on a high the next day: 'The papers full of
beautiful descriptions, and there is but one voice of praise
from all quarters.' On 3 May she wrote to her uncle, the King
of the Belgians: 'It was the happiest, proudest day of my life,
and I can think of nothing else.' Next day, in her journal again:
'My dearest Albert is so pleased at the realisation of what he
always foretold. The Protectionists who opposed the project of
the Exhibition are much provoked, and many who would not
go, so provoked at not having been there!'

The reaction of *The Times* (whose sales on the day following the ceremony climbed to a record 56,000 copies) typified
that of all the newspapers.

> There was yesterday witnessed a sight the like of which
> has never happened before. They who were fortunate
> enough as to see it hardly knew what most to admire,
> or in what form to clothe the sense of wonder and even
> of mystery that struggled within them.

That was in the news report of the opening. The leading article
let hyperbole flow still freer:

> Till this day it has never yet occurred that all the
> nations of the earth should meet by their represent-
> atives and combine in a common act. Divided by seas,
> by their still wilder passions, by language and by
> religion, the many faces of mankind have been scat-
> tered over the surface of the globe, as if over an
> illimitable waste.

What London had just witnessed was the start of 'an amicable rivalry between all nations, which shall contribute most to the happiness and improvement of the world'.

Even the sceptical French were reluctantly impressed by the opening spectacle. Jules Janin, writing in the *Journal des Débats*, expressed reservations about the quality of some of the exhibits, especially the sculpture, but was forced to conclude:

> The first of May will count among the great days of England. She has shown herself in our eyes, and in those of all of Europe, in all her majesty, in all her glory . . . This great adventure is at the moment the inexhaustible topic of conversation throughout the civilised world.

The *Illustrated London News* was quick to celebrate such rare plaudits from across the Channel.

> John Bull is no longer an ogre, but a genial and courteous gentleman. The old joke about the gloom, smoke and dirt of London, and the austerity, inhospitability and semi-lunacy of the English character, has been dissipated, and our Parisian friends confess that the 'sombre' city has produced the gayest, most fairy-like, most beautiful and original building in the world, and that these gloomy English people are positively well-dressed, as pleasure-loving, as agreeable and as polite as the French themselves.

A poem to celebrate the opening ceremony, parodying 'The House that Jack Built', was printed on silk and sold outside the Crystal Palace as a souvenir. This is the last verse:

This is our glorious Queen and her son,
Sitting with dignified grace on the throne,
And now comes Prince Albert, leading his daughter,
Who shines as a diamond of the first water,
Amongst all the ladies so charming and fair,
Who, dressed in their best, to the Palace repair,
Looking with smiles so sweet and so bland,
On all the great officers, noble and grand,
Who govern the soldiers by royal command,
Who, dressed in their clothes, so gay and so bright,
Like to play best but are willing to fight,
In defence of the police, so active and bold,
Who mind not the heat and fear not the cold,
Who aided the sappers and miners so clever,
Who opened the cases of wood and of leather,
Which held the productions of every clime,
Sent in by the merchants in pretty good time,
To please the masters with purses so long,
Who paid the men so hearty and strong,
Who thronged the building all day long,
To obey the men who handled the pen,
To help the man who drew the plan,
Of the crystal house which Albert built.

William Makepeace Thackeray, best known as a novelist but also a journalist and versifier, wrote a sentimental 'May Day Ode' to celebrate the transformation of London and Hyde Park:

A peaceful place it was but now,
And lo! within its shining streets
A multitude of nations meets;
A countless throng!

I see beneath the crystal bow,
And Gaul and German, Russ and Turk,
Each with his native handiwork
And busy tongue.

. . .

Look yonder where the engines toil:
These England's arms of conquest are,
The trophies of her bloodless war:
Brave weapons these.
Victorious over wave and soil,
With these she sails, she weaves, she tills,
Pierces the everlasting hills
And spans the seas.

In reality, as the guests would see when they made their first tour of the exhibits after the royal party had left, the busy tongues of the foreigners were more in evidence on that opening day than were examples of their native handiwork. Although nearly all the British exhibitors completed their displays on time, many of those from overseas, especially the French, Russians and Americans, were hopelessly behind, partly because of delays in the arrival of their goods. Only about a third of the foreign exhibits had been unpacked and there were large gaps in some areas, with workmen still busy with hammers and saws, building display stands. Some of the internal and external decoration of the building itself also remained to be completed.

Punch took advantage of the delays to the transatlantic shipment of some exhibits to indulge in its favourite sport of Yankee-baiting and anti-American abuse. Speculating on what might still be on its way from the United States, it made the following suggestions:

A hat stand made out of the horns of a dilemma.

A dressing-case for the mirror of nature.

The whip with which America flogs all creation – especially the coloured portion of it.

The tremendous wooden stile that separates the American from the English fields of literature.

Queen Victoria was quite consumed by the Exhibition. Nearly every day when she was in London, rather than at Osborne or Balmoral, she would go to the Crystal Palace before the public were admitted, sometimes with Prince Albert and sometimes only with her entourage. She would usually stay for about two hours, by which time that day's visitors would have begun to arrive. To their delight she would pass briefly among them, smiling and nodding, feeling more sure of herself as time went on. She recorded her impressions in further entries in her journal:

[7 May] This was an interesting morning's work. Enormous quantities of people, with differently priced tickets, come all and every day. [The daily price was still five shillings, and would not be reduced to a shilling for two more weeks. She was presumably referring to those who had bought season tickets.]

[10 May] Chubb's locks were the first exhibits we regularly inspected, and they really are wonderful, of every size and kind. He explained to us the ingenious manner by which an attempt to force the lock is discovered . . . There were 'Bowie' knives in profusion, made entirely for Americans, who never move without one . . . Every time one visits this great work one feels more and more impressed with its lofty

conception . . . The progress of the human race result-
ing from the labour of all men ought to be the final
object of the exertion of each individual. [That was a
motto that Albert had chosen for the catalogue. Reporters also noted that she seemed especially interested that day in the display of churns and beehives.]

[17 May, admiring the Sèvres porcelain in the French
section, which had only just been put on show
because of the delays in installation] The taste and
execution are quite unequalled and gave one a wish to
buy all one saw! [She did in fact buy a considerable
quantity of porcelain and other decorative items from
British and overseas exhibitors.]

[19 May, in the United States section, where she was
less impressed by the 'very curious inventions'] There
was a double piano exhibited, two people playing at
each end, which had a ludicrous effect.

[30 May, on the Swiss stand, she was enchanted by
the] . . . really exquisite watches, some very diminu-
tive, barely an inch in circumference, most beautifully
set with lovely enamelled exteriors of every kind and
shape – one being on top of a pencil case! The workmanship was most complicated and perfect.

[7 June] Went to the machinery part, where we remained two hours, and which is excessively interesting and instructive, and fills one with admiration
for the greatness of man's mind, which can devise and
carry out such wonderful inventions, contributing to
the welfare and comfort of the whole world.

While Victoria's Panglossian attitude to the Exhibition was to a large extent justified, she did leave out some of the alarming incidents, such as a fire that broke out in the Canadian section, quite close to the south entrance, just a week after the opening. It had been caused by a burning paper from the gas stove in the contractors' office being blown along a vent that had its outlet near the Canadian stand, where it ignited a basket and a box. It was quickly brought under control, but the Commissioners rebuked the contractors for installing a gas stove in their office and ordered the immediate removal not only of that one but of all stoves used for heating in the entire building, except in the refreshment rooms. They also forbade workmen from smoking in the spaces beneath the floor, where they had been detected through smoke rising between the boards.

Between May and the close of the Exhibition in October, the Queen must have spent more than fifty hours in the Crystal Palace, the equivalent of two full days and nights. Most visitors, with the exception of the season-ticket holders, would spend no more than a single eight-hour day and some, such as the group from the Surrey villages, rather less. Faced with the bewildering array of objects, ranging from huge machines – some in motion – to the very smallest artifacts, how could they decide what to see? Charles Dickens was one of several visitors who declared himself outfaced by the sheer scale of it.

For the Surrey farm labourers it was a comparatively straightforward choice. Since the primary purpose of the visit had been presented to them as educational, they would have been guided straight to the agricultural machinery. Privately, though, many may have preferred to gaze at some of the domestic gadgets, powered by gas and the new miracle of electricity, that promised to make nineteenth-century life so much easier – if not for them, then hopefully for their children, when mass production would bring the price of such devices within an affordable range.

But how were any visitors to decide whether to linger at the fine silks and ivories from India; the marvellous machine that turned out a hundred cigarettes a minute; the statues whose frank carnality – daring in such a staid era – was excused by their being art; or the splendours of Augustus Pugin's medieval court? And what were they to make of such quirky items as the lifeboat bearing a figurehead in which eight quarts of coffee could be brewed; the hollowed walking stick for doctors that contained medical instruments; and the numerous representations of Victoria and Albert, including a model of the Queen made entirely of paper by her loyal subjects in Jersey?

Many items were interesting in themselves, either because of the ingenuity of their construction or the useful function they performed, but others had found a place in the show merely because of the singular circumstances in which they were produced, despite the efforts of the Commissioners to keep them out. The correspondent for the *Bradford Observer* put it with characteristic Yorkshire bluntness: 'There are in the Exhibition diverse articles which will neither immortalise the memories nor fill the pockets of their makers . . . They are specimens neither of the useful, the beautiful nor the valuable.' He gave a few examples: miniature tea kettles made of halfpennies or sixpenny pieces; patchwork quilts sewn with millions of stitches; commonplace trifles submitted by a man with only one arm, an orphan or a blind woman.

'The Crystal Palace was not meant to be a gigantic reproduction of the Old Curiosity Shop,' he fumed, referring to Charles Dickens's novel published ten years earlier. True, it was not meant to be, but for many it was – and they thought none the worse of it for that.

CHAPTER SIX

❧ ❧

CORNUCOPIA

The public will bear in mind that on a first visit to the Exhibition, little or
nothing can be seen in detail of its marvellous contents. The mind and the
eye have both enough to do in comprehending the general design and in
becoming familiar with the coup d'oeil of the interior.

The Times, 23 May 1851

The Times calculated that to give every exhibit in the Crystal Palace the attention it deserved would mean spending 200 hours in the building. It would therefore take more than a month of daily visits to complete a thorough circuit. Even Queen Victoria did not come close to achieving this, and since it would be impossible for most other visitors they 'wander aimlessly through the building, astonished but confused, greatly delighted but little edified'.

Since ours is to be a virtual tour, we need not bother about such limitations of stamina. I shall lead us round the whole building in one visit, starting from the south entrance at the centre. There was no compulsory route and the contingency plan to introduce one in the event of serious overcrowding never had to be put into effect. The official guidebook suggested that visitors should follow the course of the sun, which would work only if we entered from the east entrance and, taken literally, would forbid any back-tracking. A popular route from the main entrance, at the centre of the south side, was to turn left on entering the building, just in front of the equestrian statue of the Queen. In this way visitors first got to see the British and colonial exhibits in the western half, before tackling the rest of the world to the east. (Prince Albert's original idealistic plan to have British products displayed alongside their overseas rivals had long been abandoned, in part because each country wanted to arrange its own displays to highlight its national strengths.)

We shall broadly follow this itinerary, using as our guide *Hunt's Handbook to the Official Catalogues*. Robert Hunt was a writer about science and an expert on mining, and although his 948-page handbook laid stress on those technical aspects of the displays, he also had some apt comments on other, less earnest exhibits.

Our route takes us straight to one of the most notable and extensive areas, showing products from India. The star items were four elaborate gifts to the Queen from Nawab Nazim of Bengal; the most spectacular a throne, its purple velvet canopy supported by four silver poles, its seat in scarlet velvet with a gold and silver embroidered border, and more silver and gold used in the frame. There were two palanquins – covered conveyances like large sedan chairs but carried by four or six bearers: one of ivory, with a gold embroidered canopy. The fourth gift was a highly decorated howdah, which looked a little out of place in the opening weeks before a stuffed elephant – loaned by a museum in Saffron Walden, Essex, after a plaintive appeal by the organisers – allowed it to be displayed to proper effect. These, along with a tent spectacularly furnished with carpets and cushions, were the eye-catchers; but there were many hundreds of other Indian exhibits, among them rich silks and cottons, splendid furniture, minerals, medicines, cereals, dyes, India rubber, foodstuffs, leather, ceramics, simple agricultural machines and models of traditional boats.

The Canadian section.

Beyond India were three more colonial sections: Canada, Australia and the West Indies. Canada sent large quantities of minerals and food products, but what intrigued visitors were devices, not usually seen in Britain, designed to cope with the cold and rugged conditions in this largely undeveloped territory. There were snow shoes and sleighs, about which Hunt enthused:

Seated in one of these light and elegant carriages, wrapped in the warmest furs, ornamented with the gayest colours, and tempted abroad by a sky that equals that of Italy in brilliancy, the Canadian thoroughly enjoys himself, even though the thermometer sometimes be 30 degrees [Fahrenheit] below the freezing point.

There was a large canoe used for shooting the rapids and examples of American Indian dress, as well as mats made by the Indians from porcupine quills.

The Newfoundland stand was devoted entirely to that useful but unglamorous product cod liver oil. The West Indies concentrated on flowers, fruit and natural products. Australia showed the skins and meat of some of its distinctive animals – the kangaroo, the possum, the duck-billed platypus – along with the teeth of the sperm whale and the feathers of the sooty petrel. From the Cape of Good Hope (South Africa) came more such exotica, including an elephant's tusk weighing 103 pounds and some ostrich eggs, said to be considered great delicacies by the Hottentots, who cooked them by plunging them into the live embers of a wood fire.

Separating the colonial exhibits from the domestic British stands on the south of the aisle was the British sculpture room, and on the north Pugin's medieval court. The main subjects of the sculptures were classical or biblical, and several commentators were shocked and offended by some of the nude figures, here and in other parts of the Exhibition. Depictions of the female form in 1851 were less common, and therefore more provocative, than they would become during the following century and a half. Cupid was a recurrent figure, as was Eve with the forbidden fruit, and there were portrayals of Ophelia, Pluto and Proseprine, Ariadne, Titania and nymphs of various descriptions, as well as more of the royal portrait sculptures that proliferated all over the building.

In the medieval court, Pugin's purpose was to showcase the products of skilled craftsmanship for comparison with those made using the new mass-production methods celebrated in other exhibits. On one side were ecclesiastical ornaments, including a giant cross that angered some Protestants, still fearful that the Roman Catholics might seek to restore their hold on the English church 300 years after they forfeited it. On the other side were domestic furniture, tapestries and ornamental tiles, all in the heavy Gothic style that future generations would identify with Victorian taste and which Pugin set out in 1841 in *The True Principles of Christian or Pointed Architecture*. The style was controversial among Pugin's contemporaries. Ralph Wornum, keeper of the National Gallery, called it 'dead and bygone' and 'only a cowl to smother all independent thought'. One hundred years later the writer Osbert Lancaster would describe it as 'the last frenzied writhing of an exhausted rococo'. Today, opinions on its merits are still divided.

Immediately after Pugin's exercise in costly self-indulgence, visitors were brought face to face with the contrasting products of the Industrial Revolution, beginning with those from Birmingham, a city that had emerged during the century as the country's leading manufacturing centre. Here was an array of gas fittings, brass bedsteads, buttons, needles, pins, steel pens and countless other domestic items that added to the comfort and convenience of middle-class life and were now, thanks to mass production, within the price range of many more people.

Starting here, and arranged along the centre of the aisle all the way to its western end, was a large display of farm machinery, of intense interest to country visitors even though the machines in this section of the building were not shown in operation. Most were still designed to be powered by men or horses, but steam engines were beginning to be developed for agricultural purposes, and Hunt was enthusiastic about their possibilities, making the point that the physical and moral condition of farm labourers would be improved if they were no longer hired primarily for their physical strength. Smaller items such as churns and cider presses were included, as well as a range of beehives, one designed to resemble an elegant contemporary three-storey villa.

Along the south side of this aisle were examples of British minerals, from precious gemstones to artificial and natural fertilizers, suitably deodorised. On the north side were exhibits of cast iron and brass and intricate padlocks, and behind them part of the display of British furniture, upholstery and wallpaper. The most ostentatious pieces of furniture were usually dedicated to the royal family. A state bed made by H. Scrymgeour of Edinburgh had the royal Scottish arms and Scottish crown embroidered on the headpiece, and the Victoria crown on the footboard. On the canopy, a crown was supported by four palm trees held aloft by a lion and unicorn, and above the cornice were figures representing agriculture, commerce, the Army and the Navy. Sarah le Mercier of Hammersmith, a teacher of tapestry work, showed a chair in honour of Prince Albert, embroidered with a plume and coronet and symbols of England, Scotland, Wales and Ireland.

The Times reflected a widely held view when it found much of the British furniture clumsy and vulgar compared with that from other parts of the world. While it was certainly solid and well constructed, it lacked elegance of design. 'It is as well that things should be made to last and stand wear and tear, but durability combined with unsightliness is an infliction sincerely to be deprecated.' The English furniture would 'appeal more to the parvenu, who wants to get his house flashily decked out, than the man of elegant tastes or moderate means'.

Next came the products of Sheffield, dominated by steel – not just cutlery but also stoves, grates, saws and other tools and springs for coaches and railway carriages. Exhibitors included names destined to survive into the twenty-first century, such as Spear and Jackson, and Wilkinson's. Modern

Sportsman's knife, containing eighty blades and other instruments with carved mother of pearl handle.

tableware, using the newly invented technique of electro-plating, was shown alongside such ingenious devices as multi-bladed penknives and implements that went back as far as the 'Sheffield whittle', a large knife mentioned in the reeve's story in Chaucer's *Canterbury Tales*.

From Sheffield and its hardware we move to another part of Yorkshire to enjoy the luxurious softness of woollen and worsted fabrics. This was the area that the visitors from Mr Priestley's Bradford savings club would have been drawn to, along with their counterparts from Leeds, Huddersfield, Halifax, Dewsbury and smaller woollen towns in other regions. Each manufacturing centre had its separate display, and there was intense competition between them. Bradford's stand was better received than that of neighbouring Leeds, which one critic dismissed as being 'more like a woollen draper's shop'.

Hunt was less partisan, commenting about the whole woollen section:

> Had this Exhibition done nothing more than bring together the many excellent specimens of manufacture here displayed, and thus shown to manufacturers of this great community the reliance they may safely place on their own energies, it would have done a great national service.

Assessing Bradford's contribution, he singled out Titus Salt's alpacas and moreens (heavier fabrics used for upholstery), and added: 'The worsted yarns of Bradford are famous wherever the manufacture is carried on.'

Beyond here we pay homage to the other side of the Pennines, with cotton goods from Manchester and the rest of Lancashire. Flax and printed fabrics were the last two sections in this aisle, sealed at the western end by a display of stained glass. Turning north, we can now look back towards the east along the main avenue and, for the first time, gain an impression of the immense length of the building seen from one end. The Main Avenue was where some of the most spectacular exhibits were sited and we are now going to walk along it, back towards the centre of the building, admiring the assorted marvels as we go.

That extraordinary model of Liverpool docks was the first of them, and beyond it some of the many busts dotted around the building. The first three depicted Prince Albert, the Duke of Wellington and Sir Robert Peel, next to a huge metal head of a horse. Then came a limestone model of the breakwater across Plymouth Sound, completed in the early years of the century, alongside a silver model of the lighthouse at one end of it.

More models followed: one showing the geological composition of the Undercliffe on the Isle of Wight, with its contrasting strata of sand and rock, and another representing 3,000 square miles of northern England in relief. Then came several modern feats of engineering, notably the newly opened Britannia railway bridge, designed by Robert Stephenson as two parallel tubes across the Menai Strait linking Anglesey with the mainland, and the British-built bridge over the Dnieper at Kiev in Russia. Nearby, on a more modest scale, were two royal exhibits – a jewel case lent by the Queen, and some cashmere fabrics made from the wool of goats kept by Prince Albert in Windsor Great Park.

The variety of things on show here was bewildering: eclecticism gone mad. A model of a Gothic church in Bolton was placed next to a large montage of ostrich feathers, with skins and furs hanging from above. There was a collection of early photographs alongside an educative display of lamp systems for lighthouses. An electroplated vase bore the figures of Prince Albert, Sir Isaac Newton, William Shakespeare, Francis

Bacon and James Watt; equating the Prince's achievement with those other intellectual giants. Britain's imperial adventure was celebrated not only on the stands of the colonies themselves, which we have already seen, but in exhibits such as a statue honouring the controversial achievements of Lord Ellenborough, who had been recalled from his post as Governor-General of India because of his repressive policies and his refusal to take instructions from London. This statue's centrepiece was supported by three recumbent elephants, while around the pedestal an Indian soldier, in the service of the Raj, gloated over captive Africans and Chinese. Above them Britannia embraced Asia, who in turn placed a laurel wreath on Britannia's helmet.

The Coalbrookdale ironworks had crafted a much-admired cast iron dome, thirty feet high and twenty feet in diameter, while not far away was an unfinished statue of Shakespeare by John Bell, one of the leading sculptors of the day, who had several works on display here in the Crystal Palace, including *The Eagle Slayer*, which stands today outside the Bethnal Green Museum of Childhood in east London. Later he would contribute to a number of heroic sculptures in the capital, including the Albert Memorial in Hyde Park and the Guards Crimea Memorial in Waterloo Place.

Near his Shakespeare statue was a cast iron altar rail designed by Henry Cole. A large slab of Honduras mahogany dwarfed a combination games table for cards, bagatelle and chess, called 'Multum in Uno' – many in one. After some specimens of polished marble and a statue of Rosamonda came further models of bridges, of another church and of the new county assize court in Cambridge. Still more statues surrounded an imposing monument made from logs and planks of Canadian timber, alongside the tall trunk of a petrified tree and the lower jawbone of a sperm whale, both from Australia.

Beyond these was another large monument of softer aspect – the Silk Trophy, assembled by D. Keith and Co. of London's Cheapside. It was a breathtaking spectacle, with swathes of fine Spitalfields silks, damasks and brocades mounted on a tall structure of plate glass.

Now we are at Osler's crystal fountain at the very centre of the building. This was a favourite place for trysts and assignations and was the single exhibit that for years people associated with the Exhibition. Though nowhere near halfway through our tour, we are certainly ready for something to drink or eat. We could, like so many others, take water from the fountain; but instead, for something rather more elaborate, we head north up the transept, between the equestrian statues of the Queen and Prince, passing two more statues and a fine display of tropical plants, through the Coalbrookdale iron gates to the Refreshment Court. I fear, though, that we are unlikely to enjoy a memorable gastronomic experience here, for the catering was almost the only aspect of the Exhibition subject to sustained criticism.

We could have a plate of ham for sixpence, with twopence extra for bread and butter. Sandwiches, buns, jellies and coffee were also available. Schweppes soda water cost sixpence: more than a million bottles of non-alcoholic beverages were sold during the Exhibition's run. Ices, frozen by a steam-driven refrigerator, were sixpence and a shilling – prices that struck many visitors as extortionate by comparison with those current elsewhere. The *Morning Chronicle* published a number of letters of complaint about both the cost and the meagre portions offered. One correspondent wrote of the 'worst and smallest sandwiches I ever tasted', but said that even these were marginally to be preferred to 'the little, dry, sixpenny dollops of pork pie', washed down with coffee that was 'always nearly cold and good for nothing'.

The appearance of the waitresses was the main concern of another dissatisfied customer:

> Pray assist to remedy a most universal complaint of all those hungry curious at the Great Exhibition, by giving the young females at the refreshment tables a hint that their personal appearances, as well as their hands and faces, would be greatly improved by a moderate use of soap. The excuse of not having had time since the 1st May to wash themselves certainly appears true, but the contractor would do well, in case of increasing business, to have relays of washed damsels if he wishes to see his eatables well digested.

Because there was no readmission once visitors left the building, the option of eating at a nearby tavern or restaurant was not a realistic one. Two Frenchmen were reported to have been so appalled at the paltry fare on offer – not to mention the unscrubbed waitresses – that they decided to leave at lunchtime with half the stands unvisited. Small wonder, then, that as word spread about the dismal catering, many people decided to bring their own picnics. Bags and hampers were not inspected at the entrance, so they could also beat the liquor ban by bringing alcoholic drinks to wash the food down. Every day hundreds spread themselves around the bases of the fountains and statues and consumed their home-made feasts. (On warm days they would no doubt have preferred to picnic in the park, but again that would have meant paying a second admission fee to come back in.)

Refreshed, at least up to a point, we can resume our tour by completing the circuit of the western half of the Palace before tackling the mainly foreign exhibits to the east. Walking west

ONE TOUCH OF NATURE
MAKES THE WHOLE WORLD KIN.

How Punch *portrayed the picnickers.*

again along the aisle north of the Main Avenue, we pass
through more Indian splendour and beyond it, on the left, the
Fine Arts Court, with an extraordinarily wide range of exhibits: a model of an Elizabethan tournament cut out of plain
paper with scissors; a design for a wrought-iron canopied

tomb; furniture made of Irish bog yew carved with scenes from the history of Ireland; flowers made from human hair; miniature playing cards; a machine for wiping shoes; and a group of stuffed partridges. The highlight was the Kenilworth Buffet, one of the most elaborate pieces of furniture on display, a sideboard cut from an oak, eleven feet in diameter, that grew in the grounds of Kenilworth Castle. It was carved with scenes from a pageant held at the castle on the occasion of Queen Elizabeth's visit in 1575.

North of the aisle began a fascinating display of machines in motion, all placed in this section to be near the steam boilers that powered them, which were housed in a separate structure just outside the Crystal Palace itself and connected to it by underground pipes. Stretching all the way to the western end of the building, and including some foreign as well as British machinery, this proved one of the most popular groups of exhibits. Visitors crowded to see and hear these magical machines that in a few short years would revolutionise their lives and their children's in ways that were only beginning to become apparent.

The most ambitious demonstration was by Hibbert, Platt and Sons of Oldham, Lancashire, who had fifteen machines in one large room undertaking cotton spinning in all its stages – processes that would formerly have involved scores of people, some of them children, doing unskilled, repetitive jobs. Hunt observed:

> Little more than 70 years since, every thread used in the manufacture of cotton, wool, worsted and flax, throughout the world, was spun singly by the fingers of the spinners, with the aid of that classical instrument the domestic spinning-wheel ... Nowadays several thousand spindles may be seen in a single

room, revolving with inconceivable rapidity, with no hand to urge their progress or to guide their operations, drawing out, twisting, and winding up as many thousand threads, with unfailing precision, indefatigable patience and strength – a scene as magical to the eye that is not familiarised to it, as the effects have been marvellous in augmenting wealth and population.

Not many of the awe-struck spectators, pressed three and four deep behind the iron railing installed to keep them at a safe distance, were likely to be pondering the long-term social ramifications of the shift from manpower to automation that was implied by this impressive display. One who did was Baron Charles Dupin, the French Commissioner to the Exhibition, who wrote of the advances in agricultural machinery: 'By superseding the labour, the country is depopulated and filled with machines. I leave it to statesmen to decide whether the unlimited emigration, which must ensue, will also be part of the national progress.' Most visitors were content to abjure such far-reaching speculation and to marvel at the way the

Read's patent garden watering engine.

mechanical spinners and weavers mimicked human dexterity.

As well as the fascinating machine for making envelopes that intrigued our group of Surrey villagers, there was an ingenious device for folding paper, such as newspapers or the pages of books. The many printing presses were greatly admired. One of them, as used in *The Times* office, reproduced circular woodcuts as well as type. There was, too, an early example of that staple piece of office equipment, the copying machine.

For anyone wanting to follow the development of the steam engine from its beginnings, models made by James Watt in 1785 were shown on the stand of the company he founded, along with an up-to-date application of the principle in a 700-horsepower engine for steamships driven by the new screw-propellers, replacing the old paddle wheels. Nearby a rival company, Maudslay, Son & Field of Lambeth, showed why it was pre-eminent in the marine engine field by trumping Watt's engine with one of 800 horsepower. Even more powerful were some of the locomotives: the Great Western Railway's imposing *Lord of the Isles* claimed to be equivalent to 1,000 horsepower and the London and North Western's *Liverpool* to 1,140.

There was plenty more here for railway enthusiasts. This new form of mass transport, without which not half as many people would have been able to visit the Exhibition, was celebrated with dozens of impressive locomotives and rolling stock, devices for track-laying and signalling, as well as one design for 'railways in the streets', later known as trams. All this technology was still in an experimental stage, as Hunt observed:

Excepting in the general arrangement of the mechanism, which has not varied in one important particular

since 1829, the notions of locomotive constructors
seem to be as various as if there were nothing to guide
them but their fancy.

He cited the debate about the virtues of long trains, carrying
many hundreds of passengers, as against lighter, more frequent services, carrying fewer people and needing less heavy
engines; and there was still no universally accepted standard
gauge for the tracks.

Steam was not the only source of power for the machines
on display, although it was by far the dominant one. A few
water wheels were exhibited, and a couple of windmills, as
well as many horse-drawn carriages and omnibuses.
Although horse-drawn vehicles would never be able to compete with the railways in terms of speed, their manufacturers
compensated for this shortcoming by introducing new comfort features to cosset their passengers. One carriage had
noiseless rubber wheels and another was fitted with a trans-
parent dome, allowing views of the tops of buildings. In a
carriage designed chiefly for ladies, the wheels were placed
directly underneath the superstructure instead of stretching
out on both sides, to avoid splattering passengers with mud.
There was a fantastic phaeton shaped like a sea shell and
painted white. An omnibus had a seating area divided into
small individual compartments, 'which obviates the possibility of robbery, or infection, or annoyance of any kind', and
introduced the principle of external steps to reach the top
deck, where previously people who sat there had to clamber
up the side. This design was the basis for the double-decker
bus that would become familiar in London streets before the
end of the century.

The first omnibuses had appeared in London in 1829,
introduced by George Shillibeer, who picked up the idea on a

visit to Paris. Here at the Exhibition, Shillibeer continued his innovative ways by showing a 'patent expanding funeral carriage', though why it would need to expand is unclear. There were several invalid carriages and a few devices for moving canal boats between levels – most of them more cumbersome than the traditional locks they were designed to replace, which probably explains why they did not catch on.

Now we have reached the end of the aisle and we join the press of people staring ahead, looking at themselves. The enormous sheet of glass here was exhibited by the Thames Plate Glass Company, who claimed that it was the world's largest mirror. Reflecting the entire length of the Main Avenue, it gave the impression that the Crystal Palace was endless – and soon we might begin to believe our eyes, because we have a great deal more to see yet.

For a change of pace and aspect, this is a good time to venture up the stairs into the galleries. Here we shall see many of the smaller articles on display, including some of those quirky items which, through the years, have given the Exhibition the undeserved reputation of being something of a freak show. After climbing the north-west staircase we can pause to look over the rail at the sensational scene spread below us: a slow-moving mass of humanity, probably more people than we have ever seen in one place before. They move from stand to stand in a slightly dazed fashion, as though drugged or mesmerised, and soberly inspect the exhibits, crowding round the most popular ones. At the refreshment areas they form orderly queues. Looking upwards to the roof, we enjoy our closest look at the building's extraordinary structure, its iron and glass walls soaring upwards and curving inwards to come together at the top of the arched transept.

It may have been the view from here that inspired one

visitor in particular – William Whiteley, a nineteen-year-old lad from Yorkshire enjoying his first holiday away from home. He was a draper's apprentice in Leeds and would have been fascinated to look down on the extensive displays of cloths in the Crystal Palace. Seeing the immense variety of goods all laid out for inspection gave him the idea for a shop that would sell a vast range of items, rather than concentrating on a single category, and have as much of the stock as possible on display. He moved to London a few years later, and in 1863 made the first step towards achieving his dream when he opened a shop selling ribbons and laces in Westbourne Grove, west of Paddington Station and the splendid new Great Western Hotel. He soon expanded into neighbouring shops and by 1872 had created one of London's first department stores, calling himself 'The Universal Provider' and offering to supply anything from a pin to an elephant. (Whiteley was shot dead in his office in 1907 by a man claiming to be his bastard son.)

Returning to our own inspection of the exhibits we find, against the north wall of the gallery, more models of buildings and bridges, and opposite them part of the wide-ranging Class 10. Described intriguingly as comprising 'philosophical [meaning broadly scientific], musical, horological and surgical instruments', it occupied much of the western end of the gallery. In essence, it was an eclectic display of the products of the extraordinary mental fertility of professional and amateur inventors in the Victorian age, forever seeking new and more efficient ways of performing day-to-day functions and overcoming minor inconveniences. As new materials and power sources came on stream, these men and women turned their minds to harnessing them in novel ways. Many of the devices they produced were so complex and cumbersome that they were destined never to go into general production, but the better ones quickly became part of daily life. The objects on display were a mixture of the two.

More than 130 British clockmakers were represented, most with several clocks and watches on their stands, making a glorious hubbub of ticking and chiming. There were grandiose clocks for public buildings; elaborately decorated timepieces for the drawing room; watches specially designed for railwaymen; a stopwatch measuring time to the nearest one-sixth of a second; clocks that could go for more than a year without winding; and others that told the time and date in every part of the world. A waterproof watch was displayed in a glass of water, ticking away happily. There were several examples of clocks powered by electricity and of electric telegraph machines, both recent technological advances. (Brunel had called for all electrical devices to be barred, since he regarded them as mere toys.)

Globes, depicting the earth and the heavens – and one showing both at the same time – proved especially fascinating to visitors. An ambitious terrestrial globe, thirty inches in diameter, showed the geological structure of the earth, as well as the path of the winds and ocean currents, with isotherms mapping patterns of temperature. Its walnut stand was adorned with carved figures representing the four seasons and the indigenous people and products of the four quarters of the world. A set of portable globes was made of tissue paper, designed to be inflated when needed; another was displayed in several pieces, as a puzzle to be fitted together; while a mechanical globe revolved constantly, at one revolution an hour, to show the advance of the seasons. A device called a periphan, consisting of a globe with models of the sun and moon attached, calculated the time of sunrise and sunset and the moon's phases.

While Hunt described all these ingenious devices meticulously, there were some too outlandish even for his broad mind. He was especially severe on M. Ryles of Staffordshire, who exhibited an apparatus demonstrating the rise and fall of the tides. It worked on the assumption that the earth was a living creature encased in a shell, like a snail, and that the ebb and flow of the tides was caused by the beating of its heart. Ryles accompanied the exhibit with a plea for a patron to help him prove his novel theory that the tides made the world go round. Hunt wrote:

> This must be classed among those curiosities of the Exhibition which it would have been friendly to have excluded. There is little doubt that the exhibitor is a man of ingenious mind and much industry, but unfortunately he represents a class of men who venture to invent while yet in perfect ignorance of the truths which investigation has placed beyond all doubt.

He was more generous about other curiosities, including Dr Merryweather's Tempest Prognosticator, based on the observed phenomenon that leeches leave the water if they detect changes in the atmosphere suggesting that a storm is brewing. In the device live leeches were placed in water and a bell rang when they began to crawl to the surface. Leeches were in 1851 still used by doctors for drawing blood: in the nearby display of surgical instruments, alongside glass eyes, false teeth and artificial limbs, was a mechanical leech which did the job quicker than the real thing and with less mess. Another innovation in health care, for doctors who wanted to be ready for emergencies without making their calling too obvious, was a walking stick containing medical instruments, medicines and an enema.

One of the half-dozen exhibits that most caught the public

imagination, during the Exhibition itself and in the many accounts of it written subsequently, was a mechanism for tipping people out of bed at a set hour. The most common story has it that the occupant of the bed was ejected into a bath of cold water – but this was merely one suggestion by the inventor, not actually demonstrated in the Crystal Palace: if it were, it would have been harder to find volunteers to submit themselves to the device among the policemen patrolling the Palace, some of whom seemed rather to enjoy the novel experience and the chance, however fleeting, to take the weight off their feet. A more practical bedroom gadget, shown nearby, was a bedstead for immobile invalids that lifted them up so that the bed could be made beneath them.

Here too were lenses, microscopes, magic lanterns, eye glasses, barometers, thermometers and a rain gauge that told the user what angle the rain fell at, as well as how much of it there was. An exhibit that defied easy categorisation was a mechanical human figure, made up of 7,000 small pieces of steel, that could expand or contract to correspond to anybody's measurements, allowing tailor-made clothing to be tried on and altered without the customer having to be present at every fitting.

One of the most exciting and significant inventions of the mid-nineteenth century was photography, and more than a dozen exhibitors showed the latest advances. It was only twelve years since the French pioneer Louis-Jacques-Mandé Daguerre – who died aged sixty-one in July 1851, during the course of the Great Exhibition – announced the first successful photographic process, the daguerreotype. Two years after that breakthrough, in 1841, William Henry Fox Talbot patented a more viable process, the calotype or talbotype, which laid the basis for the development of the craft. (Hunt was keen to claim it as a British invention.) More than 700 photographs, both daguerreotypes and talbotypes, were exhibited in the Crystal Palace, by British and overseas photographers. There were fewer actual cameras on display, but they included two portable models, looking forward to the day when they would become indispensable accessories for holidaymakers.

Walking back east along the north gallery, before crossing over to the south, we pass musical instruments on our right. Barrel organs, on which a selection of pre-set tunes could be played by turning a handle, had been popular since the late eighteenth century, not just with street entertainers but also, by the time of the Exhibition, in churches that could not run to a full-scale organ. Several on show here boasted suitably ecclesiastical Gothic adornments. The classic model worked by having pins, precision-fitted on to the barrel, operating levers that let air into the organ pipes. A variation on show here, called the Autophon, used instead sheets of perforated board that were fed into it, like the punched tape used on telegraph and telex machines in the twentieth century and the cards that operated early computers.

No fewer than thirty-eight exhibitors showed pianos, those essential adornments of any self-respecting Victorian middle-class drawing room. A collapsible piano, designed for 'gentlemen's yachts, ladies' cabins, saloons of steam vessels, etc.', measured only thirteen and a half inches from front to back when folded. Another had the instrument concealed inside a drawing-room table, springing into place when the table top was opened. Hunt was especially enthusiastic about a new range of low-cost pianos designed to spread the musical habit to the less well-off:

> The spread of taste among the humbler classes must ever be regarded as the most humanising of all good

gifts. With a keen relish for music amongst them, which is now rarely realised but by listening to the abortive attempts of an itinerant fiddler or organ-player, how much more might this taste be indulged if it could be gratified in a higher manner.

Cost had been a barrier, but 'it has remained for the exhibitors to remove this objection, by the manufacture of instruments which are by no means inferior to the best in tune and touch, but greatly so in price'.

Still heading back east, towards the centre of the Crystal Palace, we come on our right to Class 24, for objects made of glass – characterised by the ever-enthusiastic Hunt as 'one of the most extraordinary substances ever manufactured by the hand of man'. He was not convinced, though, that the objects on show did justice to this remarkable commodity. The repeal of the glass duty in 1845 had encouraged bottle manufacturers to experiment with a variety of shapes and sizes, of which some 800 were on show here, but Hunt commented: 'Art has not done much to improve bottle-making, as many of the forms used are crude and shapeless, and leave much room for improvement.' He blamed the fact that workmen were paid by the number of bottles they made in a day, discouraging experimentation.

On the other side of the aisle, Class 28, for products made from animal and vegetable substances, was another miscellaneous collection of the imaginative and ingenious. One story nicely illustrates the determination and commitment of the thousands of small traders and craftspeople who supplied the bulk of the British exhibits. In the 1820s Thomas Smith of Herstmonceux, in East Sussex, went into business making trugs – baskets formed from willow and chestnut in the shape of a coracle boat. They soon became popular, mainly for carrying garden produce, and he was delighted when they were admitted to the Great Exhibition where, despite being described as 'truck-baskets' in the catalogue, they won a gold medal. Better still, they caught Queen Victoria's eye on one of her walks round the gallery and she ordered several as gifts for her staff. When Smith had fulfilled the order, adding appropriately regal decoration, he and his brother piled the trugs in a handcart and delivered them personally to Buckingham Palace, covering the sixty miles on foot.

Here too were wigs, brushes and items made from various kinds of rubber, whose uses had only recently come to be appreciated fully. Several waterproof coats and fabrics were on display, including some from Mackintosh and Co., the company founded by Charles Macintosh, who invented the raincoat and whose name has since become a generic word for it. A craftsman from Clerkenwell showed a meticulously constructed model of a tower, with minarets, carved out of a thousand pieces of a material known as vegetable ivory – the seed of a Peruvian pine tree. Hats made from cork and a chandelier from straw were among other unusual exhibits.

The gallery over the north transept was filled mainly with British porcelain and other china. All the big names of Staffordshire pottery were represented: Minton, Copeland, Mason, Ridgway, Wedgwood, as well as Chamberlain's Worcester Porcelain factory and many smaller manufacturers. While they may not have been able to compete in terms of refined taste with the exhibits in the overseas section of the Exhibition, from factories such as Sèvres and Meissen, they showed that the British manufacturers were beginning to catch up with their European rivals.

There was a huge array of porcelain figures representing the royal family, other eminent people and scenes from history and mythology, plus something else that caught the Queen's fancy, on a somewhat grander scale than the Sussex trugs: a sumptuous dessert service that she bought for 1,000 guineas to present to the Austrian Emperor. In white, turquoise and gold, it comprised seventy-two dessert plates with paintings of birds, flowers and fruit, plus a range of elaborate baskets, wine coolers and centrepieces. The wine coolers had relief decoration representing a bear hunt, while on the top Bacchus, the god of wine, pressed the grapes. Minton showed a pair of enormous porcelain vases, one in turquoise and the other in blue, with silver and ormolu handles.

Next to the china was Class 29, for miscellaneous objects that would not fit easily into any other category. Umbrellas, parasols, walking sticks, pencils, pins and needles were jumbled together with fishing tackle, rocking horses, cricket equipment, candles, wax flowers and fruit. Some items of food and drink qualified to be exhibited here, because they involved novel production techniques: biscuits, lemonade, confectionery and even a few wedding cakes made with preservatives that allowed them to be sent long distances without deteriorating.

Among an array of stuffed birds and animals, one that stood out was a dodo, the flightless bird from Mauritius that became extinct in the seventeenth century because of the combination of its lethargic gait and the appetising flavour of its meat, which the island's Dutch settlers were unable to resist. A stuffed dodo was one of the highlights of John Tradescant's pioneering Museum of Curiosities in South Lambeth in the early seventeenth century, but much of the collection was destroyed when acquired by the Ashmolean Museum in Oxford more than a hundred years later. This Crystal Palace dodo was constructed on the basis of contemporary accounts of Tradescant's bird.

Still in the gallery, we have turned round and are making

our way back now to its western end for a final circuit that will allow us to complete our look at the British exhibits before plunging into the foreign half of the building. As we go, we can take the opportunity of admiring the carpets, tapestries and tablecloths suspended from the girders just above us. The far western wall accommodated naval architecture and military engineering, including those weapons of war that were admitted despite the stated aim of the Commission that the Exhibition's primary purpose should be to foster peace.

Larger models and equipment were shown on the ground floor, but the bulk of Class 8 was here upstairs, including models of historic ships such as Henry VIII's *Henry Grace de Dieu* and the Admiralty barge, as well as another made from wood taken from famous warships such as the *Victory* and *Temeraire*. There were scores of model lifeboats, including one made of rubber that inflated the moment it was released from its holder, in the manner of the airbag in a modern automobile.

Other items related to seafaring were also grouped at this end. There were some ingenious devices for preserving life, notably an unsinkable deckchair for passenger ships, a watertight trunk that could hold fifteen people and remain afloat, and a pair of swimming gloves shaped like webbed feet to give better flotation and propulsion – the same principle as in flippers for snorkellers. The telescopic sight was one of the innovations included in the display of rifles and small arms. Hunt marvelled at the wide range of price and quality in this section. Some splendidly ornamented guns would sell for hundreds of pounds, others for a few shillings:

> These low-priced guns, from the extreme cheapness with which the barrels are made, have received the name of 'park paling', for which they are well suited.

They are sold in vast numbers to the Brazilians, who exchange them for slaves in Africa.

Now we are walking back east along the southern side of the gallery. On our left is Class 23, works in precious metals and jewellery, and on our right 3 and 4 – substances used as food, and vegetable and animal products used in manufacture. Garrard's, the renowned West End jeweller, mounted a large display of gold and silverware and other priceless trinkets. The fabled Koh-i-Noor diamond took pride of place on the ground floor, near the crystal fountain, but up here in the gallery were a number of gems of almost equal – some say greater – splendour.

Principal among them was the blue-tinted forty-five-carat Hope Diamond, which had a romantic history. It was originally part of an immense 112-carat stone taken to France from India and bought by Louis XIV in 1668 to form part of the French crown jewels. He had it cut down to sixty-seven carats but it was purloined during the Revolution and reappeared in its present reduced but still magnificent state in 1830, when it was bought by Thomas Hope, a London banker, author and collector. Much later, it was acquired by the Smithsonian Institution at Washington, DC. The black Bahia Diamond, from Brazil, was even larger. Spectacular settings of small diamonds included one representing a bouquet of flowers, made up of 6,000 stones, and a portrait in relief of Louis XVI.

The food substances area was principally of interest to visitors engaged in farming. Many exhibits were of improved strains of domestic cereals and hops, developed to meet the needs of Britain's rapidly growing population, along with imported products such as cocoa, coffee and tea. Perishable food was not exhibited, but there were examples of recently perfected techniques of preservation, among them a canister of boiled mutton supplied to an Arctic exploration expedition in 1824 and found in perfect condition by another expedition twenty-five years later. Fortnum and Mason, then as now a prestigious London provision merchant, showed a range of nuts and dried fruits. The inclusion of tobacco products (including several Havana cigars) as a food crop was something of an anomaly even at a time when to chew tobacco was a popular alternative to smoking it. Hunt commented that the smoking habit 'has now grown almost into a necessity, despite the fiercest opposition'. Not much has changed there, then.

Class 4, for vegetable and animal substances used in manufacture, was dominated by timber, wool and flax. A Wiltshire farmer enlivened these somewhat staid exhibits by showing a stuffed Southdown ewe, which died aged seven without ever being shorn, and whose wool was twenty-five inches long. Beyond this was Class 2, for chemical and pharmaceutical products, where phials, tubes and bottles filled with multicoloured crystals and mysterious liquids gave the appearance of a sorcerer's laboratory. As well as medicines, some only recently discovered, there were many examples of colourful dyes. Rhubarb was shown here rather than among the food products, being valued in those days chiefly for its medicinal qualities.

On the other side of the southern gallery was lace – much of it from Honiton in Devon – embroidery, silks and velvets. Most of the silks were manufactured in Spitalfields, just east of the City of London, a centre of silk-weaving since French Huguenots established the industry there in the late seventeenth century. There were sixteen exhibitors from Paisley in Scotland, showing shawls in a variety of fabrics in the distinctive Paisley design, originally inspired by cloths imported from India. Here, too, were Irish poplins and ribbons from Coventry.

The last British display on this level was also one of the most fascinating – articles of clothing, representing items in common everyday use as well as novel variations, not all of which would catch on. From St Albans came a range of fancy headgear, including a Wellington hat (one of many articles of clothing, in addition to rubber boots, then named after the popular duke) made from a Brazilian palm leaf; a 'Chinese hat' and hats made of straw and willow. A ventilating hat admitted air through channels cut in cork, and let it out through a valve at the top. An inventor from Newark was showing a waistcoat that held up trousers without the use of braces, while others experimented with elastic, a new combination of cloth and rubber that allowed garments such as corsets and bodices to cling to the body without their wearers having to go through the laborious process of lacing.

London's Regent Street was keen to burnish its reputation as the leading centre of men's clothing and innovation. Wheeler and Ablett introduced 'the bachelor's shirt, of peculiar construction, without buttons'. A neighbour, S. Powell, was fighting a losing battle to gain acceptance for his word 'bisunique' to denote reversible garments. W. Reid, whose shop was just off Regent Street in Conduit Street, offered a shirt described as 'sans-pli', perhaps the forerunner of non-iron garments in the ensuing century. Scottish tartans proliferated – one pair of tartan socks was studded with 1,300 diamonds – as did patterned woollens from the Shetland Islands. Much was made in the catalogue of items knitted by 'peasant girls in their own home' and 'poor girls only nine months under tuition'.

At the halfway point on our journey around the Crystal Palace, we have inspected a comprehensive array of British products and inventions, both traditional and innovative, from great machines to trivial fripperies, as well as learning about the natural resources that fuel our role as a leading manufacturing nation. Now it is time to discover what our neighbours and competitors have to offer.

CHAPTER SEVEN

❧ ❧

AROUND THE WORLD
IN HALF A DAY

*Its grandeur does not consist in one thing, but in the unique assemblage of
all things. Whatever human industry has created you find there . . . It
seems as if only magic could have gathered this mass of wealth from all the
ends of the earth.*

Charlotte Brontë, 1851

*The exhibits . . . included perhaps the most eccentric collection of
ornate but tasteless objects in the way of furniture and manufactured
articles ever assembled together.*

J. M. Richards, in *Modern Architecture* (Penguin, 1956)

The overseas exhibits were grouped by country rather than
category, giving them a more random aspect than the
British and slightly reducing their overall impact. All the
same, the unfamiliarity and exoticism of many of the items on
show excited the curiosity of visitors. Crowds gathered
around those that especially captured the imagination, and
this in turn drew more onlookers, keen to see what the excitement was about. The display areas were divided between the
countries broadly by imaginary north–south lines, meaning

that the same country usually occupied space on both sides of the main east–west avenue, as well as in the galleries above.

So as our virtual tour continues, we shall seldom see all the products of one country in one go. The displays in the eastern half of the gallery, where we now stand, are in effect extensions of those immediately below them, showing smaller items from the same countries. They serve as a suitable hors d'oeuvre to each country's more important exhibits at ground level. As we begin to move east from the centre, along the southern gallery, we come first to our neighbouring super-power, France. Showing mainly clothing and textiles, the French exhibitors suitably complement the last British section that we saw, giving us the chance to make invidious comparisons.

The received opinion was that French silks and fancy fabrics were of finer quality than those made in Britain, in terms of both texture and design. British manufacturers conceded this and insisted that their strength was in mass production, enabling them to dominate an overwhelmingly price-conscious market. Up here was an opulent display of superb French fabrics, chiefly silks from Lyons, from which Queen Victoria had already selected liberally when choosing gifts for her household staff and relatives. Perhaps anticipating her interest, Lemonnier and Co., a Paris firm that specialised in making ornaments from human hair, exhibited a hair portrait of the Queen. If we look down over the railing to the French section of the ground floor, we see another tribute to her – an eighteen-foot-high statue in zinc that received a mixed reception from the critics.

We move on to the textiles of Austria, the richest country in continental Europe and almost at the peak of its imperial grandeur, embracing such fabulous cities as Venice, Milan, Prague and Budapest as well as Vienna, its capital. The chief

A photograph of Victoria and Albert taken in 1861, the year of Albert's death

The Royal Commission. Standing, left to right: Charles Wentworth Dilke, John Scott Russell, Henry Cole, Charles Fox, Joseph Paxton, Lord John Russell, Sir Robert Peel, Robert Stephenson. Seated, left to right: Richard Cobden, Charles Barry, Lord Granville, William Cubitt, Prince Albert, Lord Derby. (Only about half the Commissioners are depicted here, and Fox and Paxton were not in fact members.)

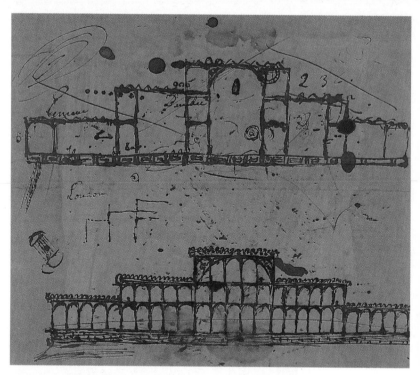

Paxton's original idea for the Crystal Palace, jotted on blotting paper at a meeting in Derby

This painting by C. Burton shows how close the finished building was to the early design

Two views of the opening ceremony. Above: Selous's famous painting, showing Queen Victoria with Prince Albert and her family in the centre. The uninvited Chinese 'ambassador' can be seen in the foreground. Below: This view by Nash shows the Crystal Fountain and details of the structure

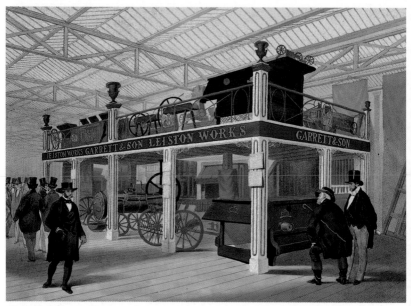

Garrett & Son's display of power-driven and manually operated agricultural machines

The Indian Court, showing the magnificent howdah adorning the stuffed elephant borrowed from an Essex amusement park

Louis Haghe's painting of one of the refreshment areas, showing two of the elm trees enclosed by the domed roof of the transept

The stained glass gallery. Although paintings were not allowed to be displayed at the Exhibition, stained glass was accepted as it was a manufactured product

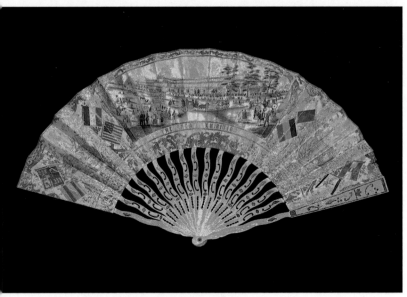

The Great Exhibition proved an inspiration for many decorative objects including wallpaper (left) and a souvenir fan (above)

Minton, one of the country's leading porcelain manufacturers, produced many royal commemorative items for the occasion

PRESENTED BY HER MAJESTY'S
COMMISSIONERS FOR THE
EXHIBITION OF M.DCCC.LI.
TO THE DEPARTMENT
OF PRACTICAL
ART.

COUNCIL.

EXHIBITORS.   JURORS   SERVICE

PRIZE.

A set of the medals awarded to winning exhibits

Rear view of the Crystal Palace as seen across the Serpentine

Austrian exhibits were downstairs, where its furniture, sculpture and machinery were shown. Up here were some of the traditional linen goods of the region, although this industry had in the preceding few years been hit by the growing popularity of cotton. There were rich ecclesiastical raiments in fine silk, manufactured in Vienna but using raw silk produced in Hungary. Leather goods included bridles, saddles, boots and gloves.

Most of the independent German states exhibited under the banner of the Zollverein, otherwise known as the Prusso-Bavarian League, a customs union established in 1834. Confusingly, though, the catalogue listed them under the names of the individual states, and it was hard to tell precisely which class of goods was exhibited where. The official plan of the gallery said that musical instruments and 'apparatus' were among the items shown at the upper level. Germany has a long tradition of making musical instruments, especially pianos, and of the several on show here the most remarkable was an aeolodion, resembling an organ in which bellows operated metal springs or tongues to produce the sound. The inventor, A. Baltzer of Frankfurt, also demonstrated a clock that displayed the correct time in twenty world cities.

Toys and models, mainly in tin and wood, are another German speciality, and there were enough on show here to delight the most demanding child. Some, though, were so elaborate that they must have been meant to impress rather than be used for active play. Grandest of all was a tableau containing more than 400 movable figures representing a garden fête at Castle Florence in Saxe-Coburg, Prince Albert's birthplace. Another tribute to the strong ties between Britain and Germany was a representation in pewter of an English regiment on parade in front of Queen Victoria. Then there was the so-called Philharmonic

Chandelier, decorated with portrayals of musicians in a well-known band.

Ploucquet's furry teacher and pupils.

The models that future generations would seize on to typify the Exhibition's strong undercurrent of high kitsch were the 'comicalities' of Hermann Ploucquet of Stuttgart. These tableaux, featuring several hundred stuffed animals in human situations, made a big impact, too, on contemporary visitors: Hunt devoted more than a page to describing them and reported that they drew large crowds daily. In 'Mrs Partington's Tea Party', stuffed ermine sat round a table, two holding mugs of tea to their lips, while another sat playing the harmonium and apparently singing along. Another tableau was made of stuffed frogs, one shaving another while a third walked behind carrying an umbrella. A hunting scene showed martens firing at hares, with weasels acting as beaters, while in a schoolroom another marten played teacher to four rabbit pupils. Hunt commented: 'The expression and attitudes of these little figures, while they have all the characteristics of the respective animals, are ridiculously like those of human beings in the same circumstances.'

Another item that attracted attention was on the stand of A. Koppe of Berlin: a Christmas tree, topped with a cupola lit by an internal lamp. The illuminated Christmas tree was a German tradition only introduced to Britain in the decade prior to the Exhibition, reputedly popularised by Prince Albert's insistence on including a tree in the royal Christmas celebrations.

We reach the east end of the southern gallery and make two left turns to go back along the north wall. Here are more exhibits from the Zollverein, interspersed with small collections of items from Russia and the United States, the bulk of whose displays were on the ground floor. We have our first look at a few of the products of Belgium and Italy, the latter including a dazzling silver filigree column from Sardinia in honour of the Great Exhibition. It was mounted on a pedestal adorned with a portrait of the Queen and the Union Jack, and on the top was a globe straddled by the allegorical figure of Fame. Next to it was a large filigree figure of Christopher Columbus – after Victoria and Albert, possibly the most popular subject for statuary in the Exhibition.

Now we return briefly to the British gallery exhibits, with displays of stained glass and wax flowers and fruit, before descending to make our way once more to Osler's crystal fountain at the centre of the building. We are going to walk east down the Main Avenue, to complete our look at the most important statues and other popular objects before we tour the eastern half. Quite close to the fountain was a gigantic sample of gold ore, from the Mariposa mine in California, exhibited by the wife of a gold-digger who was reported to have turned down an offer of £3,250 for it. Next to it were portraits of Queen Victoria and Prince Albert done on Sèvres china, based on original paintings by Franz Winterhalter, and John Bell's popular bronze statue of Andromeda, which Victoria bought for £300.

Beyond this was the Koh-i-Noor diamond, one of the big crowd-pulling attractions, although some visitors found it a let-down. Because the stone had been cut so poorly it sparkled less than people felt it should, and even placing it on black velvet did not give it the expected allure. Of ancient origin, the precious 191-carat jewel changed hands repeatedly through conquest in India and Iran, and was placed among the Crown Jewels only in 1849, when it was seized by the British army on the annexation of the Punjab. Because it disappointed so many people at the Great Exhibition it was recut in 1852 and slimmed down to 109 carats. Queen Elizabeth, mother of Elizabeth II, wore the reduced jewel in her crown at the 1937 coronation of her husband King George VI.

Not far away, in a cage resembling the one that enclosed the Koh-i-Noor diamond, was another spectacular collection of precious stones belonging to Alexander Hope, an author and Conservative Member of Parliament, the son of Thomas Hope who owned the Hope Diamond that we saw up in the gallery. Here was the largest known pearl in the world, two inches by four and a half inches, weighing three ounces and shaped something like a clenched fist. Alongside it were the largest known emerald, splendid sapphires and opals, more pearls and diamonds and a sword handle made of a single aquamarine.

We pass a large quartz crystal – contributed by the Duke of Devonshire, Paxton's employer – and still more statues of the living, the dead and the fictional: Zephyr and Aurora rubbed cold stone shoulders with the Marquis of Bute, the Provost of Eton College and Edward Jenner, pioneer of vaccination. After a formidable display of Spanish firearms and ammunition we come to sculptures from France, Belgium and Italy, mainly with classical subjects: Venus and Cupid disarmed; Psyche calling on Love for help; the torments of Cain. The zinc statue of the Queen, which we have already looked down on from above, was also hereabouts, near the largest figure in the Crystal Palace – a Belgian equestrian statue of Godfrey de Bouillon, an eleventh-century crusader. He was flanked by two small figures, also from Belgium, representing the happy and the unhappy child – the latter having just put his stick through the skin of his toy drum. Their cherubic style was reminiscent of Manneken-pis, the famous seventeenth-century fountain in Brussels.

A little further on was the German sculptor August Kiss's depiction of an Amazon on horseback attacked by a tiger, whose combination of energy and delicate modelling made it many people's favourite work in all of the Crystal Palace. The tiger's claws were embedded in the horse's body while the Amazon held her spear aloft, ready to deliver the decisive blow. Another German work, *The Boy With the Swan*, had been loaned by the Prussian King, while the Bavarian Lion, a plaster figure nine feet high and fifteen feet long, was destined to be placed on top of a triumphal arch in Munich. Beyond the next fountain were some huge Swedish vases made of porphyry, a reddish-purple mineral. Nearby were two large bouquets of artificial flowers made from feathers – the only contribution to the Exhibition from Brazil.

Soon we reach the first two American exhibits, a model of Niagara Falls and a mass of zinc weighing 16,400 pounds. Then came two widely praised marble statues by Hiram Powers, *The Greek Slave* and *The Fisher Boy*, and another

American work, *The Wounded Indian*. The reason why there were so many statues in the Crystal Palace was that paintings were not admitted, because it was supposed to be an exhibition of industry rather than art. Since sculpture involves a manufacturing process it qualified for inclusion, as did woodcuts, etchings and lithographic prints.

Now we are in the American section itself. In some senses the United States was the big winner at the Crystal Palace. When the Exhibition opened, the American display was the object of some derision, partly because, then as now, the British love taking a rise out of their transatlantic cousins and partly because transportation difficulties had prevented some of the items from arriving on time, leaving large gaps in its allotted space. Some of this empty expanse was filled by a statue of an Indian chief and his squaw, colourfully adorned with fur, feathers and paint, which shocked some critics because it contrasted so blatantly with the cool pallor of most of the other statues in the building. Soon more American goods would arrive – nothing fancy or spectacular, but for the most part useful and sometimes ingenious devices for performing everyday functions.

Agricultural implements figured strongly. In general these were of lighter construction than their British equivalents and for that reason were at first derided by farmers; but an American exhibitor wrote to the London papers to maintain that they did just as good a job and were a lot cheaper: 'The cost of a set of English farm implements would buy a farm, and a good one, in America.' Not just that, but the unnecessary weight of British tools and agricultural clothing slowed the work down.

When tested competitively towards the end of the summer, the American devices generally performed the better.

With the Exhibition on the point of closure, *The Times* magnanimously congratulated the Americans on recovering from their poor start, and commented that the 'mortifying but useful defeats we [the British] have received from our children across the Atlantic . . . will keep our manufactures utilitarian in their character and strengthen vastly the mechanical and inventive genius of the country'.

One of those defeats concerned two British locks, made by the prestigious London firms of Chubb and Bramah, and considered so unpickable that Bramah had offered a prize of £200 to anyone who could open theirs. An American locksmith named Hobbs picked both devices, although he took several weeks on Bramah's and had to send for new tools halfway through. Edward Bramah objected to this, in effect accusing Hobbs of cheating, and the matter was referred to an impartial committee – among its members the engineer Joseph Bazalgette – who decided in Hobbs's favour. Then Hobbs offered a £500 prize to anyone who could pick his American lock, but nobody dared to try. Game, set and match to the Americans.

Horace Greeley, founder and editor of the *New York Tribune*, spent much of that summer in London, acting as a judge for some of the Exhibition awards. He wrote a reasonably impartial account of his countrymen's efforts in letters to his newspaper, later published as a book. The letters were, he wrote,

> mainly written when the persistent and unsparing disparagement of the British press had created a general impression that the American exhibition was a mortifying failure, and when even some of the Americans in Europe, taking their cue from the press, were declaring themselves 'ashamed of their country'

because of such failure . . . More recently, the tide has turned, until the danger now imminent is that of extravagant if not groundless exaltation . . . The truth lies midway between the two.

Writing in the opening week, he noted:

Punch this week reiterates *The Times*'s slurs at the meagreness and poverty of the American contribution. This is meanly invidious and undeserved . . . The American genius is quicker, more wide-awake, more fertile than the British; I think that if our manufactures were as extensive and firmly established as the British, we should invent and improve machinery much faster than they do; but I do not wish to deny that this is quite a considerable country.

He reported a visit to the American section by the Queen and the Prince, when they spent over an hour there and said they were surprised by the variety of the American exhibits and the quality of some of them. He went on to explain the importance of this apparently quite modest royal endorsement: 'No American who has not been in Europe can conceive the extent of royal influence in this direction. What the Queen does, everyone who aspires to social consideration makes haste to imitate if possible.'

The two American exhibits that made the most impact were the McCormick reaping machine and the Colt revolver. Samuel Colt, born in 1814 in Hartford, Connecticut, began his working life as a seaman, and in his free time during one long voyage he carved a wooden model of a pistol with an automatically revolving chamber that would allow several bullets to be fired in quick succession without reloading. He stuck with the idea and by 1835 had made and patented a single-barrelled weapon whose cartridge cylinder rotated each time the hammer was cocked, bringing a new bullet into the barrel.

McCormick's American reaping machine.

Americans were slow to accept the new-fangled device and the first company that he formed to produce them soon went bankrupt. But army units operating against American Indians and Mexicans found them effective and the Government began to put in large orders, allowing Colt to resuscitate his business in the late 1840s. After the Exhibition he donated fifty revolvers to British army officers to persuade them of their effectiveness.

In a thoughtful leading article *The Times* pointed out that the revolver, reported as having been used in fifteen out of twenty recent murders in the untamed western state of California, was a mixed blessing. 'The invention supplies both temptation to the offence and certainty in its execution; for it must be bad shooting indeed if one shot does not tell out of five.' While it had proved useful in skirmishes on America's southern frontier, 'we very much question whether Mr Colt's discovery has not cost the Americans more lives than the Mexicans' – a judgement that would unhappily be confirmed in the American Civil War a decade later.

Much of the wealth of the United States, in these its pioneer years, derived from discovering and mining its seemingly limitless resources of minerals, and many of its exhibits reflected that. Lumps of quartz, copper, limestone, lead, tungsten, zinc and iron ore were everywhere. Although some were of an impressive size, they did not amount to a gripping visual experience for visitors untutored in their significance – not even for this audience, seemingly prepared to gawp at almost anything. The machinery, though, was a different matter. A small sewing machine, about a foot square, excited a great deal of interest, as nothing like it had been seen in Britain before. 'It is worked by a small girl,' Hunt enthused, 'and makes a saving of not less than six to eight girls by each machine.' Isaac Merritt Singer had not yet brought to market his domestic sewing machine that would become part of the lives of millions of women across the world.

There were machines for cutting stone, and for making nails, spikes and candles; all of them replacing repetitive manual labour. These were the seeds of the American industrial revolution that within half a century enabled the United States to lead the world in the manufacture of such products as steel, automobiles and later aircraft. The country's native ingenuity was shown in devices including a ship's barometer that struck a gong to alert the helmsman to a reduction in barometric pressure; a process of making animal feed into long-life biscuits; several adjustable reclining chairs; a round office table with revolving pigeon-holes; a device for turning the pages of sheet music automatically; another for opening gates without getting up from your horse-drawn carriage; a bed that folded into a suitcase; and a vacuum coffin that preserved the body for long enough to allow far-flung friends to attend the funeral. There were technologically advanced machines for printing books and newspapers and making banknotes, as well as some admired examples of photography.

The Americans continued to add items to their display until the very last weeks. In September came some dazzling dinner plates made from gold dug up in a California mine only three months earlier. At the same time an artificial leg arrived, patented by a Mr Palmer of Philadelphia, who had himself lost a leg and who was publisher of the annual *Palmer's Patent Artificial Leg Reporter and Surgical Adjuvant*. The leg was reported to be 'a great boon to suffering humanity' and remarkably lifelike: 'A lady may wear silk hose and slippers without betraying the loss she has sustained.'

Hunt was bemused by the large collection of American novelty soaps, shaped as portrait busts, flowers and letters of the alphabet, and one taking the form of a stained-glass window. But he adopted a superior tone when discussing the range of soaps alleged to be used by prominent people, pointing out sniffily that he could not comment on their quality, 'not having had the opportunities of testing their cleansing properties that Jenny Lind [the internationally renowned singer] and other celebrated persons have enjoyed, as set forth by their certificates exhibited on one of the stalls'. The nascent Yankee skill of marketing through celebrity endorsement had yet to take hold in Britain.

Now we shall head back towards the centre of the building. For the sake of the coherence of this description we have to imagine ourselves zig-zagging from north to south across the Main Avenue as we walk west, because many countries' exhibits are displayed on both sides. To fortify ourselves before we begin this final assault on the remainder of the Exhibition we can visit the second refreshment area, in the north-west corner, where we might also take advantage of George

Jennings' much-lauded toilet facilities.

After this break, we reach the small but impressive and quite valuable display of goods from Russia. The most interesting were in malachite, a carbonate of copper with a greenish sheen, mined in Siberia on land owned by Count Demidoff. He had a room constructed and furnished almost entirely in malachite. The folding entrance doors, thirteen feet high, were made of wood covered with copper, with a quarter-inch layer of malachite on the surface, decorated and panelled in gilt bronze. The room contained eight chairs, four tables, a mantelpiece, a clock, vases, paperweights and table ornaments, all in same material.

The names of the Russian exhibitors, as printed in the catalogue, gave clues to the hierarchical nature of the society. Many were imperially controlled factories – the Imperial Cannon Foundry, the Imperial Copper Works, the Imperial Mining Works and suchlike. The Tsar himself lent a fabulous collection of jewellery and silver, notably an ebony jewel box ornamented with precious stones shaped as fruit: the grapes made of amethyst, rowan berries of coral, pears of agate, plums of onyx and cherries of cornelian. Next to this was a candelabra formed from two hundredweight of silver, depicting the Battle of Koulikoff, at which Russia defeated the Tartars in 1380. At the other extreme were several more modest exhibits: a goat's-hair shawl from 'a Cossack's wife', spun camel's hair from a 'tribe of Bashkirs', ornamental head-dresses from 'peasant women, Kherson'.

The Scandinavian countries were less well represented. Sweden, Norway and Denmark (including Iceland) managed to muster fewer than one hundred exhibitors between them, peeved as they were by the decision not to allow goods to be priced. Sweden concentrated chiefly on the products of its thriving steel industry, from razors to swords. Along with the porphyry vases in the aisle, its most eye-catching item was a colossal cross hewn from a single block of granite, but this was shown outside the Crystal Palace. Denmark's most unusual entry was a rifle with an oval barrel for firing cone-shaped bullets.

In discussing a new Danish typesetting machine, Hunt demonstrated the peril of making definitive predictions about technological advance. While the inventor seemed to have made progress in the technique of sorting type mechanically into individual letters, Hunt observed that there were some functions that machines would never be able to take over from humans, among them the skill of 'justifying' lines of type, or adjusting the spaces between words so that the letters on the right of the text lined up as straight as those on the left: 'This a rational being only could accomplish, it being an operation requiring judgment as well as sight.' Tell that to your twenty-first-century word-processor. Dazzled by the inventiveness of the myriad items that filled the Crystal Palace, Hunt made the same error as many other visitors in thinking that human ingenuity had gone about as far as it could, and that few further significant advances were possible. 'State-of-the-art', as a concept and a phrase, had not yet been dreamed up; nor had the realisation that wonders would truly never cease.

The German states came next. Here, alongside the minerals and agricultural products, were exquisite jewellery and other precious objects, many displayed in a specially constructed octagonal room, with a small fountain that dispensed not water but eau de Cologne, in which ladies were invited to dab their handkerchiefs. The gold and silver pieces of a chess set were done as miniature portraits of European historical figures – the two kings being Charles V of Austria and Francis I of France. There was some fine Dresden china, an allegorical inkstand in gold and silver gilt, a dazzling jewel casket that doubled as a music box, ivory goblets carved with battle scenes, and a filigree tower, set with garnets, described in the catalogue as 'similar to those used by the Russian Jews in the celebration of the Sabbath'.

Three pendulum clocks, each less than an inch wide, aroused much curiosity; but the most elaborate piece of silverware was a huge fruit dish, four and a half feet high, adorned with figures symbolising man's progress towards civilisation. Nomadic tribes occupied the base, the first farmers were just above them, then the symbols of industry, the sciences and the arts. At the top was intelligent man, with a raised torch, standing on top of a palm tree with a subjugated serpent beneath: man conquers his basest passions.

German furniture, too, was extravagantly decorated, for the most part in characteristic heavy Gothic style: there was even a Gothic birdcage. A round rosewood table was inlaid with a portrait of Shakespeare surrounded by scenes from twelve of his plays, while an eye-catching display of walking sticks was arranged in the shape of a star. A wall ornament in the octagonal room was an extraordinary jumble of cornices, mirrors, brackets and shelves mounted with statuettes of muses, angels and European royalty, inevitably including Victoria and Albert.

Sculptures of prominent people and allegorical scenes – made of marble, plaster, cast iron, zinc and copper – were scattered through the large German exhibition area. Some were symbols of German unity. Cupid appeared frequently, while Beethoven stood on a pedestal, surrounded by figures representing joy, sadness, religion and chivalry. There was a collection of heads of hunted animals, modelled in imitation bronze – a less grisly alternative to the actual heads of the beasts mounted on so many huntsmen's walls. Nearby was a stuffed horse, with no detectable seam in the skin.

Austria came next, with exhibits of a grandeur befitting an empire that then included much of the Balkans and parts of what would eventually become northern Italy – notably Venice, with its outstanding decorated glass, and Milan, traditionally a centre of fine art. An entire room was devoted to sculpture, nearly all of it from Milan, and this proved so popular with spectators that barriers had to be erected and a one-way system enforced.

Another crowd-puller was a suite of four decorated rooms from Vienna – dining room, library, drawing room and bedroom – complete with inlaid wood floors and elaborately carved furniture. The dining table, in locust wood, seated forty people, and the same wood was used for the enormous bedstead, hung in crimson and gold. The neo-Gothic bookcase in the library had already been presented to Queen Victoria by the Austrian Emperor. A clock in the dining room had seventy-two dials, showing the mean time in all European capitals, and alongside it was an eight-day clock showing the day and the month. Here, too, was another eau-de-Cologne fountain, larger than the one in the German section.

From Budapest came an embossed silver tableau made up of 217 figures of men, elephants and horses, representing Alexander the Great's capture of Porus, King of India, in 326 BC, with a companion piece in copper depicting Alexander and Darius at the Battle of Arbela five years earlier, with hundreds of figures punched out in relief. The catalogue noted that their creator, J. Szentpeetrij, was self-taught, and worked on the pieces over a period of five years.

On a more down-to-earth level, the Austrian empire was an important producer of matches, originally known as 'Lucifer matches' – a recent invention, in common use for no more than twenty years. One Viennese manufacturer made a montage of matches with different coloured tips, arranged so as to depict the imperial eagle. Smokers were well catered for here: no fewer than twenty-nine Austrian exhibitors showed tobacco pipes, from cheap clay to expensive meerschaum, in a variety of novel shapes. L. Franz of Vienna had a hollow walking-stick that could double as a pipe, for those tobacco addicts unable to resist a puff on their perambulations.

The Imperial Printing Office in Vienna, employing nearly a thousand people, mounted one of the few Austrian exhibits that aimed to be instructive, as well as displaying national products and skills. This huge undertaking printed material in most of the languages of the world, and showed specimens of 104 distinct alphabets and the machinery used to produce them. A supporting display explained how the various families of scripts and languages had developed over the years, each being modified as it came into contact with another. The Lord's Prayer was shown printed in 608 languages or dialects that employed Roman typefaces, and in 206 languages using more exotic characters. Advanced lithographic techniques of reproducing art works were demonstrated, with the original picture hung beside the printed version to show how exact a copy it was.

Holland had one of the smaller national displays, with only 114 exhibitors taking part. At its entrance, though, was one of the most glittering of all the objects on show, the Knyphausen Hawk, another loan from the Duke of Devonshire. The life-size model of the bird was covered with precious stones such as rubies, amethysts and carbuncles, as was the rock on which it stood. There is a legend that it was made to celebrate the end of a feud between two Dutch families, and removing the hawk's head revealed a gold cup from which the squabbling noblemen were said to have drunk their toast to peace. While most of the Dutch exhibits were in this decorative vein – they included cloaks, muffs and ruffles made from the feathers of the great crested grebe and marabou stork – there was an impressive practical display of the world's most powerful magnets, one of them capable of lifting weights of 500 pounds.

Belgium made a greater effort than its neighbour, with 512 exhibitors in its section. Many were showing sculptures, adding to those that we already came across in the nave. Victoria and Albert were represented in porcelain, the Belgian King and Queen in bronze and Princess Charlotte in plaster. *The Lion in Love* depicted the beast foolishly allowing the object of his passion to cut off his claws. There were large quantities of machinery and furniture – among the latter a revolving library table that rotated vertically like the wheel of a paddle steamer. A student needing many books on hand for reference could turn the wheel until the appropriate shelf – which always stayed horizontal – reached eye level: another bright idea that never caught on.

Now we reach France, the largest and most significant of the overseas sections, with 1,740 exhibitors, destined to win a raft of prizes. No country in the world had better learned how to combine fine art, superlative design and sophisticated manufacturing processes. Sèvres porcelain, Gobelins tapestries, Limoges enamels, Parisian bronzes and clocks are among the classes of French production that had even then become bywords for taste and quality, and all were represented here, along with some extremely stylish furniture and wallpaper. Despite their sophistication, though, the French were as prone as other nationalities to succumb to the lure of novelty, as in a desk whose drawers all flew open at the turn of the key and a 'California bedstead' that could be folded and carried under the arm, designed for emigrants who wanted to travel light.

French sculptures often featured movement and drama. A plaster statue of St Michael wrestling with a dragon proved popular, as did two groups depicting children in peril – one being defended by a dog from a poisonous snake, and another attacked by an eagle. French jewellery and silverware was much appreciated: they were especially good at making 'paste' or fake jewellery for the theatre and for women to wear on occasions when they did not want to risk exposing their genuine gems. An imitation table napkin in silver, as an adornment for a dinner table, gained particular praise. Bookbinding was another area where France led the world: there were books bound in velvet, morocco leather, ivory and carved wood.

The French, though, wanted it all ways, and were unhappy that there was so little appreciation of the many items of farm and other machinery that they transported across the Channel. 'Crude', 'heavy' and 'inconvenient' were just three of the epithets that Hunt ascribed to these. Nor was he impressed with the French pianos, which 'want sufficient softness and delicacy of touch and sometimes are defective in harmonious sound' – undeniably a serious fault in a musical instrument.

Continuing towards the centre of the Crystal Palace, the next country we reach is Italy, split into three separate areas as Sardinia (then including Piedmont and Savoy), Tuscany and Rome. The highlights here were marvellous displays of mosaics from Rome and Florence, all executed with meticulous craftsmanship, some set into tables and others presented as art works in their own right. Subjects included buildings and landscapes in Italian cities, as well as animals and birds. Another Roman skill on display was that of engraving cameos on shells and onyx, while the Florentines sent some splendid carved furniture: a chair gilded to look like porcelain and a casket symbolising the glory of Britain, with a figure of Britannia and scenes of naval and military triumphs. A large plaster figure depicted Columbus unveiling America to the world, and, by minuscule contrast, a cherry stone was intricately carved with a figure of St George and the dragon on one side and twenty-four human heads on the other. The Sardinian section likewise celebrated the skill of miniaturisation, with examples of printing from microscopic typefaces. Here too were a stuffed elk and a foldaway bed disguised as a sideboard.

On to Spain, Portugal and their colonial possessions, especially Cuba and the Philippines, where the air was laden with heady aromas. The path leading to the section was lined with barrels of several varieties of fine snuff, with cigars from Havana and cheroots from Manila completing the assault on our nostrils. Furniture made from tropical timbers was inlaid to form intricate patterns, and from Spain itself came a carved wooden model of the Madrid bull-ring, filled with several thousand spectators wearing Spanish provincial dress. There was a piece of the original wall of the Alhambra, the Moorish palace at Granada. Portugal showed a sword presented to Field Marshal Viscount Beresford, its scabbard illustrating battles fought under his leadership in the Peninsular War.

Across the avenue, the Swiss were playing to their strengths, showing some cleverly carved wooden models, toys and furniture, including white wood tables painted with local views. A model of a Bernese farmhouse had a roof that could be removed to allow the detail of every room to be examined. But it was the clocks and watches that dominated this stand. They came in an extraordinary variety of settings – in bracelets, brooches, lockets, rings, or attached to thermometers and compasses. Many were miniaturised, the smallest having a face less than a quarter of an inch in diameter, on which it told the month and the day as well as the hours and minutes. These were the watches that so fascinated the Queen, as she noted in her diary.

Hunt explained why Swiss watches were not only delicately crafted but also comparatively cheap. It was because a system of home working was employed, in which the individual parts were made by the out-workers, often members of the watchmaker's family, who 'employ their long winter evenings in the construction of various parts'. These were then sent to the towns, where the watchmaker himself assembled and sold them.

Greece, Persia, Turkey and Egypt shared the north-east corner of the junction between the transept and the Main Avenue, with China and Tunis across the avenue to the south. The Greek presence was small, with only sixty-one exhibitors, and consisted mainly of the marble sculptures for which the country has been known since ancient times. On the Persian, Turkish, Egyptian and Tunisian stands were characteristic Middle Eastern carved boxes and spoons, hookahs for smoking tobacco, decorated swords and pistols, jewellery and ornaments in silver and precious stones. Turkey mounted an impressive display of animal skins used in the fur trade. In all the variations of smoking accessories that we have seen in the Crystal Palace, the Turks came up with the most ingenious: a pipe that doubled as a crutch for a lame man. The Egyptians showed many examples of their agricultural produce, including cereals, beans, cotton, sugar, tobacco, flax, lentils and even lupins.

The Chinese section (which incorporated some items from Japan) deservedly occupied a prominent position near the centre of the Exhibition, and always drew a good crowd. Most of the goods were provided not by Chinese traders or officials but by London merchants engaged in the China trade. As we would expect, fine porcelain claimed pride of place –

not only a selection of exquisite wares but also a display of the techniques involved in their manufacture. Other Chinese products included silks, bamboo and lacquered furniture, lanterns, fans and many samples of tea, with paintings on rice paper that illustrated how the tea is harvested and processed. Another exhibit explained the origin of rice paper itself – the pith or tissue from the stem of a tree in the ginseng family, pressed into very thin sheets.

Hunt was intrigued by what he called the 'edible bird's nest', the basis for bird's nest soup. 'This substance, so valued by the epicures of the Celestial empire, is apparently in part of animal and in part of vegetable origin.' In fact it is largely composed of the saliva of the swiftlet, a species of humming-bird. Hunt was slightly outfaced by the Chinese tradition of grotesque carvings, using the gnarled roots of trees to heighten the sinister effect. 'The Chinese toys exhibited would be enough to frighten any European baby,' he complained. There was some delicate miniature furniture, and bottles carved from peach stones. A curious sword had been construc-ted from Chinese coins of the type that have holes in the middle, strung together to form the blade and hilt.

We have now completed our tour of the highlights inside the Crystal Palace, but our visit is not quite finished yet. Some bulky items, impervious to the weather, were kept outside, and we are going to make a quick circuit of the perimeter before we leave. At the eastern end were just five exhibits: the large cross hewn from a single block of Swedish granite; a French lifeboat; a cast-iron fountain, also from France; an Indian tent; and a thirty-foot weeping cypress tree from China.

There was a great deal more to admire on the western side, especially for those who enjoyed looking at gargantuan pieces of stone and minerals. There were eighteen large lumps of coal, from fields in England, Scotland and Wales, including the one whose slow progress to London from Swansea was reported in detail by the newspapers in the weeks before the Exhibition opened. A cross-section of a Staffordshire coal seam was brought here to show the various strata of soil and minerals in a typical pit formation. Thirty exhibitors showed big blocks of cement and stone, both natural and artificial, and there were three tall granite columns.

Glazed stoneware jars and other vessels, mainly for use in the chemical industry, were shown here, as well as high-capacity drainage pipes made of the same material, much in demand as towns and cities hastened to install modern sewer systems. Doulton's of Lambeth, one of the principal manu-facturers, claimed to be making five miles of sewage pipes a week. Three anchors, big enough to secure the largest war-ships, impressed with their enormous scale, while a pair of automatic level-crossing gates helped meet growing concerns about rail safety. On a smaller scale was a display of clay flowerpots.

A few yards from all this stood Marochetti's equestrian statue of Richard Coeur de Lion – later moved to its present site outside the new Houses of Parliament – making a fittingly heroic final image as we finally tear ourselves away from Paxton's palace of glass. If we still have an ounce of energy left we could walk a few hundred yards to the Guards' Barracks to inspect the model workers' dwellings designed by Prince Albert – a block of four flats that stand today, forlorn and isolated, in Kennington Park. Otherwise we could join the throng trying to find an omnibus or a cab to take them home, or maybe, if the wait seems too long, we might cross Knightsbridge to Gore House, on the site of the present-day Royal Albert Hall, and treat ourselves to a supper that should prove more sustaining and delectable than what we were able to find in the refreshment courts.

This former home of the bankrupt Lady Blessington was where Alexis Soyer, the first French chef to make a name for himself in London, opened in 1851 'The Symposium of All Nations', an extensive international restaurant with a banqueting room big enough for 1,500 people. The house had an eventful history. Built in the 1750s, its early owners included Admiral Lord Rodney and William Wilberforce, the campaigner against slavery. In 1836 Lady Blessington (née Marguerite Power), a colourful and beautiful Irish writer and a close friend of Lord Byron, moved here and established a famous literary and political salon attended by such luminaries as the Duke of Wellington, Benjamin Disraeli, Louis Napoleon and Charles Dickens. Twice married (the first time at the age of fifteen), Lady Blessington was by then living with her lover, the French dandy Count d'Orsay, the husband of her stepdaughter. Their extravagance led to bankruptcy, and in 1849 they were forced to leave London for Paris, where she died of apoplexy the same year.

By 1850 the house stood empty. Soyer and his partner in the venture, the cartoonist George Sala, spent a fortune on equipping it as a luxury restaurant and banqueting house, hoping to attract the cream of the Exhibition's élite visitors. First we shall wander through the grounds, where we might come across a strolling entertainer or two as we admire the statues, fountains, lights and a banqueting table 300 feet long, covered but open to the elements on the sides. We pass through the entrance hall and absorb its vast mural depicting the statesmen and leading writers of the age – many of whom used to be regulars at Lady Blessington's salon – in the company of real and legendary beasts. Tearing ourselves away, we enter the sumptuously decorated dining room, where we should have no difficulty in finding a table: the establishment would close in October, having lost Soyer and Sala £7,000. For some of the visitors who chose to sample the restaurant's delights, it may have been their first taste of the gastronomic specialities of the nations whose products they had just come from admiring. Although a commercial failure, Soyer's Symposium was a significant landmark in the introduction of continental influences to the English palate.

❦ ❦

CHAPTER EIGHT

IN FOR A SHILLING

Never before in England had there been so free and general
a mixture of classes as under that roof.

John Tallis, *Tallis's History and Description of the Crystal Palace, and the*
Exhibition of the World's Industry in 1851 (London, 1852)

For most of May, the upper classes had the Crystal Palace to themselves. On the Friday and Saturday after the opening the admission price of £1 a head kept out all but the very wealthy: just over a thousand attended over the two days. For the next three weeks the fee was five shillings – not prohibitive, but a distinct deterrent given that it had already been announced that the charge on Mondays to Thursdays would go down to a shilling on 26 May. It would be up to two shillings and sixpence (half a crown) on Fridays and five shillings on Saturdays, for those who wanted to avoid contact with the lower orders. The Exhibition was closed on Sundays – a costly tribute to the influence of the Sabbatarian groups campaigning to keep the Lord's Day holy.

For the first three weeks the average daily attendance was under 10,000, so by the time the cheaper admissions came into effect, fewer than 200,000 people had been to see the show. The result of this deliberately slow start was that it was not possible in those first weeks to gauge for certain whether the Great Exhibition was going to live up to its name, or be a gigantic flop.

The first reaction of visitors, to judge from correspondence in the newspapers, involved the traditional British pastime of complaining about the amenities. It was not just the catering. There were many protests about exploitative cab drivers, with one correspondent indignant at being charged three shillings for the journey from Holborn to Knightsbridge, half as much again as it usually cost. Moreover the journey was now taking much longer, because of the traffic jams along Piccadilly and Knightsbridge – with the result that some cabs and omnibuses were dropping their passengers a good quarter of a mile from the entrance so that they could find new fares more quickly.

Profiteering by the omnibus companies and the insolence of their conductors were the most frequent complaints. On wet days they refused to take passengers for less than a shilling, no matter how short the distance they wanted to travel. Indeed, it was hard to go any distance into the suburbs, for buses whose routes notionally took them as far as Kennington in the south and Islington in the north found it more profitable to shuttle between Hyde Park and Charing Cross, where passengers would have to find another conveyance – and an additional fare – to take them further.

Deploring such abuses in a leading article, *The Times* commented: 'The relation of the metropolitan cab-men to foreigners, strangers and ladies is simply that of the wolf to the sheep tribe.' To help counter this exploitation, it published a list of authorised cab fares to the Exhibition from all parts of London; but that did not deter the cabmen and bus conductors from taking advantage of the ignorant yokels when they could.

On the positive side, the paper reported that several

clergymen from working-class districts had enquired whether arrangements could be made to bring in parties from their parishes. 'A general desire seems felt that every facility should be given to the industrial classes to see and enjoy the magnificent spectacle which their labour has created.' And there was more good news: contrary to fears, the Exhibition was not frightening the horses. Rotten Row, Hyde Park's famous ride, was functioning normally. 'Horses gallop past the Exhibition without starting, and the numbers and fashion of the habitués appear to have undergone no significant diminution.'

So far so good, but on 17 May, nine days before the price of admission was due to be reduced, *The Times* wondered if sufficient thought had been given to making provision for the expected hordes. 'The building is calculated to hold 60,000 people – a large number, certainly, but hardly sufficient if the humbler classes show a curiosity about the contents of the Exhibition at all proportionate to that displayed by their superiors.'

Fears of a large and unruly gathering of the great unwashed still haunted respectable Londoners, and on 19 May William Mayne of the Metropolitan Police wrote a letter to the Commissioners that reflected his incipient panic. A prudent man, he thought that the gates should be closed when 45,000 or 50,000 people were inside. 'If the numbers are so great that they cannot move about, they will become discontented and uncontrollable.' Extra police should be deployed to manage the queues outside. Other measures to combat overcrowding could include asking the railway companies to sell reserved tickets for the Exhibition in advance, and instituting a separate entrance for ticket-holders. Inside, a one-way system should be introduced to ease traffic flow, and a method established for the police to inform to their colleagues when any of the aisles was blocked.

Alexander Redgrave, the official charged with overseeing the arrangements for working-class visitors to London, was concerned about what might happen elsewhere in the city. He feared that Whit Monday and Tuesday, 9 and 10 June, being holidays in many manufacturing areas, would see a huge influx of people on excursion trains, putting perilous pressure on the Crystal Palace. He wrote to Lord Granville suggesting that, to head off this threat, Londoners be provided with alternative entertainments to divert them from going to the Exhibition on those two days, leaving it all to the out-of-towners. He proposed military parades and displays by artillery and cavalry in different locations around the capital – although he was careful to insist that a regiment of Guards remain in their barracks, on alert to quell any disorder.

Horace Greeley, reporting back to his *New York Tribune*, made some astute and far-sighted observations about these fears of the mob:

> Faith in man abstractly is weak here, while faith in the police, the Horse Guards and the gallows is strong. There are always 200 soldiers and 300 policemen in the building while it is open to the public, and in case of any attempt at robbery every outlet would (by means of the telegraph) be closed and guarded within a few seconds, while hundreds if not thousands of soldiers are at all times on call. But they will not be needed.

On Friday 23 May a number of newspapers, noting that there were only two more visiting days before 'King Mob' took over, urged all those who could afford five shillings to hurry to see the Exhibition in serene conditions. They needed no encouraging. That day some 16,000 people were admitted, and

20,000 on the Saturday – the highest figure yet. The railway companies were already reporting double the usual traffic on their trunk routes. 'This is really a prodigious success,' *The Times* decided, although it had some stern words for those many visitors appearing not to give the exhibits the attention they deserved:

> The aristocratic, the fashionable and the well-to-do portions of the community have had the privileges of their station in life amply provided for during more than twenty days of leisurely inspection . . . We fear, however, that they have made indifferent use of their opportunities. The nave is filled day after day with loungers, who appear to come there with no other object than to see and be seen.

Sometimes the behaviour of the well-to-do was frankly appalling. On the last five-shilling Saturday in May, the paper reported that a Spanish family, wearing national costume, had been brought to the Crystal Palace by Lord Ranelagh. 'They were stared at and crowded round with a perseverance and impudence which, considering the charge for admission, and the presumed presence of a rather select assemblage, said very little for its good breeding.'

The leader writer hoped, if with limited confidence, that the shilling-payers would take it all rather more seriously, by using the Exhibition as a springboard for a general improvement in public education and awareness. This is what he wrote on the morning when the lower fee came into effect:

> Among millions there will, of course, be a great deal of ignorance and dullness. To the end of time, the cobbler will always be a poor creature beyond the

> reach of his last. His criticisms, if he criticises or
> notices at all, will not be worth much . . . That is the
> work which we hope to see beginning in good earnest
> this day – the gradual rising of our industrial classes
> from lamentable incultivation, ignorance and moral
> debasement.

Against this background of high-minded altruism, mingled
with a vague dread of the unpredictable, the first shilling
customers were admitted to the Crystal Palace at ten a.m. on
26 May. The 300 policemen inside and outside the building
included some loaned by foreign cities to identify known
troublemakers, and wooden barriers had been erected to control the crowds. Placards announced that the doors would be
shut after the first 60,000 people had been admitted. As the
Daily News observed: 'As many precautions were taken as if an
irruption of the Huns had been anticipated.' The Queen and
Prince Albert had timed one of their regular visits so as to be
there when the doors opened, but security was more tightly
controlled than in the earlier days, when the crowds had
parted spontaneously to let the royals walk through unmolested.

The anticipated flood of visitors did not materialise, and it
all proved a colossal anticlimax. By opening time, scarcely a
thousand people were waiting to be admitted. No doubt
deterred by the predictions of uncontrolled chaos on this first
popular day, the lower orders revealed their native good sense
by biding their time until the novelty began to wear off. Only
21,258 turned up – scarcely more than on the previous five-
shilling Saturday. *Punch* reported:

> On reaching the doors of the Exhibition, we found
> massive barriers intended to contain the multitude:

THE POUND AND THE SHILLING.
"Whoever Thought of Meeting You Here?"

Punch *celebrates the mingling of the classes.*

but the multitude consisted of so few that they could scarcely contain themselves, for they kept bursting with laughter at the ponderous preparations for resisting their expected violence . . . They are far better behaved than the well-dressed promenaders, who push each other about and stare each other out of countenance.

As the week progressed, the numbers began to increase to something close to what had been expected, with a top figure of around 55,000. *The Times* explained the slow build by asserting that 'the industrious population of the metropolis are procrastinators in all that relates to pleasure'; but it praised their demeanour once they did get there. They inspected the exhibits with 'solemnity and attention' – so unlike the frivolous loungers that the paper had chided the week before. They were 'well dressed, orderly and sedate, earnestly engaged in examining all that interests them, not quarrelsome or obstinate, but playing with manifest propriety and good temperament the important part assigned to them at this gathering'. *The Economist* also noted the phenomenon, declaring: 'No more orderly people ever existed than the multitude of London.'

Horace Greeley concurred:

Turn into whatever corner you might, there were clusters of deeply interested gazers, intent on making the most of their day and their shilling, while in the quieter nooks from 1 to 3 o'clock might be seen families or parties eating the lunch which, with a prophetic foresight of the miserable quality and exorbitant price of the viands served to you in the spacious refreshment saloons, they had wisely brought from home.

Something else that surprised *The Times* was that the holders of season tickets – all assumed to be from the middle and upper classes – were willing to visit the Exhibition on shilling days and rub shoulders with hoi polloi:

> There is something particularly gratifying in this frat-
> ernisation of the great and the humble under circum-
> stances so unusual and, we may add, so unexpected.
> No one anticipated when the price of admission had
> fallen to its minimum that high-born ladies would
> venture amidst the thronging masses, and entrust
> themselves to the politeness of the people.

Within a few weeks, the Queen herself felt confident enough to dispense with her tight security detail as she wandered through the low-born crowd. On 24 June she performed what was probably the first-ever royal walkabout – in retrospect a key moment in relations between the monarchy and the people. The crowd reacted with respect and courtesy, but were at first unsure exactly what degree of loyalty to display. A few people began cheering but quickly lapsed into silence when not many others joined in. Most felt instinctively that it would be wrong to respond to what was clearly meant to be an informal gesture in the same way as they would when the Queen was driving past in an official parade.

The novelty of this new royal accessibility was quick to wear off. The exhibitors were the first to take advantage of it by boldly seeking to draw Victoria and Albert's attention to the goods they were displaying, sometimes with farcical effect. On 5 July the royal pair, inspecting the large array of surgical instruments and medical devices, were besieged by a bevy of dentists, many clutching false teeth in their hands. Nearby, the manufacturer of an infant's cradle seized a tea kettle from a neighbouring stand and made it play the role of the baby, vigorously rocking it back and forth. The Queen and her consort could scarcely fail to take notice, and the enterprising exhibitors would have taken full advantage of the incidents in their subsequent publicity.

* * *

Inevitably, there were some exceptions to the prevailing atmosphere of good cheer. On the first shilling day two pickpockets were arrested inside the building. Sir John Bowring, reporting the arrests to Colonel Grey, hinted at the existence of a master criminal in London resembling Fagin in Charles Dickens' *Oliver Twist*, written fourteen years earlier:

> You will probably have heard of the first capture of pickpockets yesterday by the Belgian police in the building, in the shape of two women. I believe that many suspicious characters were observed there – in particular the gentleman who keeps the great training school for young thieves.

Despite that initial alarm, only twelve pickpockets were arrested during the Exhibition's five-and-a-half-month run, though presumably many more escaped with their loot. The police believed that 'the swell mob' – thieves who dressed like swells so as to put people off their guard – had decided to keep away from the Crystal Palace because of the effective policing arrangements. Both foreign and British policemen worked conscientiously in the background to deter miscreants and head off any of the plots and outrages that had been the subject of so much advance trepidation. They filed daily reports, offering rare insights into the louche and shady criminal underworld of Victorian London.

The reports from the foreign policemen are especially illuminating. After a day at the Crystal Palace eyeing up suspected revolutionaries and pilferers, these budding Inspector Maigrets would head for the dimly lit backstreets of Soho, and other areas with a large expatriate population, whose bars and cabaret houses provided meeting places for ne'er-do-wells, and where vices such as prostitution and gambling thrived.

Agent Henri Galbie was the senior Parisian police officer in London and was meticulous about filing reports. On the opening day, 1 May, he spotted a few known thieves and some Greek card-sharps patrolling the Exhibition. 'I shall keep an eye on them,' he promised his superiors. The following week he advised the German police to keep a close watch on a public house at 20 Great Windmill Street, in Soho, where German and Polish agitators were gathering regularly. In nearby Cranbourn Street a low cabaret run by a Mr Kessler attracted 'incipient revolutionaries'.

By 9 May Agent Galbie's survey of West End night life was broadening. He spotted prostitutes operating at midnight in arcades in the Haymarket, close to the Theatre Royal. They doubled as pickpockets and had stolen £4 from a French visitor. A French pickpocket named Coulmon was living in Golden Square with a group of French and Irish prostitutes, along with a blackmailer called Gustave Costain, and Fanny de Villars, a confidence trickster who pretended to be a countess. A known French criminal, Delannay, was living in the Hotel de Normandie nearby. The underworld was clearly in ferment.

On 22 May Galbie's investigations took him to the race meeting at Epsom, which he was sure would attract low-lifers and swindlers of every kind; but he was disappointed. 'Thieves from France have been kept away by reports of security measures by the French police,' he wrote – in other words, Galbie's own high reputation had frightened them off. The only substantive event he could report was an injury to a jockey.

Back in Soho, he had discovered that the Bal du Casino Laurent in Great Windmill Street (later the site of the Windmill Theatre, famous for its posing nudes) was a haunt of dangerous radicals, and he kept it under regular surveillance. On 2 June, when the orchestra played the National Anthem at the end of the performance, everybody stood up except one man, who was beaten up by the rest of the audience for his insolence. Mercifully he was not French but 'an English demagogue or Chartist'.

Agent Galbie spent the rest of the summer in like fashion, his days in the Crystal Palace and his nights in Soho, reporting on the comings and goings of known French criminals. Occasionally he would record snippets of information about the Exhibition itself – rain in early June came through the roof and damaged some exhibits; high winds in July broke some of the glass. By August there was little to report except the odd overcharging cab driver, and he was clearly becoming frustrated at the lack of work for a conscientious policeman to do. 'Always the same order, the same tranquillity,' he reported, with a distinct hint of despair.

The visit later that month of M. Barouche, the French Minister of Foreign Affairs, seems to have given him a new sense of purpose. Only days after he was part of the Minister's security detail on his tour of the Exhibition, Galbie was on the scent of two French social democratic leaders, although he failed to find them. September was a busy month. It began with the arrest of Baroness Albertine de la Genandière, a French noblewoman, for non-payment of a debt. Then he began to watch an old Catholic chapel in Webb Street, where a bookseller called Lindsey was discovered to be holding secret meetings of social democrats, many of them French. Towards the end of the month, he reported an evil-looking drunkard slipping into the Crystal Palace and making a scene before being arrested.

In October he was asked to look out for some gold and silver optical instruments stolen in Paris and thought to have been sent to Jewish dealers based in London. By now, though, his thoughts were set on his return home. On 11 October he reported, with an almost audible sigh of relief, that 'foreigners are beginning to leave London', and he signed off two days later with an affecting report of Prince Albert being cheered to the echo as the Exhibition closed.

Other European policemen, less resourceful in finding ways of occupying their time, discovered little to report except the occasional distribution of xenophobic tracts calling down curses on the heads of the French, Belgians or whoever. Soon they were being summoned home. Galbie's compatriot, Chief Inspector de Busigny, from Lyons, left with his men in June, reporting that 'before leaving London, the police officers from Lyons expressed their regret to the British Government at not having proved more useful'.

Most of the German police also left in June or July, but one of them from Berlin, Officer Wilhelm Stieber, made good use of his time, finding frauds and complex conspiracies everywhere. In May he helped locate a Berlin banker named Philippe, who had quit the Prussian capital in haste with debts of £20,000. Stieber tracked him down on behalf of a creditor and showed no mercy in returning him, now ill and penniless, to face the music at home. At the same time he noted the presence in London of Hartmann, a former lieutenant in the Prussian army who was now a professional gambler. Using the social connections of his beautiful sister, Hartmann – tall, about forty, with a small moustache – would never play at the table himself but employed card-sharps to do it for him.

Stieber was good with corrupt card players. Before long he was on the trail of 'a very dangerous person named Arnheim, a Jew . . . a cheating gambler who does much mischief'. Arnheim was short, with a small black moustache and a scar on his cheek, customarily wearing a light grey cloak with a long collar. At the same time Stieber was keeping an eye on Carl Hunn, an eighteen-year-old painter's apprentice and 'a violent Republican', as well as von Bulow, a 'dangerous character' employed by the German Commissioner to the Great Exhibition. His inquiries took him to Ascot races, on the lookout for forgers of Prussian banknotes and other suspicious persons. In mid-June this frenzied bout of detection came to an end when Stieber returned to Berlin, where his wife was having a baby.

Three New York cops – Captains Leonard and Hopkins and Officer Bowyer – came to look out for North American villains, including some who had been transported from Britain to the US and had returned at the end of their sentences. Like their European counterparts, the policemen decided that race meetings would be suitable places to conduct their researches. Bowyer went to Ascot on 3 June and reported: 'Saw a number of pickpockets but only recognised one as being from New York. He was convicted there for forgery in the year 1834 under the name Bill Abby, alias Fish, alias Anstrewher.' He pointed the villain out to British policemen, and his report so excited his superiors, Leonard and Hopkins, that, two days later, they went to Ascot races themselves, where they too spotted Abby, but took no action.

A few days later Leonard and Bowyer were in Fleet Street, where they recognised George Mason, a criminal who had been transported from Britain and found his way to the United States, which he had left hurriedly five years earlier, suspected of having robbed a Philadelphia bank of $8,000. He now kept the Crown Tavern in Fleet Street. They reported this to the Metropolitan Police, who said they knew that Mason was a returned transport but that he now appeared to be going straight. Bowyer saw him again in the Crystal Palace in

September and kept him under observation, but could detect no sign of fresh criminal activity.

Around 58,000 foreigners travelled to London in 1851 – nearly three times as many as in 1850, but still only a small percentage of the six million visitors to the Exhibition over the summer. About half were from France, 12,000 from Germany and 5,000 from the United States. Some shops in the West End and the City welcomed them and solicited their custom by putting up signs in foreign languages. The Society for Promoting Christian Knowledge gave them a more ambiguous welcome, issuing pamphlets, again in several languages, exhorting them to respect the Lord's Day by refraining from travel on Sundays and from making any but the most essential demands on hotel staff:

> In London, with its two million inhabitants, you may meet with many thousands who spend the day [Sunday] as it ought not to be spent; but do not mistake this disorderly multitude for the people of England, and we entreat you not to swell that tide by your influence and example.

That aside, the attitude of the natives in a jingoistic age was scarcely welcoming. *Punch* and other journals ran cartoons lampooning foreigners, especially the French, who were depicted without exception as sporting beards and whiskers before facial hair had become fashionable in nineteenth-century London. The French were thought, too, to have unclean habits – although London in 1851 could itself scarcely be termed a salubrious city. One *Punch* cartoon showed two bewhiskered Frenchmen passing a stand at the Crystal Palace that offered the use of soap and water in a jug and basin, and wondering aloud what it could be for. A press report asserted that foreign visitors were so mean that when they took tea in a café they would empty the sugar bowl into their pockets. (The Scots were thought to be even meaner: the owner of a Greenwich tea shop reported that six of them had come in and ordered a pot of tea for two.)

There were exceptions to all this xenophobia. Richard Cobden, the free-trade campaigner and a member of the Commission, told a public meeting in Birmingham in advance of the Exhibition: 'We shall by that means break down the barriers that have separated the people of different nations, and witness the universal republic.' The inventor Charles Babbage wrote:

> One of the great advantages of the Exhibition will arise from the interchange of kindly feelings between the inhabitants of foreign countries and our own. The classes who visit us will consist neither of the very elevated nor of the very low. . . They will probably possess above average information and instruction.

Another group that welcomed the foreigners, for less elevated reasons, were the London cab drivers. Locals complained that late at night, outside popular attractions such as Vauxhall Gardens, drivers would accept only foreign passengers because it was easier to charge them extortionate fares.

The impact on London of the foreign influx was well observed by a French visitor, John Lemoinne, writing in the *Journal des Débats*:

> This pacific invasion of all nations has changed the aspect of London. In this immense city . . . the presence of foreigners is, in general, rarely observable. At

present, however, one's ears never cease to be struck with all dialects, known and unknown. From the Chinese true and false, to the serfs of Russia, all races are represented, and are walking about in all costumes, to say nothing of the beards and moustaches, which here in England are still a foreign adornment. The English have on this occasion abandoned their usual habits. In very truth, I think they are becoming social and familiar. They have always been polite and hospitable to those who bring proper introductions to them, but now one actually meets some who enter into conversation without that preliminary condition. Decidedly, British manners are altered.

By the middle of the summer the Exhibition, clearly an unalloyed success, was dominating all aspects of London life. Attendances on shilling days were regularly exceeding 50,000. Hundreds of commemorative books, pamphlets, poems and songs were being written and sold all over the capital. No musical performance at a tavern, a concert hall or the newly emerging music halls was complete without a song celebrating the great event, ranging from the sentimental to the frankly bawdy – and many of these, too, such as 'The National Exhibition', made fun of the foreigners:

There's Welshmen, Prussian, Spanish, Greek,
Swiss, Flemish, Turks and Frenchmen,
The wondrous Exhibition seek –
'Cos it won't go and fetch them.
The Chinese talk of ladders long
Such as were used for Babel
With pig-tails, genuine from Hong Kong,
As many as they're able . . .

> The Russians mean to bring bears' grease
> The Yankees quids for all, sirs.
> So what with Dutch and Nepalese,
> 'Twill be a fancy ball, sirs.

Others treated the overseas visitors with greater awe.
'Britannia's Sons' contained this verse:

> It is a glorious sight to see so many thousands meet,
> Not heeding creed or country, each other friendly greet.

Not all the songs played on the prevailing obsession with
foreigners. The first of them, such as 'In Great Hyde Park',
were written while the Crystal Palace was still being built.

> In great Hyde Park, like lots of larks they work with
>   expedition.
> Like swarms of bees among the trees at the Great
>   Exhibition.
> Talk of Mount Vesuvius or the tower of Babylon-e
> Is nothing to it – or Noah's Ark or the whale that
>   swallowed Jonah.

One of the liveliest was called 'Come, let us go and see the
Exhibition for a Shilling':

> If I sell the pig and donkey, the frying pan and bed,
> I will see the Exhibition while it is a bob a head.
> Never mind the rent or taxes, dear Polly come with me,
> To the Great Exhibition, all the wonders for to see.
>
> There we may see King Alfred and Billy Rufus bold,
> Prince Albert all in silver and Victoria made of gold.

Queen Anne made out of beeswax on a wondrous pillar
    perch'd
With her nose stuck in a gin shop and her rump against
    the church.

There's syllabubs and sandwiches, bath buns and nice
    cheese cakes.
Sew up your trouser pocket, Tom, some people make
    mistakes.
Nanny hold your bustle up and do not let it drop -
It's only twopence halfpenny for a bottle of ginger pop.

Tie up your garters, Caroline, the Exhibition for to see.
I have pawned my coat and trousers to pay for you and
    me . . .
Isabella, love, get ready, along with me to trip,
And you shall see the foreigners with their funny hairy
    lips.

And as the great event neared its close, there appeared several
songs and poems that mourned its passing. 'Lamentation of
the Exhibition' was written as though spoken by the Crystal
Palace itself:

Naught in the world can me surpass,
Body and breeches made in glass.

and contained the ritual put-down of the foreign visitors:

Hundreds of thousands on me smiled,
They came from England and the Nile . . .
Foreigners to me did throng,
Hair round their mouths twelve inches long.

It went on to suggest that some visitors had used the occasion for something other than self-improvement and intellectual gratification:

> Five hundred maidens got with child
> At the National Exhibition . . .
> Many a pretty damsel kind,
> Oh, lack a day! In nine months' time,
> In a truss of straw will be confin'd
> With a national exhibition.

> Some got squeezed and some got hobbed,
> Some got kicked and some got robbed,
> Some got barked at by the dogs
> And some got smothered in smoke and fogs.
> Some pretty maids got in disgrace,
> Lost what they never can replace,
> And thousands went with a dirty face,
> To see the Exhibition.

The poem ended with a regretful farewell:

> Oh dear! Oh crikey! Crack my nob,
> By me they have raised many a bob,
> I'm coming down – what a dreadful job!
> They've ruined the Exhibition.

Many books and pamphlets gave satirical accounts of the adventures of fictional characters making the journey to London. One of the most appealing, clearly based in part on personal experience, was the anonymous *Tom Treddlehoyle's Trip to Lunnon to see Paxton's Great Glass Lantern, Dedicated we' all t'pleasure i' t'world to Prince Olbert*, published in Leeds and written in an approximation of Yorkshire dialect. Treddlehoyle describes his train journey to London – where someone stole the pork pie he had brought for his supper – and the rough lodging he found in an inn near Tyburn (now Marble Arch), where he claims to have bedded down between two Chinese. Next day he made for Hyde Park:

> The streets were crowded like a fair with folks from all parts of the country and foreign parts. Some were black, some brown and some a mixture of all colours and dressed in all manner of cuts and fashions, with beards, moustaches and hair of varying length, through the tail of a winter fowl to a shoe-brush, and spluttering all sorts of gibberish talk – like a regular Babel.

When he first saw the Crystal Palace 'it was glittering as brilliantly as if all the sky-lights and cucumber frames in the country were piled in a heap'. The flags flying around the roof reminded him of wash day. Inside, the mass of men's hats and women's bonnets 'looked for all the world like a swarm of midges dancing in a sunbeam'.

He was unimpressed with the Koh-i-Noor diamond – 'wouldn't give sixpence for it' – likening it to the stopper of a vinegar cruet in a wire mousetrap. He was much taken, though, with the model of Liverpool Docks and its surroundings, where the houses were so realistic that you could almost hear the postman knocking at the doors. And, with his local interest in mind, he spent time at the stalls of Bradford and the other Yorkshire woollen towns:

> John Rand and Titus Salt had some of the prettiest dresses for ladies I ever saw. Titus had some bed-hangings that would keep people awake for a week,

they were so butterfly-winged . . . If a bachelor hung his bed with this stuff he'd be in such a hurry to get to bed every night that he'd forget to grate the ginger into his gruel.

It was not that the pseudonymous Treddlehoyle's judgement had been affected by his Yorkshire patriotism, for less partial observers also had high praise for Bradford's efforts. The *Morning Chronicle* reported: 'Bradford has risen from the obscurity of a mere manufacturing village to the position of one of the busiest and wealthiest communities in the country... The manufacturers of Bradford have done them-selves infinite honour by their displays.'

Treddlehoyle also admired the samples of coal from Barnsley, 'the best in England, geologists say, for making a good winter fire and frying pancakes over'. When he reached the overseas exhibits, he singled out the model of the Spanish bull-ring for praise, but he was horrified at the way the crowd treated the Chinese man on his country's stand: 'Poor fellow he were shamed, for folks did nothing but talk and laugh at him.'

By now it was time to take some sustenance:

I went into the Refreshment Room and it was almost like being in a field of battle, for the corks of the soda water and ginger beer bottles were flying about on all sides, and cups and saucers rattling like horses' feet cantering. A chap was grinding ice and ladling rasp-berry and pineapple ice cream out of tin saucepans.

After his snack he 'felt as lively as a bee and as light as a feather, and upstairs I cut like a lamplighter into the north-east galleries'.

Soon after he got there the Queen and Prince Albert

arrived below. 'I must have a look at her or it will be no use me going back to Barnsley,' he told himself. The royal pair were 'hurrying like two good 'uns to get out of folks' way – bless her little face and her, she was all smiling . . . I think she shot a glance at me'.

With that excitement over, he had time to admire the view from the gallery.

> Looking right and left among organs, looking-glasses, statues and temples, you'll be almost riveted to the spot, it's so grand. And to see thousands of folks walking backwards and forwards and all ways, of every shade and colour and nation and shape – it really looks like machinery work.

Apart from complaining that the glass roof was dirty, Treddlehoyle was greatly impressed by what he described as 'an astounding piece of structure and management; for the building, and everything in it, seems as if they had all been cast in a mould at one time; all fits and harmonises so nicely together'.

He did not stay at Harrisson's Mechanics' Home in Pimlico but he appears to have visited it, for he describes its 'factorified' look and wonders what it must sound like at two in the morning with all the thousand beds occupied. (Sadly for Harrisson, that hardly ever occurred.) And he celebrates the cosmopolitan nature of the potential clientele.

> The eating part will be most amusing for there'll be Norfolk chaps with their dumplings; Denby-dykers with their tatty-pie; Huddersfielders with their braweys; the Lancashire lads with their churned milk; Dewsburians and Holmfirthers with their oat cake

and thickans; and some with some thing and some
with another – it would be as good as any play to see
them.

He offers some cautionary words of advice to visitors who may
follow in his footsteps: 'Take care, for there will be temptations
as rank as locusts, and in a thousand shops, different from
whatever you've seen before.' He advises northerners to enjoy
'a good tuck in' before they leave home, because London food
is different from theirs and 'milk is like starch water, three-
quarters made of chalk'. But he concludes:

Never mind this for I shouldn't want anybody – a
Lancashire or Yorkshireman – to be left out . . . Make
the best haste you can to have a peep at Paxton's Great
Glass Lantern. Nah, off we go – never mind shutting
the door, for it's the grandest sight a man ever saw –
hey, or woman either.

The most accomplished of all the satires was Henry Mayhew's
1851, or The Adventures of Mr and Mrs Cursty Sandboys . . .,
already mentioned in earlier chapters. Mayhew began by
describing the mood in London that spring:

The Great Exhibition was about to attract sightseers
of all the world . . . The African had mounted his
ostrich, the Crisp of the Desert [an invented eastern
potentate] had announced an excursion caravan from
Zulu to Fez, the Yakutskian Shillibar had already
started the first reindeer omnibus to Novorogod . . .
In London, Alexis Soyer was about to open a
restaurant of all nations, where the universe might
dine from sixpence to a hundred guineas, off *cartes*

ranging from pickled whelks to nightingales' tongues
– from the rats *à la tartare* of the Chinese to the
turkey and truffles of the Parisian gourmet . . .

But the excitement was not confined to London:

While these gigantic preparations for the gratification
of foreign visitors were being made, the whole of the
British provinces likewise were preparing extensively
to enjoy themselves. Every city was arranging some
monster train to shoot the whole of its inhabitants, at
a halfpenny per ton, into the lodging houses of
London . . . Not a village, a hamlet, a borough, a
township or a wick, but each had its shilling club for
providing their inhabitants with a three-day journey
to London, a mattress under the long arches of the
Adelphi and tickets for soup *ad libitum* . . . Bradshaw's
Railway Guide had swelled into an encyclopedia . . .
Omnibus conductors were undergoing a polyglot
course on the Hamiltonian system, to enable them to
abuse all foreigners in their native tongues.

Mayhew's plot concerned a farming family from Cumbria
whose head, Mr Sandboys, had originally vetoed the idea of
going to London for the Exhibition. 'He had lived all his life in
a village with fifteen houses and seven families and was unlikely, in his fifty-fifth year, to take up abode with a thousand
people under one roof.' But after he had taken his family to see
the rest of the village leave for their communal trip, they
found that they were almost isolated. Because every other
villager had left, all the shops were closed and they could not
buy the basic necessities.

So Sandboys and his wife decided that they had little

alternative but to follow the crowd to London, taking their two children with them. The journey was a series of misadventures. They began by mistakenly travelling north, to Edinburgh, instead of south. After they had found the right train, Mr Sandboys fell prey to a confidence trickster who extracted all his money from him. In London, there was no room at any legitimate inn, and all they could find was a hammock in the cellar of a lodging house: the landlady told them that her neighbour had put a feather mattress in the bath and let it to a young East Indian for a guinea a week. Finally they found a more spacious room in Wimbledon, in a house occupied by forty-seven French guardsmen who never washed their clothes.

After more financial and personal disasters the family did not actually get to see the Exhibition, losing their nerve when they stood before the Crystal Palace and saw the enormous crowd. Instead, they thankfully took the train home.

In nearly every such account, the fictional visitors not only suffer various mishaps on the way, falling victims to robbers and swindlers, but most, for good measure, have bruising encounters with foreigners, too. In Thomas Onwhyn's *Mr and Mrs Brown's Visit to the Great Exhibition*, the Browns were horrified by the oddly attired strangers. One of its illustrations depicts three cannibals at a restaurant table making an offer for a toothsome English child sitting opposite.

In an anonymous skit called *Chaff and the Nigger*, an American major finds himself sharing the same boarding house, and occasionally the same bed, with a black former slave and an English country doctor. After much argument about the institution of slavery, the doctor says of the major:

I rather like him. He has got one good Anglo-Saxon

'Perfidious Albion lets his drawing-room floor to a distinguished foreigner'
– a cartoon from Punch.

characteristic. He is game, either to liquor or fight. I
think they will be an ornament yet to the Anglo-
Saxon race, if we can cure them of chewing, spitting,
bolting their food and talking through their noses.

But what did the foreigners think of their hosts? A purported
answer came in a pamphlet called: *A Frenchman's Visit to
England and the Chrystal Palace: All he Saw There, with his
General Remarks upon England and the English People* . . . In an
open letter to 'Monsieur Anglais', the author declared: 'As a
Frenchman, I cannot say I ever liked you, still I will endeavour
to do you strict justice.'

Although he found England generally an industrious
nation, with little time for repose and leisure, he stated:

The manners of the English generally are not
good . . . There is a rudeness in style, a coarseness of

expression, an overbearing manner about a genuine
John Bull, that to a foreigner is unpleasant . . . Their
amour propre makes them consider all strangers fair
game for the exercise of their wit.

They are also pugnacious: 'If an Englishman plants himself
before you and fixes his legs wide apart, with his arms squared
and his fists doubled, get out of his way.'

The anonymous writer was dismissive of British cultural
pretensions: 'In the west end of London, fashion rules all. If a
screech-owl could get an engagement at the opera and call
itself Signora Hootani Italiano, the audience would be half
mad with delight and admiration.' He ridiculed the class
system ('Everybody is afraid of everybody'), the food ('Everybody eats too much beef') and the hypocrisy ('Cant and hum-
bug is very prevalent amongst a certain clique'), and he
concluded: 'We must all have our hobby-horse to ride; the
German his pipe, the Italian his fiddle, the Frenchman his
revolution and the Englishman his umbrella.'

Despite this discouraging evidence to the contrary,
Charles Dickens thought that foreigners' exposure to British
ways would in the long term be for the good. In his *Household
Words* he wrote:

I am of the opinion that the editors of foreign newspapers will no longer declare that we live on raw beef-
steaks and occasionally eat the winners of our
Derbies; that every nobleman takes his 'bouledoge' to
court with him; that we are in the daily habit of
selling our wives in Smithfield market; and that
during the month of November three-fourths of the
population of London commit suicide. Altogether I
think that a little peace, and a little good-will, and a

little brotherhood among nations will result from the foreign invasion; and that it will in future no longer be a matter of course that because 50,000 Frenchmen in blue coats and red trousers meet 50,000 Englishmen in blue trousers and red coats, they must all fall to and cut or blow each other to atoms.

The Great Exhibition did not, as it happened, set the stage for world peace, as Dickens and many others had ardently hoped. But it did herald changes in British society far more profound than its promoters could ever have imagined.

CHAPTER NINE

❧ ❧

THE EXCURSIONISTS

'Talking of World's Fairs, Exhibitions and what not,' said the old gentleman, 'I would not go round the corner to see a dozen of them nowadays. The only exhibition that ever made, or ever will make, any impression on my imagination was the first of the series, the parent of them all and now a thing of old times – the Great Exhibition of 1851 in Hyde Park, London. None of the younger generation can realise the sense of novelty it produced in us who were then in our prime . . . It was exhibition hat, exhibition razor strop, exhibition watch; nay, even exhibition weather, exhibition spirits, sweethearts, babies, wives.'

Thomas Hardy, 'The Fiddler on the Reels' (1898)

Even if the experiences of the Sandboys family owed more to Mayhew's vivid imagination than to reality, there can be no doubt that the book accurately reflected the fears of country people travelling to London for the first time. Certainly, many did fall victim to sharp Cockney swindlers. Several incidents were documented in newspaper reports throughout the summer and autumn, but these must have constituted only a fraction of those that occurred in the teeming city. Most victims would have accepted their losses ruefully, without informing the police or the press.

On 28 June the *Leeds Intelligencer* published a report headed: 'Caution to Persons Visiting London'. It described the experience of William Symington, a Bradford merchant, who 'suffered great inconvenience in London last week and was kept one night in prison through a false charge having been made against him of having attempted to pass a counterfeit sovereign at a stall in the Thames Tunnel'.

The world's first underwater tunnel, linking Wapping with Rotherhithe down river from London Bridge, was the marvel of the capital – or at least it had been until the Crystal Palace was built to rival it. Today part of the Underground railway system, the 400-yard Thames Tunnel was designed by the engineer Sir Marc Brunel, who invented a shield that could be moved along the tunnel as each section was completed, to reduce the danger of a cave-in. All the same, many lives were lost in its construction before it was completed in 1843, by which time Sir Marc's son Isambard had become chief engineer. It was originally intended to be used by horse-drawn vehicles but money ran out before the necessary ramps could be built, so it was opened as a foot tunnel and soon became a tourist attraction, lined with stalls selling souvenirs, knick-knacks and refreshments.

Places that attract visitors also draw crafty local tricksters, bent on taking advantage of them. Symington had gone into the tunnel with a group of acquaintances and bought a sixpenny notebook from a stallholder named Elizabeth Cox, adept at sleight of hand. 'He tendered her a sovereign in payment and by some trick of what is known by the name of "ringing the changes" the good coin gave place to a counterfeit one and Mr Symington was given into custody.' Next morning the magistrates dismissed the case. The paper commented: 'His reputation stands too high in Bradford for him to suffer in the opinion of his fellow townsmen . . . The offence with which he stands charged was wholly incompatible with his previous history.'

The *Dumfries Standard* reported another instance of

trickery, this time in the Crystal Palace itself. The victim was a farmer from Kircudbright who visited on one of the days when the Queen was walking amongst the crowd. A young girl standing beside him asked him to lift her above the heads of the people in front so that she could get a better view. The 'rustic haggis-fed' – as the paper, quoting Robert Burns, described the farmer – complied. 'Higher! Higher!' cried the little girl, and he did his best to fulfil her demands until the Queen had passed. When he put her down she scurried away and he quickly found that his pocket had been picked, presumably by an adult accomplice standing alongside them.

To prepare against such hazards, prudent visitors from the provinces equipped themselves with guide books that gave them tips both on how to see the sights of the capital and on how to counter the wicked ways of its citizens. Sometimes, as in the case of Tom Treddlehoyle, the advice was contained in a fictional account of a visit. One of the more conventional guide books, also aimed at a northern audience, was the twenty-eight-page *Yorkshireman's Guide to the Great Metropolis and the Crystal Palace*, published by M. Bell in Richmond, North Yorkshire.

The hard-headed advice in Bell's booklet won it a favourable review in the *Leeds Intelligencer*: 'The compiler of this guide is well acquainted with the metropolis and its "lions" and he has put a great deal of useful information as it were into a nutshell.' Like other guides, in addition to advising its readers how to take care of themselves, it provided details of sights they might see after they had done justice to the Crystal Palace. Attractions including the Tower of London, St Paul's Cathedral, Westminster Abbey, the National Gallery and the British Museum, as well as stately homes such as Northumberland House in the Strand, had extended their opening times and reduced their admission prices (if any) for that special summer. They were complemented by several impressive panoramas of the world's great sights, a popular form of attraction at the time, as well as two major installations in Leicester Square: Wyld's Globe, a giant reproduction of the planet, and Cantelo's Hydro-Incubator, where hundreds of chicks were hatched daily for the entertainment of onlookers.

The booklet also offered advice to the rail traveller on the complicated journeys involved in the early days before all the major mainline through routes had been constructed. From York or Leeds, readers were advised to take the North Midland line to Derby, then the Midland Counties to Rugby to join the North Western. There was an alternative route via the Great Northern line, changing at Burton Salmon, but the author seems to have preferred the first option, chiefly because of the catering facilities: 'At Wolverton he [the traveller] will find refreshments served by several beautiful young ladies and be enabled to refresh the inner man with coffee, soup, pork pie, bottled porter or ale, as he chooses.'

As the North Western train neared London it would pass by Primrose Hill – 'the Cockney's Sunday walk' – before arriving at Euston, then on the northern fringe of the capital. Here the visitor could get on an omnibus for sixpence a mile or a cab for eightpence, but, as we have already seen, he had to be careful: 'The drivers are proverbial for extortion, so that the Yorkshireman must use his native cuteness and not be done, the first moment he arrives in the Great Metropolis.'

Railways were crucial to the success of the Great Exhibition. The first public railway in Britain opened in 1825, carrying mostly freight between Stockton and Darlington, using a steam engine designed by George Stephenson. The first line dedicated primarily to passengers opened five years later, between Liverpool and Manchester. London's first railway, from Greenwich to Bermondsey, began operating in 1836, and the following year a route to Birmingham was completed by a company controlled by Robert Stephenson, George's son. New termini were established at St Pancras and King's Cross, a few hundred yards east of Euston, as rival companies opened long-distance lines to the north. In 1838 the Great Western built a terminus close to the present Paddington station – completed by Brunel in 1854 using techniques pioneered at the Crystal Palace – so that by the time of the Great Exhibition a network of lines, owned by numerous competing entrepreneurs, criss-crossed the country.

Although at first the long-distance steam trains were used principally by businessmen or the wealthy gentry, it became apparent that if they were to become commercially viable they would have to reach out to a broader, less prosperous travelling public. The idea began to take hold of running special excursion trains for day or weekend trips, with much lower fares than on the regular scheduled services. Properly marketed, and with the likelihood of nearly every seat being filled, these could be run at a considerable profit.

The pioneer of excursions was Thomas Cook, whose name lives on today in the international travel firm that he established. Born in Melbourne, Derbyshire, in 1808, he left school at ten to become an estate worker at a penny a day, to help support his widowed mother. Later he trained as a wood turner and moved to Market Harborough in Leicestershire. A passionate teetotaller, he became secretary to the local branch of the South Midland Temperance Association, and in that capacity organised an excursion from Leicester to Loughborough for a large temperance rally on 5 July 1841 – the first public rail excursion in Britain. It carried 570 passengers and caused a great stir in both towns: a band played as the train set off from Leicester, and a large crowd had gathered to see it arrive at its destination.

This success encouraged other organisations to turn to Cook when they wanted to arrange group trips, until eventually he moved to Leicester and set himself up as probably the world's first public travel agent, recruiting people for trips by train and steamboat in Britain and overseas. By 1850 his business was well established – and in the autumn of that year he was involved in yet another of the encounters at railway stations on which much of the story of the Great Exhibition hinges.

He had decided to travel to America to investigate the possibility of running organised tours across the Atlantic. On his way to Liverpool, where he was to discuss his idea with the steamship companies, he changed trains at Derby and there met Joseph Paxton and John Ellis, the head of the Midland Railway. Construction of Paxton's Crystal Palace was already under way and Ellis had ordered 100 new passenger carriages, anticipating a huge demand for travel to the Exhibition. The two men suggested to Cook that he should organise excursions for the Midland Railway. Immediately spotting the potential of the idea, he needed little persuasion.

Soon Cook was holding meetings in large population centres of the Midlands and north, encouraging the creation of savings clubs to raise the fifteen-shilling fare that the company had said would be a flat fee for excursions to London from all stations in the areas it served. He promised that all trips would be accompanied either by him or his son, who had now joined him in the business, and said he would produce a guide to accommodation and the sights of London that would be given free to all passengers.

He did not initially meet with the success he had hoped for. As Alexander Redgrave told the Commissioners in the run-up to the opening of the Exhibition, many people were reluctant to commit themselves to the regular subscriptions that they would have to pay if they became club members. In part this was because the Midland was competing fiercely with other lines for traffic from the industrial areas, and people were learning from experience that this kind of head-to-head combat invariably led to deep price cuts. As the tussle for passengers reached its peak in July, the *Leeds Intelligencer* reported:

> The working classes seemed to have a kind of pre-science that the competition for their patronage would be so strong between the rival railway companies as to cause the fares to be reduced much below the scale which was then stated to have been agreed upon by the respective boards of directors, and hence they did not generally chime in with the plans propounded for their consideration and adoption, but showed an inclination to wait and take the chances of making better terms. The spirit of competition has done even more than those shrewd working men ventured to anticipate.

The most ferocious bout of price-cutting began on Monday 21 July. After scenes approaching frenzy at railway stations in Yorkshire and other parts of the north, the excursion fares to London were reduced dramatically within days, and remained at rock bottom for the remainder of the summer and autumn. The railways were in competition not only with each other but also with the steamships operating regular services between London and Hull. The latter took much longer than the trains but cost less. By the previous Saturday, the Midland and Great Northern railways had already cut their third-class excursion fare from the north to eleven shillings from the fifteen shillings envisaged originally (second class was £1 4s and first class £1 12s). On Monday the Midland put the price down to nine shillings, and by Tuesday crowds had gathered around the stations of the north, sensing that there were even greater bargains to be had.

Representatives of the rival companies paraded with placards advertising the latest offers. At Bradford, Thomas Cook's son led a brass band round the town announcing every new cut in the Midland's price. The Great Northern declared that it would carry excursionists for sixpence less than whatever price the Midland was offering. Finally, when the Midland went down to just five shillings the Great Northern called a truce, and both companies agreed to stick at that price until the Exhibition closed. A Midland train carrying 350 people at that fare, organised by Cook and accompanied by his son as a guide, left Bradford on the Wednesday. The shrewdness and prescience of the northern labourers had paid handsome dividends.

According to one estimate, Cook organised travel to the Exhibition for 165,000 people. His largest excursion involved ferrying 3,000 Sunday-school children to London from Derby, Leicester and Nottingham. He laid on transport from Euston to the Crystal Palace, and got them back in time for the night train. He also organised a trip for his fellow teetotallers from Leeds and the West Riding, who were embarking on a 'Grand Temperance Excursion' to London to join other abstainers for a great rally inside the Exhibition building. There were so many of them that they travelled on two days – Saturday 2 August and the following Monday. On the Tuesday they joined many thousands of other teetotallers, mostly women, in the Crystal Palace, where they halted everyone else in their tracks by bursting into a Welsh song. This sparked a near-disaster when a man (a teetotaller himself, as it later transpired) became so emotional that he attacked three of the singers and knocked them to the ground, before being restrained by the police. As a consequence of this disturbance, the Exhibition's executive committee issued an edict banning singing on the premises.

The enterprising Cook did not confine himself to running excursions to the capital. From his office in Seymour Street, north of Oxford Street, he offered Londoners and overseas visitors a trip to Chatsworth, Matlock and Derby from Euston. The cost of 12s 6d (first class 17s 6d), included entrance to Chatsworth, where visitors could see Paxton's great lily house, the forerunner of the Crystal Palace. But Cook was unable, despite his persistence, to persuade the Commissioners to allow him to include the price of admission to the Exhibition in his excursions to London.

Although the principal organiser of travel to the Exhibition, Cook was not the only one. One of his rivals, H. R. Marcus of Liverpool, organised a trip for several hundred members of The Liverpool Excursion Club on a train that left Edge Hill station at six a.m. on Saturday 5 July, allowing the excursionists to stay for one week or two. He gave all of them a copy of his own accommodation guide and offered help in finding lodgings. Members were advised to provide themselves with a stock of provisions so that the Liverpool shops instead of the grasping traders of London would benefit from their custom.

The many industrialists and landowners who paid for their employees to visit the Exhibition also used the excursion trains. One of the most ambitious trips was sponsored by the fourth Duke of Northumberland for 150 workers on his extensive estates in and around his seat at Alnwick Castle, more than 300 miles north of London. On 6 June the Duke's

EXHIBITION of the INDUSTRY OF ALL NATIONS, 1851.

Liverpool Excursion Club

·FOR ENABLING THE·

WORKING CLASSES

TO VISIT LONDON IN 1851.

The Worshipful the Mayor,
The Venerable the Archdeacon Brooks, } PATRONS.
The Rev. Augustus Campbell, Rector of Liverpool.

AND UNDER THE MANAGEMENT OF THE

Liverpool Executive Committee for the Exhibition.

Mr. John Finch, and Mr. John R. Isaac, Auditors.

Bankers : Messrs. Heywoods & Co.

THE principal Railway Companies having decided on sending Excursion Trains during the Exhibition, for the benefit of such as belong to Subscription Clubs, those who wish to avail themselves of this privilege in this Town and Neighbourhood, are invited to a consideration of the plan now suggested.

The Excursion Trains will not commence running before the *First of July*, 1851, nor until the price of admission to the Exhibition is reduced to One Shilling.

Attention is directed to the following clauses published by the Railway Companies :—

"That in order to encourage the early formation of 'Subscription Clubs' in the country, to enable the labouring classes to travel to London and back during the Exhibition of 1851, the Railway Companies have undertaken to convey all persons so subscribing to local clubs at a single railway fare for both journeys, up and down.

"That 250 passengers for the whole journey must be secured, in order to engage a special train, the hour of arrival in London being made as convenient as possible for the Excursionists, and the time of departure for the return journey being previously arranged according to circumstances, but in no case to exceed six days from that of arrival.

The Fare from Liverpool to London and back will not exceed 15s. 6d.

REGULATIONS OF CLUB.

Subscriptions to be paid weekly, at the places appointed as described below, and in sums of not less than One Shilling from each party.

Each person to pay Twopence, on receiving his Card.—The payment of Subscriptions to commence on the 1st January, 1851.

No Depositor allowed to be in arrears more than four weeks at any one time. Should any discontinue his subscription, his money not to be returned until the Club is closed, unless by special permission of the Committee.

No one to be entitled to the benefits of this Club who has not subscribed for Three Months previous to starting the Excursion Trains.

The Committee shall have the power to refuse admission to improper characters, or expel them from the Club.

Due Notice will be given when the period arrives for commencing the Excursion Trains.

It is the intention of the Committee to endeavour to assist the Working Classes by affording them information respecting Lodgings while in London, and engage to furnish each Member with instructions for his journey, and during his stay in the Metropolis ; but on this subject, and on all other points connected with the regulation for the journey, &c., the Committee will give more particulars as the arrangements are made.

Members of BOTH SEXES will be enrolled, and subscriptions received as follows :—

Savings' Bank, Bold-street, DAILY, from 10 o'clock to 5, commencing the first Monday in Jan., 1851.
District Provident Society, at Queen's-square, on MONDAYS, from 5½ to 7 in the Evening.
Ditto, at North Church of England School, Bond St., Ditto.
Ditto, at 33, Bispham-street, MONDAYS, 2 to 3 in the Afternoon.
Ditto, at 7, Bedford-st., Toxteth Park, MONDAYS, from 5½ to 7 in Evening.

And for the advantage of COUNTRY MEMBERS,

At the DISTRICT PROVIDENT SOCIETY'S OFFICE, QUEEN'S SQUARE, EVERY DAY, from 11 till 1 o'clock.

Further particulars may be obtained from MR. JOHN R. ISAAC, 62, *Castle-street* ; Rev. Mr. BISHOP, 7, *Bedford-street, Toxteth-park* ; Mr. JOHN GALE, 20, *Brooke's Alley, Hanover-street* ; *and from*

JOHN GRANTHAM, Hon. Sec.,
[R. PINKNEY, PRINTER, BIRKENHEAD.]   ORANGE COURT.

A flyer urging Liverpudlians to join the club.

chief agent sent a circular to the agents of all his properties in the area, and they in turn consulted their tenant farmers as to which of their workers would gain most benefit from the trip, scheduled for the week beginning 19 July. Arrangements at the London end were handled by Thomas Williams, the Duke's London agent, based at Northumberland House. The week before the visit he wrote to Alnwick asking for the names, addresses and occupations of all those travelling, 'and will you, entre nous, give me the names of one or two of the most intelligent among them' – perhaps so that they could play a liaison role between the London sophisticates and the visiting Northumbrian rustics.

They must have spent at least a week in London, probably paying more than one visit to the Crystal Palace: the newspapers reported their presence there on 23 July. Their leaders and guides carried banners emblazoned with the Duke's coat of arms, for easy identification. According to the Alnwick ledger book, the bill for their tavern accommodation and expenses came to £396 5s 8d and their rail fare to £198 9s 5d, with £26 9s 7d paid for refreshments en route: all in all a generous gesture by the Duke.

The facilities on the excursion trains were basic and the seats uncomfortable. Thomas Hardy gave a vivid description of them in his story 'The Fiddler on the Reels', published in 1898 in his collection *Life's Little Ironies*. Hardy was eleven years old in 1851, and the passage appears to be based on an eye-witness account of excursions leaving Dorchester, where he went to school. The story concerns Ned Hipcroft who, thwarted in love, moves to London from his Wessex village and finds work as one of the builders of the Crystal Palace. When the Exhibition is in full swing he receives a letter from the Wessex woman who spurned him, saying that she now wants to accept his proposal. She comes up on an excursion train and he goes to the station to meet her:

> There had just begun to be run wonderfully contrived special trains, called excursion-trains, on account of the Great Exhibition; so that she could come up easily alone . . . The 'excursion-train' – an absolutely new

departure in the history of travel – was still a novelty on the Wessex line, and probably everywhere. Crowds of people had flocked to all the stations on the way up to witness the unwonted sight of so long a train's passage . . . The seats for the humbler class of travellers in these early experiments in steam-locomotion were open trucks, without any protection whatever from the wind and rain.

Thus the arriving passengers were 'in a pitiable condition from their long journey; blue-faced, stiff-necked, sneezing, rain-beaten, chilled to the marrow'.

As autumn approached, Exhibition fever increased. Under their agreement with the administrators of the Royal Parks, the Commissioners were obliged to close the Crystal Palace by 1 November. Some weeks in advance, they announced that the last public admissions would be on Saturday 11 October, that exhibitors and their guests would be allowed in on the following Monday and Tuesday, and that there would be a formal closing ceremony on the Wednesday in the presence of Prince Albert, but not the Queen. The announcement had a dramatic effect on attendance figures, as people realised that time was running out for them to witness what by general consent was now recognised as the great event of their lifetime.

Some had delayed their visit hoping that the price of admission would be reduced to below a shilling for the final few weeks – a course recommended by Paxton, Dickens and several newspaper leader-writers. By the beginning of September the Commissioners had made it known that, despite the large profits they were amassing, there would be no reduction – in part because they feared that the Crystal Palace could not accommodate any larger crowds.

On 2 September more than a thousand people from Sunderland made a mass invasion. The following week a group of 400 from the carpet-making town of Wilton included 120 workers from the factory that had made the Great Windsor Carpet lent to the Exhibition by Prince Albert. One Saturday in early September a pawnbroker in Leeds reported that he had paid out on a bushel and a half of watches before the departure of the excursion train to London, attributing the phenomenon to the desire of people to visit the Crystal Palace while there was still time, even if they could not really afford it. So the music-hall song about selling the pig and donkey was not far wide of the mark.

'The crowds are now the main attraction,' wrote *The Times*, as the final weeks began to slip away.

> The six railway termini are regularly choked up with arrivals from the country. Omnibuses are filled inside and out with a rapidity which far outstrips the zeal of their conductors . . . Cabs are frequently not to be had on the best attended stands and the thoroughfares leading to Hyde Park are swept throughout the day by a continuous and inexhaustible stream of public conveyances . . . Till long after midday the pavements on either side along Piccadilly and from Hyde Park Corner up Sloane Street to Knightsbridge are swarming with dense black columns of pedestrians.

Inside the Crystal Palace, the nave and transept resembled 'a stupendous beehive'.

In the closing weeks the crowds included many thousands of schoolchildren on visits paid for by charities and wealthy philanthropists. Nearly 500 school parties visited throughout the summer. On 18 September, thirty-three schools sent groups on the same day, making a total of 2,729 children. At the other end of the age scale was a party of eighteen old people from Bletchingley in Surrey whose combined ages totalled 1,141 years.

John Lemoinne, in the *Journal des Débats*, described a typical Monday-morning scene, as groups of countryfolk and schoolchildren arrived at the entrance to the Exhibition:

> Four-horse coaches, such as were used before the establishment of railways, carrying four inside and about twenty outside passengers, are again brought into requisition for this occasion. From these elevated vehicles descend multitudes of females in very gay toilettes. Being safely landed, they leisurely arrange their dresses . . . After these arrive large wagons, with a series of seats, bringing the young folks from the boarding or charity schools. It is somewhat curious to see this general landing. I could never have conceived, without the evidence of my eyes, that so many living beings could be packed into so small a space without being suffocated. Out they come, fifty at a time, and when you imagine the vehicle has delivered all its load, out pours a new batch.

Not everyone travelled in groups. The railway companies quickly abandoned the original plan of offering their lowest fares only to organised parties, and allowed individuals to buy cheap tickets. The *Bradford Observer* reported that people were leaving daily in their hundreds, and some factories closed for a few days so that all their workers could make the journey.

Last week a power-loom weaver, when she had

received her wages, observing a crush at the station, took it into her head to visit the Exhibition just as she was, without either bonnet, cap or change of linen, having nothing over her head but a handkerchief.

Most factory workers were paid on Saturdays, so she probably spent two days in London and returned on Monday night.

A man from Huddersfield, according to the *Daily News*, went down and back by the night train on two weeknights, taking his own sandwiches and drinking from the crystal fountain, thus avoiding having to find a bed in London and spending nothing there except the admission fee. The *Illustrated London News* told of a man from Peterborough who may have been Britain's first long-distance commuter. He came down on a morning train, visited the Exhibition but was unable to find suitable lodgings, so took a late train back. As he still had more to see at the Crystal Palace he took the train from Peterborough again next day.

The large and sudden increase in passenger demand exerted tremendous pressure on a railway system that was still in its infancy. People who were not going to the Exhibition, but who had become accustomed in the last few years to using the trains for business and leisure travel, complained vigorously in letters to the press about delays and disruption to regular services caused by the need to accommodate the excursionists. One fumed:

The whole duty of the line is dislocated and disorganised to make way for these interlopers, who in their turn are decoyed [meaning lured or enticed] in such prodigious numbers that it is found utterly impossible to keep faith with them.

Two serious train crashes in September – at Bicester in Oxfordshire and Hornsey in north London – were partly caused by congestion within the system. On 24 September the Great Western Railway had advertised a 6.30 a.m. excursion from Bristol to London, and because of the overwhelming response, they had to borrow an extra twelve carriages from the Midland Railway in addition to the sixteen they had already provided. The train carried more than 2,000 people but still over 700 were left behind at the station, and all trains on the line were delayed by an hour or more. On the same day the London and North-Western Railway announced that since May their receipts had increased by between £10,000 and £15,000 a week. Unofficial calculations put the extra revenue accruing to all the operating companies during that period at around £500,000. However, the cut-throat competition meant that their profits from this greatly increased traffic were minimal. The share price of the Midland Railway, which had stood at above 55d in May, was down to 37d by the end of August.

Without the railways, the Exhibition would probably never have been mounted, and would certainly not have enjoyed anywhere near the success it did. As *The Times* pointed out: 'When it was rumoured during the struggle over the Reform Bill [in 1832] that 50,000 men from Birmingham were coming to London to present a petition, a "great authority" wondered: "Where will they find shoes?" ' Now, nineteen years on, 'the artisans of Birmingham have achieved their threatened march on the metropolis on shoes of iron'.

There were some who felt compelled to see the Exhibition, under the lash of overwhelming public recommendation, but for whom even the five shilling round-trip by rail was too expensive. From time to time the newspapers would publish accounts of long, adventurous journeys to London made by other means, involving feats of stamina and a high level of ingenuity. The *Leeds Intelligencer* reported that three youths from the district of Armley set off on Whit Tuesday, 10 June, telling friends and relatives that they were going to a gala celebration at the city's botanical garden. No word was heard from them for more than a week, until a letter was received from the outskirts of the capital asking for money to be sent to them at a London post office.

After nine days on the road, walking on average twenty-three miles a day, the trio reached their destination on Thursday 20 June. Finding that the admission price on Friday and Saturday was more than they could afford, they had to wait until Monday to visit the Exhibition – presumably sleeping rough over the weekend, although this is not recorded. On Tuesday they caught a steam packet to Hull and walked the sixty miles home, which they reached, 'much to the joy of their parents', after an absence of sixteen days.

The most publicised pedestrian feat came towards the end of September when Mary Kerlynack, an eighty-four-year-old fisherwoman, was reported to have taken five weeks to walk the 265 miles from Paul, near Penzance, on the furthest point of the Cornish coast. In London she went to visit the Lord Mayor at the Mansion House, telling him that she had already visited the Exhibition and intended to return home, but only had fivepence-halfpenny left to her name. He gave her a sovereign, along with a warning to keep it safely from his larcenous fellow citizens. She wept and said: 'Now I'll be able to get back,' before being taken by the Lady Mayoress for tea in the housekeeper's room.

However, she did not go home immediately, because she became caught up in what today we would call the celebrity circuit. Someone impressed by her grit offered her a place to stay in Marylebone, and for the last few weeks of the Exhibition she was taken up by fashionable society. On the day before the closing ceremony in October she was on hand at the Crystal Palace when Queen Victoria came for her final look round, primed to shout 'God bless your Majesty' as the monarch went past.

While the excursionists were homing in on London from all parts of the country, the Exhibition's organisers went off on a little trip of their own. The municipal authorities of Paris, in a gesture of goodwill, had invited the Commissioners, the jurors and many other grandees, including the mayors of important towns and cities, to spend a week in the French capital at the beginning of August. The highlight was to be a grand *fête*, involving a banquet and a display of arms. Prince Albert declined gracefully, saying that the Commissioners would be admirably led by Lord Granville. Well before the visit was over, many of the invitees were to wish that they had followed that princely example of self-denial.

On Saturday 2 August the Parisian authorities had organised a special train from London Bridge station to Dover, where it would connect with a steamer to Boulogne and then a train to Paris. For Henry Cole, things began to go wrong at the very start, as he recorded in his memoirs:

> My personal adventures in this visit to Paris were irksome, but farcical. Mr D— (a juror) and his wife agreed to go in the same carriage with us. Mrs Cole and myself breakfasted, and started from Notting Hill in ample time to get to London Bridge Station, for the special train leaving at 9 a.m. We called for our companions in Fitzroy Square. They were not down, and had not breakfasted! We made the mistake of waiting for them for more than half an hour, and at last got off. When we arrived at Rathbone Place, D—

found out he had left his keys behind, and we were obliged to return for them, and we arrived at London Bridge just in time to see the special train off, and thus lost all the comfortable arrangements which had been made for our reaching Paris as soon as possible.

However, when he read the account in *The Times* of the departure of the excursion, Cole will have realised that 'comfortable' was scarcely the word to describe the condition of those who managed to catch the train. 'We cannot congratulate the railway company on their arrangements for the occasion, for they were nearly as bad as they could be,' the paper commented magisterially. The first train was not big enough to take all the guests, so a second and a third had to be provided at short notice. The sea was rough and many of the party were sick. Things perked up at Boulogne, where passport and customs inspections had been waived, and an 'elegant lunch' was provided at the station.

Then confusion struck again. An empty train drew in and, recalling the scramble at London Bridge, the most assertive members of the group pushed their way on to it and found the best seats. The doors were locked but the train remained at the station until a few minutes later a second, shorter train arrived, took up the passengers who had been stranded on the platform and immediately set off for Paris, leaving those in the first train a good two hours behind them. After stopping for wine and biscuits at Amiens, the first train reached Paris at nine p.m., the second just after eleven, and those who had not booked accommodation in advance spent hours tramping the streets looking for somewhere to stay.

Meanwhile, Cole and his travelling companions had been forced to take the regular Paris train that left after the specials. As a result they missed the fine spread laid on at Boulogne and could find nothing at all to eat there, and not much at Amiens. When they arrived in Paris at midnight, Cole, in an excess of politeness, let the late-rising juror D— take the room he had reserved for himself at Meurice's, the English gentleman's Parisian hotel of choice, while he and Mrs Cole, with the aid of M. De La Rue, a French colleague, 'got a little room to be in' somewhere else.

However, this turned out to be only the first, and not the gravest, of the problems that faced not only Cole but even those guests who had managed to catch the nine o'clock special. The sheer quantity of their luggage – containing as it did their formal dress clothes for the balls and galas that they had been invited to attend – quite outfaced the customs officers at Boulogne who, apparently not forewarned of the cross-Channel influx, promptly sent the bulk of it back to Dover and dispatched part of the rest to Brussels. For an English gentleman and gentlewoman, few plights are as desperate as being without the proper dress for a formal function. As *The Times* reported sardonically: 'Even several of the aldermen felt downcast and overcome by a railway which sent them off to a foreign land without their chains and scarlet gowns.'

Cole observed that the women in the party showed greater resource in making do than the men:

The following morning, the first work the ladies did was to go out shopping and buy bonnets and trimmings. A grand banquet was to be given at the Hôtel de Ville, and the contrivances of the ladies in adorning and metamorphosing their travelling dresses to make them passable at dinner, were amusing. Every Englishman and woman we met were in the same predicament. I had to borrow clothes; Mr De La Rue, who was double my cubical capacity, kindly lent me a huge pair of black trousers, which were made to fit as best they could, and the only coat I could obtain was one from M. Meurice, with buttons under my shoulder-blades and tails coming down to my heels, which had been made in the period of the Empire [the early years of the century].

The appearance of almost every Englishman at dinner was as odd as my own, but we sympathised with each other's misfortunes and the dinner passed off well, and was of a superb kind. The company was parcelled out into parties of four, each party was served with the same courses, accompanied by no fewer than sixteen changes of excellent wine. No clothes found the next day. The cry throughout Paris during the week was, 'Have you got your clothes?'

A laconic account of this sartorial fiasco came from Lord Granville, the senior member of the British party, in a series of letters to Prince Albert's aide, Colonel Phipps. By arriving on the Friday evening, Granville had avoided the Great Baggage Disaster. Reporting on the dreadful journey, he wrote:

The principal facts concerning it that I have been able to ascertain are that the Lord Mayor is not a good sailor, that the reception in Boulogne was pretty and cordial, and that two-thirds of the baggage were lost in that town, the result of which is that some of the excursionists such as Baring [Thomas Baring MP, a leading banker and one of the Commissioners] are obliged to walk the streets in uniform, while others such as Lord Albemarle are reduced to go to the evening fêtes in shooting jackets.

The Times correspondent, who seemed already to have decided to cast the French hosts in the role of bumbling incompetents, could hardly believe his luck. Drawing on his ample reserves of wit and spite, and deploying his very purplest prose, he painted a savage portrait of the débâcle:

> After a day spent by a majority of the guests of the city of Paris in unspeakable anguish and bitterness of mind at the fatal mismanagement which had left them without bag or baggage, and in superhuman efforts to repair the loss by levying such contributions of male attire as would enable them to make some decent approach to the recognised evening costume, the apartments of the Hôtel de Ville began, at the appointed hour, gradually to fill with the strangest miscellany of costumes and personages ever assembled within the walls of the ancient municipal palace during all the vicissitudes of its eventful annals. It was a sight full of pity to see men who would, but for railway inexactitude, have appeared swelling in the magnificence of civic attire.

According to the report, they sought invisibility by dashing into the thick of the crowd or cowering in alcoves. Apart from that, though, the evening was 'a complete and brilliant success', the banquet 'beyond description and beyond pain'. Lord Granville responded to the toast in French (poor French, according to *The Times*, but Cole thought it brilliant). Then they were regaled with a performance of Molière's *Le Médecin Malgré Lui*, followed by a concert.

There was a further blip in the arrangements the next day, when guests were kept waiting for two hours before the Versailles fête could start because the guest of honour,

Alderman John Musgrove, Lord Mayor of London, was late arriving. 'Our fair countrymen are without exception monsters, but all behave well,' Lord Granville reported. 'The French are civility itself.' Things began to look up by Monday, when the wayward trunks arrived in time for the reception by the President, Louis Napoleon, at his palace at St Cloud.

Even this brilliant highlight of the visit did not wholly impress the man from *The Times*, determined to mock the behaviour of the British guests now that they were reunited with their proper clothes. In the Orangery, a splendid buffet had been set out on tables, and waiters stood by with champagne bottles poised for action. Hungry guests paced outside, peering in, but the doors were guarded by 'tall and peremptory dragoons', who refused to let anybody feed until Louis Napoleon appeared to inaugurate the reception. As soon as he did so, everyone went on the attack simultaneously:

> The rush was tremendous, the gallant soldiers of the Republic, who formed a large proportion of the President's guard, being foremost in the assault. In a moment the invading crowd had taken possession of every important post and were doing rapid execution on the *galantines de veau*, which they literally cut to pieces beneath a heavy fire of champagne corks.

The final day's programmes included war games in the Champ de Mars – a shameless display of French military prowess – and in the evening what Granville described as 'a dull French opera, with a pretty scene of the Crystal Palace'. The journey back to England went more smoothly than the trip out; but even when the guests were safely in their own beds and their fine garments back in their wardrobes, *The Times* continued pooh-poohing the event, snobbishly decrying the class of people who formed the bulk of the British representatives. The paper was outraged that civic officials should have been treated as guests of honour at a military review. Seldom has the perceived gulf between the officer class and the jumped-up trading fraternity been expressed so clearly and so viciously – and this during an Exhibition one of whose purported aims was to celebrate the worth of the manufacturing and labouring classes:

> What must be thought [in Paris] of England and the English, if a batch of aldermen and their civic fugle-man [the Lord Mayor] are accepted as specimens of the highest breeding and most distinguished manner extant in this country? . . . We should as soon think of sending a hippopotamus to preside over a parish meeting, or of sending a parish beadle to inspect a squadron of firstrates [warships] at Spithead, as of inviting the Lord Mayor to be present at the relief of a corporal's guard in England . . . We freely admit that where eating and drinking were the main and principal objects of a public ceremony, the Lord Mayor and aldermen of the City of London might be supposed to be in their especial element. What do they represent except jobbery and good living, not to say gluttony and corruption?

It is hard to imagine what poor John Musgrove and his fellow aldermen could have done to warrant such abuse.

Like nearly every English summer, that of 1851 offered extremes of weather, from heavy, drenching rain to a few days of tremendous heat. The roof of the Crystal Palace was never made totally waterproof, and before the close several exhibitors would claim that some of their prize artifacts had been badly damaged by rain. Heat was a potentially graver problem. Although the canvas awning on the roof modified the worst effects of the sun in the middle of the day, the glass walls made it much hotter inside than out.

The first really hot day was a Saturday, 28 June, when only 11,501 people were prepared to pay the higher weekend tariff for the privilege of being slowly frizzled. Many of them clustered round the fountains, where the air was slightly cooler, while others poured bottles of water over themselves. There were long queues for ices and cool drinks. The decorative fans exhibited by the Chinese, Indians and Tunisians were removed from display and used by the assistants on the stands. Over the weekend, staff took out some of the glass panels so as to provide a better air flow, and it was more comfortable on the Monday, although attendance was again poor. The heat wave ended on 1 July with a burst of heavy rain.

With every newspaper printing almost daily reports from the Crystal Palace, attention-seekers and pressure groups of various kinds found it a productive venue for staging demonstrations. A group of about eighty artisans from Sardinia handed out leaflets complaining that the island was being oppressed by neighbouring powers. One of the biggest stirs was created by a party of young women dressed in the distinctive outfit devised by Amelia Bloomer, an early American feminist and dress reformer who gave her name to a particular style of loose trousers, gathered in at the ankles.

The unusual mode of dress was a clever way of drawing attention to a cause that was not to become politically fashionable for nearly half a century. It had already provoked a minor sensation in London. A show called *Bloomerism: or the Follies of a Day* was playing at the Adelphi Theatre, featuring the Bloomer Polka. Bloomer costume balls and transatlantic soirées were organised, while bloomers abounded in the lyrics of comic songs at the music halls. Mlle Rousseau, a noted equestrian, was adding zest to her performances at the Drury Lane Theatre by wearing the outrageous articles during her appearances on horseback.

Miss Bloomer herself had not come to London but a few of her supporters had, led by Emily Griswold of Baltimore, and they had recruited a small cell of backers from among the nonconformist section of the London élite. Lectures were given in venues designated 'Bloomer Hall' for the occasion. On 26 September *The Globe* reported the appearance in Hyde Park, just outside the Crystal Palace, of 'three ladies, attired according to the Bloomer fashion, accompanied by two gentlemen wearing the habiliments of the new sect'. They 'appeared to be people of some station and bore taunts with good humour'. Two of the women were identified as being from 'a respectable family in Torrington Square' – the other one could have been Ms Griswold. They attracted a large crowd of onlookers as they handed out leaflets inviting people to a lecture the following week at the Bloomer Hall in Finsbury, north London. A few days later another bloomer-clad woman was reported, this time having penetrated the Crystal Palace itself.

On Tuesday 7 October, the last shilling day but two, 109,915 people were admitted – the largest single day's attendance. Until that extraordinary year, nobody would have dreamed that such a crowd, including people of all stations and persuasions, could have gathered without any hint of disorder. There was just one worrying moment that day. The Duke of Wellington, paying his farewell visit, almost came to grief among the adoring fans who surrounded him. As Cole described it, the Duke insisted on walking up the nave among the crowd, although the police had warned him that it could be dangerous.

What actually happened could not have been predicted. The Duke, as he must have known he would be, was cheered to the echo; but people in distant parts of the Crystal Palace knew nothing of his visit and, hearing a commotion, began to panic. Rumours spread that the building was so crowded that it was on the point of collapse. Everyone rushed down the nave to the exit, and the Duke was swamped. Fortunately six policemen had followed him on his triumphant progress. They scooped him up, fearful and protesting, and carried him bodily to safety through the passages that led to the executive offices. It might have been an appropriate death – suffocated by an implacable mob of hero-worshippers – but the hero of Waterloo was to enjoy several more months of life and fame.

Officials readied themselves for an even larger crowd on the last of all the shilling days, 9 October, but the weather intervened. Heavy rain kept the number down to a modest (by recent standards) 90,813. Once inside the Crystal Palace they were comparatively dry, but getting there was the problem. Only hardened country-dwellers seemed unworried about riding on the uncovered tops and sides of the omnibuses, which splattered the clothes of passers-by with mud from the gutters.

You get what you pay for, and the gods were more considerate to the 53,061 who had stumped up the higher admission fee for the very last public day, Saturday 11 October. It was the highest turnout on a non-shilling day and it took the total number of visitors since 1 May above the six million mark, to 6,039,195. The weather could not have been better. 'The sun looked down warmly upon the only great building in the world which does not inhospitably exclude its rays,' reported *The Times*.

Not all the visitors were from the moneyed classes. Some of the less wealthy had thought it worth paying the extra for the excitement of being in at the death of the most successful public spectacle yet held in Britain. A band of hop-pickers, for instance, were parading up and down the aisles, wearing wreaths of hops as necklaces. There was anticipation in the air from the very start of the day. The organs played throughout the morning, as people hurried to get their final glimpse of those objects that had impressed them most. In the afternoon, as the five p.m. closing time approached, the music stopped and visitors began to move away from the galleries and peripheral gangways, to congregate near the centre of the building.

A few minutes before five o'clock, the crystal fountain spluttered as its water was switched off for the last time, and the crowd fell silent. An official appeared in the gallery with a red flag. As the clock struck five he raised the flag and the organs burst into life again, playing the National Anthem. The men removed their hats and everyone joined in the singing wholeheartedly – if not always tunefully, for it was hard to keep in time with the contrasting rhythms of competing organs. When the music stopped, cheers rang out for several minutes, followed by the mass stamping of fifty thousand pairs of feet. In the gallery, someone unfurled a piece of cloth bearing the lines from *The Tempest* that begin 'Our revels now are ended . . .' and close with '. . . like this insubstantial pageant faded, leave not a rack behind'.

There was a further short silence before bells began to ring out over the building, soon supplemented by Chinese gongs and drums from India. This was meant as a signal for everyone to leave but still the crowd lingered, until gradually the trickle towards the exits became something like a current. Night was falling and the gas lamps were being lit. As they moved out of the building the crowd spontaneously delivered three cheers for various people whose names had become associated with the Exhibition – Paxton, Prince Albert, the contractors Fox and Henderson. A mischief-maker suggested three cheers for Louis Kossuth, the exiled Hungarian revolutionary who would arrive in England later that month, but there was no enthusiasm for such an accolade amongst a crowd that had just acted out so potent an endorsement of Britain's monarchy.

A few stragglers congregated around the silent fountain, some filling bottles – which they would take home as souvenirs – from the rapidly depleting bowl beneath it. The police and army engineers moved in and, without any overt show of force, persuaded the last of them to leave by six, when the bells finally stopped ringing.

CHAPTER TEN

❧ ❧

THE PARTY'S OVER

This will long be remembered as a singularly happy
year of peace, plenty, good feeling, innocent pleasure,
national glory of the best and purest sort.

Lord Macaulay, 14 October 1851

The destruction of such a building is itself a catastrophe,
for so is death itself, though ever so anticipated.

The Times, 6 October 1851

The most vainglorious actor could not have hoped for
better reviews. Even those newspapers that had originally
been hostile to the enterprise had to agree, when the curtain fell,
that the Exhibition had been a triumphant success. *The
Standard* conceded that it had been 'more successful than we
anticipated and . . . highly honourable to the character of our
countrymen'. Most of the other papers went further, though
none quite so far as the *Morning Chronicle*, which characterised
it as 'not only the noblest exhibition of the results of human
ingenuity, but an important chapter in the history of the human
race', adding: 'As a people, we are not what we were.'

It was universally celebrated as a triumph of British
phlegm, resourcefulness and tolerance. A common theme

among the obituaries published on and after the final days was how none of the worst fears of social disorder – nor, more prosaically, of the building's destruction by extreme weather – had been realised. The summer of 1851 had brought the nation together; artisans rubbed shoulders with aristocrats without robbing them (at least not often), insulting them or otherwise disturbing the peace. Still more amazingly, the lower orders even appeared to show interest in the exhibits and to understand them. As *The Globe* put it:

> The prophets stand abashed, and the universal voice proclaims the gladdening triumphs of genius and nature over the dreams and delusions of prejudice . . . The great gratifying and crowning fact and glory of the Exhibition is that the mechanics and artisans, the labourers and clodhoppers of England, have availed themselves of this opportunity of acquiring knowledge, and conducted themselves with the ut-most propriety, despite the unfavourable anticipations which were too generally formed of them.

The *Daily News* wrote:

> The English are accused of being brutal in their pleasures, of loving drink and low excitement. Hyde Park in 1851 gives the lie to such a calumny, and proves that no population can more fully appreciate an intellectual pleasure, or enjoy it with greater decorum and with greater mutual courtesy.

If it had been an educational experience for Britain's workers, their perceived betters had equally learned a great deal about them.

The Illustrated London News stressed that the nation could be proud not just of the people's behaviour in unprecedented circumstances, but of the content of the Exhibition itself:

> It has served its end and stands upon record as the most gratifying and surprising event of our time. As a mere show, the history of the world offers no parallel or rival to it . . . The result of the Great Exhibition has been to disabuse the mind of much of the stupid prejudice, handed down from father to son and re-peated by traveller after traveller, of the infinite superiority in point of taste of the foreign producer.

The Times, more eloquent and less chauvinistic, took a broader view of the phenomenon that had changed the nation's view of itself:

> The pageant terminates, the doors of the Crystal Palace no longer yield to the open sesame of money, and in a few days hence thousands of hands will be busily engaged in removing all those triumphs of human skill, and those evidences of natural wealth which the world was assembled to behold . . . The ephemeral existence assigned to the Exhibition has all along been fully recognised, yet it was impossible that so marvellous an undertaking could run its brief career without gathering around it many attachments, sympathies, and associations which at the last it proved difficult to sever . . . With a large proportion it was the edifice itself which took the firmest hold upon their hearts. Its vastness, its simplicity and regu-larity of structural details, and a certain atmosphere of mysterious grandeur which pervades it, are features

which harmonise so perfectly with our character as a
people, that they must have left a strong impression.
If the whole country does not now protest against the
wanton and aimless destruction of the Crystal Palace
we shall be very much surprised.

The future of the building had already become a matter of
heated debate, but before it could be resolved there were
still some last rites to be performed on the pageant itself.
The official farewell ceremony was scheduled for 15 October,
the Wednesday following the closure to the public, with the
Monday and Tuesday set aside to allow exhibitors and their
friends a free run. This was a goodwill gesture, recognising
that the people who had performed a central role in the
Exhibition's success may not have had the chance to
appreciate it in its entirety. Exhibitors would also be allowed
to attend the closing ceremony, along with leading public
figures invited by the Commissioners. Apprehensive to the
last about the potential behaviour even of people so closely
involved in the enterprise, the Commissioners issued an edict
that, over the three days, 'no person is to stand on any counter
or stand, and exhibitors are earnestly requested to protect each
other's property'.

The Queen, who would not be taking part in the closing
ceremony, visited the Crystal Palace on both Monday and
Tuesday mornings, scarcely able to tear herself away from her
husband's triumphant brainchild. On the first day she looked
at some of the items that had been introduced in the closing
weeks, including the gold plates from California, which
gleamed seductively in the autumn sunshine. On the Tuesday
she was presented with bound copies of the *Official Illustrated
Catalogue*, just published as a permanent record of the event.
She recorded that final visit in her journal:

It looked so beautiful and I could not believe that it was the last time that I should behold this wonderful creation of my beloved Albert's . . . The view from near the end, close to the last entrance, one can never carry in one's mind – each time one is amazed afresh at the immense length and height and the fairy like effect of the different objects that fill it. Walked in fact through the whole building, bidding it regretfully adieu.

She was unhappy at being excluded from the closing ceremony, as she wrote the next day, 15 October:

I grieved not to be able to be present, and yet I think Albert was right, that I could hardly have been there as a spectator . . . To think that this great and bright time is past, like a dream, after all its success and triumph, and that all the labour and anxiety it caused for nearly two years should likewise now be only remembered as 'a has been' seems incredible and melancholy.

Many others also resented the Queen's absence, and the superstitious among them thought that it was to blame for the weather turning nasty again on Wednesday morning. The Commissioners having decided that their President, Prince Albert, should do the honours, the ceremony was set deliberately in a low key, so as not to compete in anyone's memory with the splendour of the opening. The result was a tawdry ceremony that, by common consent, failed to do justice to the significance of the occasion. The roof of the Crystal Palace was still leaking, and some of the 20,000 or so people who attended had to bring out their umbrellas to keep themselves dry as they stood in the transept to watch. Some prominent exhibits had already been removed to make way for the dais on which the proceedings were to take place. Most notably, the crystal fountain was missing, as were Keith's Silk Trophy and the Canadian timber monument.

The platform was covered with a scarlet cloth, and on it stood the Indian throne that the Queen had used at the opening ceremony in May, now to be occupied by Prince Albert. At noon the Prince Consort led the procession of officials towards the dais, with the robed Bishop of London at his side, while the attendant choir sang the first verse of the National Anthem. Viscount Canning, on behalf of all the juries, presented a list of the awards made to the exhibitors. Of more than 17,000 who took part, 164 were to receive the top-rated Council Medal and 2,918 the lesser Prize Medal. Some others received honourable mentions, the rest nothing. Canning spoke of the dilemmas that the juries had faced in selecting the winners – probably anticipating the many disputes that were to come over their selections.

Prince Albert, who had difficulty making himself heard over the rain beating down on the glass roof, thanked Canning and reiterated the core theme of the Exhibition – the improvement of design and taste in manufactured goods. He concluded by expressing the hope that

> this interchange of knowledge, resulting from the meeting of enlightened people in friendly rivalry, may be dispersed far and wide over distant lands; and thus, by sharing our mutual dependence upon each other, be a happy means of promoting unity among nations, and peace and goodwill among the various races of mankind.

When he sat down, the final verse of the National Anthem was sung, the Bishop of London led a prayer of thanksgiving for the success of the event and the Hallelujah Chorus rounded off the ceremony. By half past twelve it was all over. The procession regrouped and marched out and the guests left the building – some for the last time, although most exhibitors would be returning over the ensuing weeks to oversee the removal, and in some cases the sale, of the items they had contributed.

The Times, discussing the jury awards, was in philosophical mood:

> It is a saying of statesmen that by every single act of patronage they make ten bitter enemies and one ungrateful friend. If this be true, a distribution of three thousand prizes among seventeen thousand competitors may be expected to procure the indifference of the three thousand and the hostility of the remaining fourteen thousand . . . Were the jurors angels, their awards would be disputed.

And so they were, heatedly. Even before the official announcement of the winners there had been rumblings based on rumours that this or that significant contribution to the well-being of humanity would not be recognised by the juries, while some exhibitors complained that their products had not even been inspected. Even many who won Prize Medals felt they had been slighted by not being awarded the higher accolade. The criterion for distinguishing between the two levels of award was that to win a Council Medal an exhibit was supposed to represent a real technological advance, whereas a Prize Medal winner merely had to be an exceptional example of its kind. Interpreting those definitions provided ample scope for challenging the jurors' decisions.

It was not only the exhibitors who protested. Some members of the thirty-four specialist juries complained that their recommendations had been overruled by the council of jury chairmen that had to endorse each award. Others noted that, with only two levels of award on offer in each class of exhibits, absurdities must inevitably arise. How could you compare a well-built steam engine with an ingeniously designed pair of boots or a jar of unusual pickles? Yet they all qualified for the same awards. The *Morning Chronicle* made the point that Osler's crystal fountain, for many the highlight of all the exhibits, rightly received a Prize Medal – but then so did a shirt from the United States. The shirt no doubt excelled in its class, but how could the importance of the two objects be compared?

All in all, the Commissioners must have been relieved that at least no money was involved: it had been decided at an early stage to scrap the original plan to award cash prizes. Yet in one sense that may have made things worse, because it meant that the exhibitors had only their reputation in the business community to fight for – and that was a matter of huge importance to them. When it came to the overseas participants, sensitive issues of national prestige came into play. Although each country had been fairly represented on the juries, there were inevitably allegations of discrimination.

Of the Council Medals seventy-eight went to British exhibits and fifty-four to France. Prussia was awarded seven, the United States five, Austria four and other countries from three to none. (No prizes of any kind went to weapons, not even the innovative Colt revolver – a deliberate omission, underlining the essentially peaceable aims of the Exhibition.) Given that only ten per cent of the exhibits were French, this might be thought a statistical triumph for our cross-Channel neighbours; but to nobody's real surprise they were not satisfied. The French journal *Constitutionnel* complained that all the Council Medals awarded to France had been for excellence in design, and that none had been given to French manufacturing industries, which had to make do with Prize Medals. The journal put this down to Britain's implacable determination to maintain its reputation as Europe's most important manufacturing country. In that respect, then, Prince Albert's dream that the Exhibition would advance international harmony was unfulfilled. Certainly the world was still a long way from the 'universal republic' that Richard Cobden had envisaged as one of the consequences of 1851. The author Charles Kingsley, preaching at St Margaret's, Westminster, said he thought the main motive of the exercise had turned out to be 'national aggrandisement, insular self-glorification and selfish – I had almost said treacherous – rivalry with the very foreigners whom we invited as our guests'.

The complaints from individual exhibitors were unstoppable. By 21 October, less than a week after the closing ceremony, *The Times* announced that it had received so many letters from those who felt aggrieved that it had decided not to print any of them. Undeterred, several complainants bought advertising space in the paper to express their outrage. Members of the musical jury protested that the council of chairmen had vetoed the Council Medals that the jury had recommended for two piano manufacturers, on the grounds that their instruments were insufficiently innovative. They complained that their opinion as specialists had been overridden by people without technical knowledge. A similar complaint came from the jury assessing astronomical instruments.

A Bond Street store asserted that it had been denied an award because the jury said it was not the manufacturer of a much-admired chandelier that hung above the gallery. It was a matter of semantics: the piece had been assembled in its workrooms. A bitter advertisement was placed by Henry Bone, by appointment painter of enamels to the Queen and Prince Albert. He observed that medals had been awarded to three enamel painters, but he was not among them. This was a 'palpable injustice' and 'an overwhelming condemnation of my professional ability'. He had therefore written to Victoria and Albert giving up the royal appointment, because the verdict of the jury suggested that he was no longer entitled to it.

A firm of hat manufacturers complained that its model of a hat factory, with a specimen of a finished silk hat, had not even been examined by the jurors, while Edward Baillie, a maker of stained glass, alleged that the jury for that section was illegally constituted in that it included Augustus Pugin, a principal of the firm that won the only British medal in the class. M. Guillerez, a French teacher from Edinburgh, was disgruntled because his display of lentils, which he had proposed as a substitute for potatoes (this being only five years after the Irish potato famine), had been passed over, although medals had been awarded to snuff and white wheat.

Some put their grievances directly to the Commissioners, even to Prince Albert himself. Frederick Fryers, the American inventor of an ice-cream freezing machine, had a sorry tale to tell of how some of his components had become misplaced on arrival at the Crystal Palace from his workshop in Baltimore. He found and fitted them just before the day appointed for the jury inspection, and bought fifteen shillings' worth of milk and sugar for his demonstration. On making the first batch of ice cream he found that one of the recovered components was a little damaged, and the jurors said they would return when it was fixed – but they did not, and when he enquired why he was told they had disbanded. Now, after five months in

London, he seemed doomed to return to Baltimore with a broken machine and no medal. Even in response to such a heartfelt plea, the unbending Commissioners merely rehearsed the official position that the award of medals had been a matter for the juries and their chairmen, not for them.

They offered the same reply to others who felt misused, such as Lieutenant Tilley (retired), who complained that his anatomised leaf arrangements had not received even an honourable mention. W. G. Begg, an Edinburgh confectioner, was angry that although his lozenges were regarded by others in the business as 'the finest specimens of hard confectionery in the Exhibition', they too had gone unrewarded. Thomas Harrington from Portsmouth claimed £65 in compensation because the jury had failed to examine his false teeth.

James Heath and Benjamin Newnham of Bath, the inventors of the Bath chair for invalids, were incensed that the award of the main prize in their section had gone to a rival chair, which they thought greatly inferior to their own and not strictly a Bath chair at all. The proper version, 'as used by the dowager Queen', should be light and easy of access, they wrote, with a shifting and folding head and an enclosed glass front for protection against the weather. 'The successful article is badly finished and without taste.' They maintained that there were few people who understood the principle of Bath chairs, and they were surprised not to have been asked to recommend experts to serve on the appropriate jury. A. and R. Thwaites of Dublin, claiming to be the inventors of soda water, were upset because they were not allowed to exhibit in Class 2, chemical products, but were consigned to Class 29, miscellaneous manufactures, where they received no award. 'We have therefore to complain of serious wrong and great injustice.'

Some felt so peeved that they refused to accept honours

they thought inadequate. P. Claussen of Gresham Street, London, turned down a Prize Medal for his new process of preparing flax, believing it merited the top award. Ridgway and Co., the Staffordshire potters, were amazed to have won a medal for their earthenware but not their porcelain, 'which everyone accepts to be a superior article'. Given that their sanitary vessels and hollow bricks, as installed in Prince Albert's model working-class dwellings, had also been passed over, 'we decline the award for earthenware'.

The other topic on which the Commissioners received a weight of correspondence was money. As soon as it was reported that the success of the Exhibition had created a healthy surplus of £186,000, letters started pouring in with suggestions on what to do with it. Several correspondents wanted to get their hands on some of the loot for themselves, claiming that their involvement with the Exhibition had left them out of pocket in various ways. Others canvassed support for charitable causes and education, not all of them in the fields of art and industry. Among the suggestions listed by Cole in his memoirs were a Museum of Aboriginal Products, a Free Hospital for all Nations, a fund for the alleviation of Irish and Highland destitution and the purchase of an Irish estate for Prince Albert.

Some local committees that had drummed up the subscriptions needed to allow the project to go ahead now wondered whether they might get their investment back. Henry Forbes, who headed the Bradford committee, was one of the leaders of this movement, claiming that it would be 'a simple act of justice'. He suggested that the cash – in Bradford's case £1,100 – could be put to good use in establishing a design school to enable local textile manufacturers to compete more effectively in international markets.

The Commissioners, determined to keep the funds under their own control, gave him and like-minded civic leaders short shrift, pointing out that it had been made clear from the beginning that no money would be refunded to the local committees. It had always been understood that their contributions were to be regarded as donations to a cause that would benefit every part of the nation, not as speculative investments in the Exhibition's success. The original intention, which they would adhere to, had been for any surplus to be put towards a project that would further the aims of the Exhibition. The provision of design schools was among the options considered, as was the establishment of a fund for mounting similar events in future years.

On 10 August, when the Exhibition still had two months to run, Prince Albert had written a memo about his plan to use the money to buy a Kensington estate to accommodate institutions fostering science and the practical arts. He summoned Cole, Playfair and Col. William Reid, the powerful head of the Executive Committee, to Osborne House to discuss it. They all expressed reservations: the scientist Playfair, for instance, wanted to establish a single college of arts and manufactures, modelled on the Ecole Centrale des Arts et Métiers in Paris.

The Prince, though, had his way. They decided to buy Gore House and seventy acres of land – much of it then used as a plant nursery – on the other side of Knightsbridge from the Crystal Palace site, and build there a complex of institutions including a museum of manufactures. The original land purchased now embraces the Victoria and Albert Museum, the Science and Natural History Museums, the Royal Geographical Society, the Royal Albert Hall and Imperial College of Science and Technology. The cost of the site was £336,000, nearly half contributed by the Government. By 1860 it was worth more than a million pounds.

264 ◆ THE WORLD FOR A SHILLING

One consequence of the Commissioners' decision was that they had to perpetuate their existence, in order to administer the newly acquired property. When the Queen established the Commission at the beginning of 1850, the intention had been that it would dissolve itself once the Exhibition was over. At the Commissioners' suggestion, she now extended the body's life in perpetuity. That is why The Royal Commission for the Great Exhibition of 1851 remains in existence today, with offices on an upper floor of Imperial College. It administers the freehold of a little less than half the original estate: the land on which the V & A, the Science Museum and the Natural History Museum now stand was ceded to the Government in 1858 and 1863 as part of a complicated financial settlement. The Commission uses the revenue from the estate and its other investments – a little over one million pounds in 2000 – to fund scholarships and projects that fulfil the criteria laid down in its charter, 'to increase the means of industrial education and extend the influence of science and art upon productive industry'.

As well as people soliciting grants from the Commission for worthy institutions and undertakings, there were those in 1851 who simply wanted a share of the kitty for themselves. Some – such as Thomas Harrisson, the entrepreneur who staked his fortune on the hostel in Pimlico, and Ann Hicks, who had to give up her Hyde Park cake stall – sought compensation for losses incurred as a direct result of the Exhibition. Others had less legitimate claims. W. Dyne from Hackney maintained that the establishment of cloakrooms and a lost property office in the Crystal Palace had been his idea, and that he was therefore entitled to a slice of the profits. The Reverend William Mitchell, the Presbyterian preacher at Hornton Street chapel, wanted payment for having performed divine services for the Sappers working on the Crystal Palace site since February. In his reply, Colonel Reid reminded Mitchell that he had performed the services voluntarily and that if he expected to be paid he should have arranged it with the military authorities in advance.

The Commissioners declined most such solicitations, including the claim by residents of Hans Town (an eighteenth-century housing development centred on Sloane Street) for compensation of at least £200 for the damage to their roads caused by the Exhibition traffic. William Roberts of Edinburgh was unsuccessful in his demand for £1 12s 6d for having sent some of his wines and spirits to London, only to learn that they would not be included in the Exhibition. James Williams, secretary of the Bath Travelling and Exhibition Fund, drew a blank when he asked for money to defray expenses he had incurred. And a different James Williams, a Dublin newspaper reporter, failed to convince the Commissioners that he should be paid for reporting meetings in the city in 1849 and 1850, which had the result of increasing support for the project among influential Dubliners.

The attendants on the exhibitors' stands did not demand financial compensation for the sacrifices they had made to ensure the success of the enterprise (they had, after all, been paid), but they wondered whether they might at least be given a medal or some other token of official approval. At the end of September some 200 of them, foreign as well as British, sent a memorandum to the Executive Committee pointing out that they had behaved with the utmost dignity and decorum throughout, even when required to work in extreme temperatures. Moreover, the steam from the constant running of engines had endangered their health: 'Many of the attendants have had various inroads made into their constitutions.' But the committee was not to be moved, pointing out that its medals were for the exhibitors only, who were in turn responsible for giving appropriate recognition to the efforts of their employees.

Exhibitors whose items were damaged, through no fault of their own, sometimes had better luck, although often they had to engage in protracted correspondence with the Commissioners and others before they received their due. The most persistent petitioner was Woldemar Seyffarth, the Commissioner for Saxony, one of the Zollverein states. His campaign began on 31 July, well before the close of the Exhibition, when he wrote to the contractors, Fox and Henderson, informing them that an important table had been damaged because of a leak in the roof during heavy rain. It was a superficially polite letter – perhaps excessively so – but it did contain a hint of menace. Seyffarth wrote that although the table maker, Mr Tuerpe of Dresden, was entitled to go to law to gain satisfaction, he was too poor to go down that route. 'But I know there is no need for that. English gentlemen, I am told, are averse to being unjust and to behaving shabbily, and I am further assured that you would rather not exist than prove yourselves an exception.'

The contractors may have been at a loss what to make of this peculiar letter. Was Seyffarth being serious, or was it just an example of heavy Teutonic irony? Perhaps for this reason, or maybe because they were just too busy, Fox and Henderson delayed their reply, and three weeks later the Saxon took his complaint to the Commissioners. He had already softened them up with a claim on an unrelated bit of damage, seeking £20 in compensation for a statue broken when it was moved from one part of the Crystal Palace to another. (The Commissioners told him to get back to them after the Exhibition closed.)

Now, though, Seyffarth was really angry at being ignored by Fox and Henderson, a cruel blow to his *amour-propre*.

He saw it as 'an insult to me and through me to the Saxon Government', and he added: 'I am not at a loss to find the German word for such conduct. I leave it to you to find the English word.' That provoked the contractors to send a reply, although not the one Seyffarth wanted. They explained the delay by saying they had been making enquiries, but having done that they denied liability. After all, if they entertained this claim they would have to pay out on countless other rain-damaged articles. This provoked the Saxon into a further emotional letter. Writing of himself in the third person, he said he would continue to have faith in the Commissioners' sense of justice 'till, disbelieving his own eyes, nothing remains for him to do but to pity his poor exhibitor and to tell Mr Tuerpe that nothing is left for him to do but to repent and to submit'.

The Commissioners asked Captain Henry Cunliffe Owen, an engineer and the general superintendent of the Exhibition, to look into the matter. He estimated the damage to the table at £25 but advised against assuming responsibility for it. 'I cannot recommend putting public funds to such an object.' However, unable to face the prospect of more pained letters from the shameless Seyffarth, the Commissioners ignored Owen's advice and paid up the £25, earning a fulsome letter of thanks.

The Austrian Commissioner, Charles Buschek, also wanted compensation for rain damage – this time to an elaborate ceiling exhibited by Montessori of Milan. In addition, he was claiming £12 2s for items that had gone missing from the Crystal Palace, including fifteen handkerchiefs, three scarves, three waistcoats and a piece of flannel. The Tuscans demanded cash for damage done to their statue of Psyche, which had been repaired poorly without consulting the sculptor, who was now 'entirely ruined because this statue was his only patrimony'. It had apparently been damaged deliberately but the culprit was not caught.

The New York sculptor George Catlin, whose work was also victim to vandalism, set his sights higher. In a letter to the Commissioners he said he had been informed by the American Commissioner that 'my two Indian figures were tumbled down and broken to pieces by a drunken woman'. He was seeking £100, because after the Exhibition he had intended to display the sculptures for sale at a gallery in London. When the Commissioners replied that they could not be held responsible for accidental damage, Catlin said he would not be claiming anything from them if his figures had been struck by lightning, but 'my loss has been of a peculiar kind'.

On a smaller scale, R. W. Savage, exhibitor of the widely noticed alarm bed that tipped people out at the chosen time, reported that the alarm clock had been broken, and enclosed a bill for £2 for its repair. Nearly all the victims of such damage received something, for on 23 October the Finance Committee was authorised to pay up to £1,000 on the various claims against it. That, though, was to be the limit of its largesse.

Then there was the touchy question of rewards for the Commissioners and others who had worked to make the Exhibition a success. In most cases these involved cash payments of various sizes, although Paxton, Fox the contractor and Cubitt and Dilke, members of the Executive Committee, were all awarded knighthoods. (Cole would have to wait another twenty-four years before he was similarly honoured, but he received a substantial honorarium and was later put in charge of the new South Kensington Museum, precursor to the Victoria and Albert, for which Parliament voted £25,000 in 1856.) Dilke was offered an honorarium on top of his knighthood, but he turned it down, saying that he could afford to give his time freely. Colonel Reid, chairman of the Executive Committee, also declined any money, on the grounds that he had held a paid government post while working on the Exhibition. John Scott Russell wrote indignantly to Colonel Grey, wondering why he had been offered nothing.

Playfair, who had performed a leading role from the very beginning, drumming up the essential support of industrialists, received a unique honour, and one that was to prove contentious. On 15 October he was invited by Prince Albert to become his gentleman usher, replacing Reid, who was going overseas. The Prince's letter explained somewhat apologetically that the salary of £100 a year was insignificant, but on the other hand the duties were light, involving only attendance at the Queen's levées and drawing rooms. It was one of several posts in the royal gift that offered nothing tangible to the holder, just the social cachet of having influence at Court.

Such positions usually went to people of high birth whose fathers may have held them before. In offering it to Playfair, a well-qualified scientist whose father had been a middle-ranking official in India, Albert was deliberately reaching out to a class of person whose position rested on merit and achievement rather than accident of birth. Although always conscious that, as a foreigner, he must tread softly when it came to breaking long-standing conventions, he was at heart a moderniser with a highly developed social conscience. The success of the Exhibition in chipping away at rigid distinctions between the classes may have emboldened him. Offering Playfair what was essentially a non-job can scarcely be classed as a revolutionary act of defiance, but it was a significant gesture all the same.

Colonel Phipps, the Prince's former private secretary, the second son of an earl and still an influential figure in the royal household, immediately recognised the significance of Albert's offer. On 17 October (by which time Playfair had accepted the appointment, although Phipps probably did not know this) he wrote a remarkable letter to the Prince which reveals a great deal about the social attitudes of the time, and the threat that the aristocracy were beginning to perceive to their traditional privileges.

> I respectfully state my opinion that this would not be a good appointment. There is no person who rejoices more than I do in all proper attention and honour being paid to men of science, but I think it should be in their own sphere, and I do not think that Dr Playfair is in any way suited by position or manners to become a member of the joint court of Her Majesty and Your Royal Highness. I do not even think it is doing him a kindness to place him in a position for which he is not suited . . . The qualities of Dr Playfair are those of a learned chemist, a geologist and a public lecturer – none of these appear to me to be the attributes that render a man fit to be gentleman usher to Your Royal Highness. Dr Playfair is a man of low birth, ordinary appearance and uncouth manners. All of these are disqualifications.

In case he had not made himself perfectly clear, Phipps reinforced the point. Reiterating that he had no objection as such to scientists and other talented people being appointed to positions in court,

> in my humble opinion these qualifications should be combined with the other necessary qualifications of birth or position in society, and I should very much regret if the society of the court were composed of or

even mixed with persons who but for their scientific achievements would not be considered eligible to be invited to it . . . A court is essentially aristocratic – and by transplanting into it persons of a different and far lower society, however personally excellent, you are more likely to lower the court than raise the individual.

Too late, the deed was done. The Prince had received a sharp lesson – if one he almost certainly did not need – in the nuances of the society he had married into. Things would have to change, and the legacy of the Great Exhibition would play an important role in bringing about those changes. But not much had changed yet, and the Phipps letter provided incontrovertible evidence that every hint of erosion of the privileges of birth, however slight, would be fought tooth and nail by those who enjoyed them. Had Albert lived longer, he might have proved an effective instrument of change. But when he died in 1861 the aristocracy was still firmly entrenched at court, and Phipps would later move on to the staff of the Prince of Wales.

Meanwhile, back at the Crystal Palace, the formidable task of clearing away the exhibits had begun. Fox and Henderson, who under the terms of their agreement with the Commissioners were now the formal owners of the building, were anxious that the process should not last too long, because they wanted to earn some revenue by admitting visitors before the end of the year and making the building available for grand functions and public events in the remainder of what they assumed would be its short life. The British exhibitors lost little time in getting most of their goods off the premises, for some were anxious to display them in their own shops and showrooms. Items that could not be moved except at exorbitant cost – such as the giant blocks of coal and granite – were presented to the Commissioners, leaving them with the disposal problem.

The overseas representatives, for the most part, were anxious to sell as many of their products as possible to avoid the expense of taking them home. Several significant sales had been transacted on the last few days of the Exhibition, and Queen Victoria had throughout its run continued to buy items that caught her fancy from both the British and foreign sections, some as gifts and some for her own use.

Henry Cole had been given £5,000 by the Treasury to buy articles from the Exhibition that were typical of contemporary taste and design. Augustus Pugin and Owen Jones – who had been responsible for the interior decoration of the Crystal Palace – helped him make the selection, and the chosen items formed the basis of a new Museum of Ornamental Art, temporarily accommodated at Marlborough House on the Mall, before being incorporated into Cole's new museum at South Kensington.

A month after the closure, few foreign exhibitors had cleared their goods from the building, with the exception of the brisk and efficient Swiss. Some had delayed moving them in the hope of making a few more sales. On 11 November the Queen, still keen to savour the last remnants of Albert's triumph, went to the Crystal Palace yet again, and wrote in her journal:

> The flags have been removed and the English side is almost entirely empty. On the foreign side there are still a good many things left, but not many in the galleries, and everywhere there are numerous packing cases. The organ is left. The canvas is entirely

removed and the beauty of the building, with the sun shining through, was never seen to greater advantage. One cannot bear to think of its all coming down, and yet I fear it will be the best and wisest thing . . . It is sad to think all is past now!

When the public were eventually admitted for one day, on 28 December, some of the objects were still there, including the giant organ, the models of the Isle of Wight and Brunel's Wye bridge and the large zinc statue of Victoria, held up by difficulties over customs duties. The building was finally cleared in the early months of 1852. For two days in March it was open free to visitors, attracting 50,000 on each day. Several large-scale concerts and other entertainments, with admission fees charged, were also staged there.

As far as the public was concerned, the fate of the Crystal Palace itself was of far greater interest than the fate of the exhibits. The Commissioners and the Government had insisted since before construction began that it was going to be a temporary building. That was how they had managed to get the plan approved by the Royal Parks authorities and – in the teeth of some doughty opposition – by Parliament. Yet at that time nobody had anticipated that the building would capture the imagination of the British public in quite the way it had.

Naturally enough Paxton, as the architect, did not want to see it demolished. While the Exhibition was under way he wrote and published a pamphlet called *What is to Become of the Crystal Palace?*. He proposed that it should stay in Hyde Park as a winter garden, providing Londoners with an alternative to the cold, murky air by allowing them to enjoy the climate of southern Italy all year round. He would fill it with tender plants and statuary and offer indoor facilities for horse riders as well as walkers. Cole supported the idea and so, amongst others, did *The Economist*, arguing that it would be foolish to destroy a building that had become a national symbol. On 3 April 1852 a large fête was held in the Palace in aid of keeping it in Hyde Park, and tens of thousands of people signed a petition in support of the idea. But local residents, who had looked askance at the project from the start, were determined to hold the Government to its promise, as were those few sceptics still convinced that the building was structurally unsound. The Government instituted a Parliamentary inquiry, which found that the Commissioners had a binding contractual obligation to restore the land to the park. On 29 April 1852 the House of Commons endorsed that decision.

Yet moving the Crystal Palace from Hyde Park did not necessarily mean destroying it. One of its virtues was that it was one of the nation's first prefabricated buildings, its glass panes and iron supports having been brought to the site ready-made. It would thus be quite easy to reverse the process, to dismantle it piece by piece and reconstruct it elsewhere. Numerous suggestions were made as to where it should go and what it should be used for. The magazine *The Builder* pointed out that the segments could be used in several ways to create a building of a different shape, and it proposed the erection of a slender glass tower, a thousand feet tall.

Many of the suggestions for new locations for the Crystal Palace involved the open spaces just outside the central area that had been mentioned as alternatives to Hyde Park when the Exhibition site was first debated in 1850. The chef Alexis Soyer came up with a plan to move it a few hundred yards south, to the land that was eventually to be occupied by the Victoria and Albert Museum. *The Times* put its weight behind moving it across the Thames to Battersea, where a strip of land almost opposite Cheyne Walk in Chelsea, surrounding two bawdy taverns called the Red House and the White House, had become notorious for scenes of working-class debauchery, especially at weekends. The paper saw the proposal as a neat way of solving two problems at once:

> The Crystal Palace might be made the medium of elevating the rude and uncivilised tastes of those swarms who, during the summer months especially, betake themselves to the river for amusement. Battersea is a favourite haunt of their class, and the spectacle which it presents, especially on Sunday afternoons, is disgraceful to the metropolis. There are collected thousands of the gamins of London, of the idle and the dissolute of both sexes, who while away their time in sports of the lowest and most vulgar kind.

The article went on to describe the saturnalia in terms that may have shocked its readers in 1851, but which 150 years later seem to indicate a lively and colourful fairground atmosphere, resembling Hampstead Heath at Easter or Epsom Downs on Derby Day. There were shooting galleries, coconut shies, donkey rides, fortune-telling, strength testing, hot pickled eels and 'vendors of unripe fruit, stale pastry and deleterious drinks'. Clearly, the élite had yet to learn to romanticise the amusements of the working class. For this reason, 'the Red and the White House at Battersea may with advantage give way to the great greenhouse which it is contemplated to send there'. In the event the great greenhouse went elsewhere, but the area was stripped of its vulgarity and its pickled eels by being incorporated into Battersea Park when it opened in 1853.

Titus Salt, the Bradford wool tycoon whose products had been so much admired at the Exhibition, toyed with the idea of buying the Crystal Palace and using it as part of the giant mill he was then building in his new town of Saltaire. He and his engineer went to Hyde Park to inspect it, but decided that it was not robust enough to withstand the vibrations from the large machines he was planning to install.

By now Paxton had calculated that if his building was to be saved he would have to play a leading role himself. On 18 May, three weeks after the Commons ordered its removal from Hyde Park, he published the prospectus of a company that proposed to buy the Crystal Palace from Fox and Henderson and move it to a site he had earmarked at the crown of Sydenham Hill in south-east London, with views of the North Downs and the Kentish Weald to its south, and of the city to the north. Francis Fuller and John Scott Russell, both of them involved in the Exhibition, were on the board of directors of the company and its chairman was Samuel Laing, chairman of the London, Brighton and South Coast Railway, which plan-ned to build new track and a station to bring day trippers to the attraction.

The dismantling of the Crystal Palace at Hyde Park began almost immediately. Never a man to think small, Paxton decided to make the Sydenham version even larger than the original. It was higher and broader, with new transepts and wings added at the north and south ends, plus a basement to cope with the sloping site. There was half as much floor space again as at Hyde Park, and twice as much glass was used. In particular the space devoted to fine arts was greatly increased, with some of the Exhibition statues – The Greek Slave and Andromeda were two – mixed in with scores of new ones purchased in Europe. Pugin's medieval court was joined by others celebrating art of all kinds – Greek, Roman, Byzantine, Romanesque, Pompeiian, Chinese, Moorish, Renaissance and Egyptian.

The Byzantine Court at the reconstructed Crystal Palace on Sydenham Hill.

The explicit nature of some of the statues provoked controversy even before the new Crystal Palace opened in the summer of 1854. Its directors received a protest from thirteen local people about the anatomical correctness of the male figures:

We are persuaded that the exhibition to promiscuous

278 THE WORLD FOR A SHILLING

> crowds of men and women of nude statues of men in
> the state there represented must, if generally sub-
> mitted to, prove very destructive to that natural
> modesty which is one of the outworks of virtue.

With an investment of over a million pounds at stake, the
directors did not want to risk offending potential visitors, so
they caved in immediately, agreeing to reduce the bulk of the
offending parts and cover them with fig leaves, although it did
not prove easy to procure enough fig leaves in time.

Musical extravaganzas were going to be an important part
of the entertainment on offer. A gigantic organ with more than
4,500 pipes was installed and a vast concert stage built
to accommodate choral performances for audiences of up to
4,000. The more sober element of the Great Exhibition was also
reflected: as well as the sculpture courts there were industrial
courts, celebrating the products of particular British cities and
regions. In the basement were machines, vehicles and carriages.
In contrast to Hyde Park, paintings were now admitted, with a
gallery devoted to contemporary work. There was a library, a
theatre and a natural history section with hundreds of stuffed
animals and birds, as well as a few live ones: an aquarium was
added in the 1870s. Interspersed with the exhibits were row
upon row of pots and planters containing exotic tropical shrubs
and trees. Osler's crystal fountain had been transferred here
from Hyde Park and occupied its original place of honour in the
centre.

On the slope of the hill outside, Paxton had designed
extensive ornamental gardens with lakes, grottos and a maze –
drawing on his experience of designing a much-imitated
urban park at Birkenhead some ten years earlier. A family of
twenty-nine giant dinosaurs, made of brick, iron and plaster,
survives today by the Crystal Palace lakes as one of the few

remnants of this ambitious showpiece – apart of course from the name given to the now heavily populated district surrounding the hill.

Queen Victoria opened the new attraction twice. The first time, on 10 June 1854, hundreds of singers performed the Hallelujah Chorus on the giant stage, harking back to that other famous opening ceremony three years earlier. Then, in 1856, she returned to switch on the spectacular fountains, incorporating 11,788 jets of water, that were to become one of the sights of the southern suburbs. Their inauguration had been delayed because of problems with the water supply, eventually solved by Isambard Brunel, who designed two 300-foot-high water towers, one at each end of the building. (These survived until 1942, when they were destroyed because of fears that they might serve as navigational aids to German bombers.)

Londoners' happy memories of the Great Exhibition ensured that for decades the new Crystal Palace would provide the most popular day out in that region of the capital, with an average of two million visitors a year for the first thirty years. Bold men in balloons ascended into the sky from it, and would take passengers who possessed the courage and the steep five-pound fare. The celebrated tightrope walker Charles Blondin cooked an omelette on a wire strung between the water towers. It became a venue for flower shows, dog shows and exhibitions of every kind. In 1868 the nation's first aeronautical show was held there, and in the same year an enthralled audience watched one of the earliest demonstrations of moving pictures. A popular series of Handel festivals was started in 1859, and six years later saw the beginning of spectacular fireworks displays organised regularly by Charles Brock, including set-pieces of famous battles. Known as Brock's Benefits, they attracted crowds of around 60,000.

Yet although visitor numbers were healthy, Paxton's company made little money, largely because in the religious climate of the time the Palace was forced to close on Sundays. In December 1866 the north transept, containing three of the sculpture courts, was destroyed in a fire and was not rebuilt. Because of the lack of money for refurbishment, the Palace, its contents and its gardens gradually began to look the worse for wear. To keep the company afloat, about half of the 350-acre site was sold off for house building. It was not enough, and in 1909 the company filed for bankruptcy. It won a temporary reprieve in 1911, the year of George V's coronation, when it was chosen as the venue for the Festival of Empire, in which three-quarter-size replicas of the parliament buildings of the colonies and dominions were constructed in the park, along with reconstructions of a South African diamond mine and an Indian tea plantation. Two years later, on the initiative of the Lord Mayor of London, the Crystal Palace became the property of the nation.

During the First World War the building was used as a naval supply depot, but in 1920 it was reopened as a visitor attraction by King George V and Queen Mary, with part of it occupied temporarily by the new Imperial War Museum. Four years later the museum moved out and the fireworks displays were resumed, now held every Thursday night. Despite their popularity, the Palace went into a decline again, its maintenance always costing more than it could earn in revenues. On the night of 30 November 1936 a fire that started in one of the administrative offices quickly spread, and Paxton's entire edifice was burned to the ground. It had its mourners but in truth it had outlived its time, and in any case the nation was preoccupied with more critical matters. Within days Edward VIII, who had succeeded to the throne that year, would abdicate. Graver still, the world was moving inexorably to a dreadful new war.

CHAPTER ELEVEN

❧ ❧

THE LEGACY

The working-class . . . raw and half-developed, has long
lain half-hidden amidst its poverty and squalor, and is now
issuing from its hiding-place to assert an Englishman's
heaven-born privilege of doing as he likes, and is beginning
to perplex us by marching where it likes, meeting where it
likes, bawling what it likes, breaking what it likes.

Matthew Arnold, *Culture and Anarchy* (1869)

Like many significant events in history, the Great Exhibition arose out of a chance combination of essentially unrelated circumstances: a Consort anxious to make his mark; a burgeoning manufacturing industry looking to expand its horizons; the dawn of the age of mass travel; a world riven by fractiousness but recognising that self-interest demanded greater levels of international co-operation. Few could have foreseen that among its lasting effects would be the furtherance of the profound social changes for which the Chartists and other radical activists had lately begun to agitate.

It was not simply that several of the heroes of 1851 – such as Paxton, Cole and Playfair – were self-made men: still something of a term of abuse rather than praise among the élite, who believed heredity to be a more reliable measure of social acceptability than mere achievement. The effect spread much wider than that. The lowering of historic social barriers in Britain – a long, slow process that is still far from complete – did not begin with the Great Exhibition, but was helped along by it. With factories and farms relying more and more on skilled and semi-skilled labour, and less on sheer physical strength, employers were encouraged by the Exhibition's organisers and supporters to recognise that an aware and well-informed work force would be an asset to their business. Inevitably there was more than a hint of paternalism involved in the 'works outings' and the groups of oddly clad villagers shepherded to London by their vicar; but such philanthropic gestures were at root an acknowledgement of mutual responsibility and self-interest. And for every worker who took part in those organised visits, there was another who struck out on his own or with his family, the railway offering for the first time an affordable means of long-distance travel as an alternative to going on foot.

All those factors came together in 1851 to vest the Great Exhibition with a significance that went beyond the event itself. Given its success, it is no surprise that there were almost immediate moves to organise another one, but none of its imitators had anything like the impact of the original. This was principally because they lacked the element of surprise that had been one of the key factors in the Crystal Palace – surprise that so inherently risky a venture should turn out so well; surprise, too, at what it revealed about the nature and character of the British.

The French, who until 1851 had been seen as specialists in the art of the exhibition, were clearly mortified that Britain had been the first to organise an international version. They followed it up as quickly as they could, with a major show in Paris in 1854, and for the next quarter-century exhibitions in Paris and London alternated every five years or so. Cole again played a leading role in London's next. It was planned to open on 1 May 1861, the tenth anniversary of the Hyde Park triumph, but was postponed by a year because of the outbreak of the war between France and Austria war in 1859. As a result of the delay, Prince Albert did not live to see it: he died of typhoid five months before it opened, to the inconsolable despair of his widow.

The 1862 exhibition was staged in the grounds of the Royal Horticultural Society's garden in Kensington – where the Natural History Museum now stands – in a building of brick, glass and iron, larger than the Crystal Palace, designed by Captain Francis Fowke, later responsible for the Royal Albert Hall. William Morris, the pioneer of the Arts and Crafts movement, contributed some of his distinctive furniture. (He had been scornful of the 1851 Exhibition, probably because he was just seventeen – a notoriously scornful age – when he visited it.) Although neither the 1862 building nor its contents achieved the popular impact of its predecessor, total attendance was in fact higher. Cole organised a further series of exhibitions between 1871 and 1874, but these were less successful.

As the century progressed, exhibitions housed in a single giant construction were superseded by more ambitious projects in which several buildings were erected on an extensive campus. The Americans took the lead in creating events in this new format, which came to be known as world's fairs. The first was the 1876 Philadelphia Centennial, celebrating the hundredth anniversary of the Declaration of Independence. Its 30,000 exhibitors occupied a site of 450 acres and attracted ten million visitors. The World's Colombian Exposition in Chicago in 1893, marking the 400th anniversary of Christopher Columbus's discovery of America, was even larger, covering 686 acres and visited by more than twenty-one million people.

Apart from its impact on American architecture and design for the next forty years, and the first extensive use of electricity at an event of its kind, the Colombian Exposition was notable for the introduction of that ground-breaking contribution to the world's entertainment, the ferris wheel – named after its inventor, George Ferris. It symbolised a tendency to turn what had begun as essentially trade shows into popular spectacles. Almost a half-century after the Great Exhibition, it was felt that the novelty of gazing at static displays of objects was beginning to wear off, and to attract big crowds it was necessary to provide something more adventurous for them to do. Subsequent exhibitions and world's fairs were essentially hybrids, in which the instructional and entertainment elements vied for dominance.

A highlight of the 1908 Franco-British Exhibition, at White City in west London, was the flip-flap, a large ride shaped like a giant V. Its passengers were enclosed in capsules at the end of two arms moving up and down and from side to side with a scary rocking motion. The British Empire provided the theme for exhibitions at Crystal Palace in 1911 and Wembley in 1924, where the attractions included a working replica of Niagara Falls and Queen Mary's Doll's House, with its miniature Art Deco furniture and decorations, now popular with visitors to Windsor Castle.

The arrival of cinema, radio and television in the first half of the twentieth century further altered perceptions of popular entertainment and placed a higher premium on novelty and excitement; yet despite this, the allure of the simple display of manufactured goods remained surprisingly strong. In September 1946, soon after the end of the Second World War, thousands queued for hours outside the Victoria and Albert Museum to see the 'Britain Can Make It' exhibition of the products of a manufacturing industry only just emerging from

the restraints of wartime. Although, due to scarcity and ration-
ing, many of the items were not available in the shops (the
exhibition's popular name was 'Britain Can't Buy It'), it still
attracted enormous interest: like window-shopping in front of
a store that you cannot afford to go into.

In 1951, when recovery from the effects of war was still
not complete, the Government decided to mark the centenary
of the Great Exhibition with the ambitious Festival of Britain.
Here the recreational and educational aspects were split. The
exhibition part was held on derelict industrial land on the
South Bank of the Thames, close to Waterloo Station, where
the Royal Festival Hall and its pier are all that remain of it
today. British technological innovation was celebrated in the
ultra-modern Dome of Discovery and next to it the elegant
Skylon, pointing to the heavens like a rocket on a launch pad.
A couple of miles upstream, at Battersea, was a giant funfair
and pleasure garden, so popular that it survived in a modified
form for a quarter of a century.

In the mid-1990s, when the Government was discussing
how to celebrate the Millennium, the idea was floated of
another huge exhibition that would, it was hoped, capture the
public's imagination as the Great Exhibition had done nearly
150 years earlier. By now, though, we were in the age of
computers, videos, mobile phones and interactive games.
More would be needed to grab people's attention than a mere
display of objects combined with old-style funfair attractions.
They must be offered experiences, not exhibits – experiences,
moreover, that fed the turn-of-the-century obsession with self
and relationships. As the official handbook put it, the themes
were to be 'who we are, what we do and where we live'. Our
minds, bodies and spirits had all to be engaged: gone were the
days when we would find it sufficiently satisfying simply to
observe and absorb.

The planning process for 2000 differed significantly from that adopted in 1851, when the nature of the Exhibition was decided first, followed by discussion of the site and the building to house it. In the case of the £758 million Millennium project, largely funded by the proceeds of the National Lottery, the site was selected first: an abandoned area around a disused gasworks by the Thames just east of historic Greenwich in south-east London. Then Richard Rogers' futuristic Dome was chosen to house the event, its roof and sides made not of glass this time but of a lightweight modern material stretched over a steel frame, as in a giant marquee. Only after those key and immutable decisions had been taken did the minds of the planners turn to precisely what was going to fill this twenty-acre space, ten times the area of St Paul's Cathedral and about an acre larger than the Crystal Palace. And it was the content, according to the Dome's critics, that was central to its being perceived as a flop.

A majority of visitors to the Millennium Dome, like many who went to the Crystal Palace, travelled by train, but of a very different kind from those open-carriaged excursions that Thomas Hardy recalled so vividly. The Jubilee Line, part of the London Underground system, had been extended to this corner of the capital especially to serve the Dome. It brought people in a matter of minutes from the heart of the metropolis to a large, airy and elegant station, just a few yards from the Dome's entrance. Some said that their arrival by train into this soaring space was the high point of their visit, that it had all been downhill from there; but these sceptics were in a distinct minority. Most visitors, asked at the end of a day at the Dome whether they had enjoyed it, said that they had, and that it had been well worth the £20 price of admission (or £57 for a family of up to five), despite increasingly negative comments in the press.

They emerged from the station through a covered walk-way into the entrance courtyard, dwarfed by the enormous Dome on the left. Straight ahead was Skyscape, a cinema where a specially written episode of the popular TV comedy series *Blackadder* was shown several times a day. There were a number of ways into the Dome itself, but the one nearest the entrance plaza took visitors almost directly to the most pub-licised of the sixteen themed 'zones' into which the space had been divided – a vast, stylised model of the human body.

In the build-up to the Dome's public opening on New Year's Day, 2000, it was the Body Zone, with its promise to explore the mysteries of the way we function physically, that captured the imagination of the public. For the first few days people queued to get into it, often for more than an hour. Entering through the right arm, they penetrated the heart, which pumped remorselessly, distending and contracting be-fore their eyes. They progressed through the womb, where sperm rushed past on their way to fertilising an egg, then to the brain, whose agility was demonstrated by a quickfire comedy routine from the late comedian Tommy Cooper. The mood changed as the route reached the eye, surrounded by touching, tear-inducing images. Close to the exit was an in-formative display on the future of medicine, highlighting new drugs and techniques.

The Body Zone was an apt place to begin a tour because it was a microcosm of the Dome itself, addressing important personal concerns in a style that sought to be accessible by engaging the emotions and using familiar symbols. Its weak-ness was a sense of trying too hard, perhaps because of a lack of confidence in the basic material – a charge that certainly was never levelled at the Great Exhibition. And as in many of the zones, the computerised electronics that controlled the displays were too often out of order.

In an exhibition aimed in part at celebrating the technological promise of the twenty-first century, the fact that so much of the sophisticated machinery proved fragile provided an easy target for critics. In a survey in February, the *Independent* found that ten of the zones contained broken equipment. Sometimes around half the computers in the side-by-side Work and Learning zones were out of action, and those that did function properly did no more than deliver pious messages about the importance of both activities. (In the Work Zone, at the time of the *Independent* survey, only twelve out of 144 mechanical hamsters were in working order and able to operate the treadmills representing the futility of repetitive labour.)

The Mind Zone, aimed at 'exploring the nature of our perceptions' through mental gymnastics, also suffered badly. A collection of robots was supposed to symbolise the working of simple minds, but they operated so spasmodically that their significance was lost. The most popular area of this zone contained 'morphing booths', where visitors could revamp their facial images on screens that let them see what they looked like when their age, sex and race were altered: the ultimate in self-absorption. These were generally working but proved so fascinating that long queues developed.

Children were especially attracted by morphing, as they were to the Play Zone, packed with novel electronic games – although again too many of them were periodically out of action. The same was true of the games at Living Island, built as a reproduction of a traditional seaside resort, with its beach, cliffs, lighthouse and amusement arcade. Its underlying message was about the future of the environment: the 'tunnel of love', through which visitors entered, was a passage through a cliff made of recycled cans. All the games in the arcade carried an environmental message, and the trees planted by the shore were there to show the effects of global warming.

The seaside theme provided a welcome dose of nostalgia, a rare emotion at the Dome because, as a general policy, the organisers discouraged too much looking back in what was meant to be a state-of-the-art attraction. The only other area where visitors could dip into the past was the Journey Zone, a fairly conventional museum-style experience that set out the history of transport, focusing on the Ford motor car, the zone's sponsor. It may have been significant that this was among the exhibits that visitors rated most highly, finding that to peer at static objects, well displayed, provided a welcome break from the repetitive clamour of high technology. Another popular section also involved transport. Home Planet was a simulated ride in a space capsule – the only ride on offer in the Dome – that 'travelled' around different regions of the earth, finally penetrating its core.

The zone called Shared Ground aimed at exploring the importance of communities and neighbourliness. It was an interactive stage set, representing an average home and neigh-bourhood, where visitors were asked questions about their family life and, under the gaze of video cameras, spoke the answers into microphones. As they left they could see and hear other people's responses to the same questions. On an allied theme, Self Portrait was a display of 400 pictures arising from a request to several thousand individuals and groups to submit an image that 'celebrates British diversity at the beginning of the new millennium'. Several of the pictures portrayed food – a sponge cake, a full English breakfast, fish and chips wrapped in newspaper.

The Talk Zone, sponsored by British Telecom, noisily celebrated the newest forms of electronic communication. To escape from the babble, visitors could slip into the Faith Zone, an essentially uninspired rundown of the world's major religions, its impact fatally diluted by the perceived need to avoid offending anybody. Here the contrast with the Great Exhibition was at its starkest. In the Crystal Palace, exhibits relating to the British Empire were based on the assumption of dozens of endlessly diverse cultures being brought together and strengthened through the firm yet benign authority of the British Raj, whose superiority went unchallenged. That was what Victorian self-confidence was about. In the intervening 150 years we have become a multicultural society that can operate only on the basis that all faiths and traditions are inherently equal and worthy of respect. That position, though the more morally defensible, effectively rules out the presentation of a consistent message powerful enough to engage the emotions.

After completing their circuit of the zones – or at least as many of them as they could manage before they flagged – visitors moved inwards to the seats around the huge arena (the size of Trafalgar Square) at the centre of the Dome. Here they watched a forty-five-minute live show that involved aerial dancing and acrobatics, clashing music and dazzling light effects. Its complex theme related how families respond to progress and change, and how love can reach beyond the barriers imposed by human prejudice. Luckily it was not necessary to catch all the nuances to enjoy the spectacle, and many rated the show best of all the attractions within the Dome.

Catering was a lot more varied than in the Crystal Palace, and, because the number of visitors to Greenwich was lower than expected, there were seldom long queues. Groups of themed restaurants offered a wide choice – hamburgers, filled rolls, eastern and continental specialities and the ever-popular fish and chips (though not wrapped in newspaper). With temperance no longer a significant social force, beer and wine could be bought with meals, and there was a modern pub within the complex, just outside the Dome itself. In 150 years, standards of personal hygiene have improved, and none of the serving men and women could be accused of needing a good scrub. George Jennings would have admired the lavatories.

Commentators on the Dome were quick to draw parallels with earlier national displays, the Great Exhibition among them. The journalist Simon Jenkins, a Millennium Commissioner and one of the chief boosters of the project in its early stages, compared the initial criticism of it with the strident voices that had opposed the 1851 initiative before it opened. In his regular column in the *Evening Standard* he predicted – wrongly as it turned out – that, like the Crystal Palace, it would triumph in the end. Rowan Moore, writing in the same paper, was more prescient: 'It is too aloof, beneath its plastic lid on a remote marsh, to achieve the great sense of national togetherness engendered by the Festival of Britain, and too derivative to match the Great Exhibition.'

In fact the Dome, with its emphasis on feelings, attitudes and ideas rather than on objects – the products of man's mind, not muscle – was in most respects the exact opposite of the Crystal Palace. It recognised that in the twenty-first century Britain lives by its wits more than by the sweat of its brow. It also aspired to 'attitude', a fashionable concept in the 1990s, usually meaning a questioning, unorthodox and self-assured approach to life. In the Dome, though, the attitude was too pious and preachy – too politically correct, in contemporary jargon. One of many teenagers asked for his reaction by the press said it was 'all shiny on the outside and nothing on the inside', while another commented: 'It's like all the worst bits of museums that try to be fun.'

Yet if the content and the overarching vision of the two grand shows were strikingly different, the organisational procedures that brought them about were in some ways comparable. Broad guidelines for the style and tone of the Dome's exhibits were established by the Millennium Commission, made up of politicians and suitable public figures, as the 1851 Commission had been. Beneath them were committees of experts in appropriate fields to rule on the fine detail of the exhibits, as there had been sub-committees for the various industries represented in the Crystal Palace.

In the case of the Dome, the committees had to include representatives of the all-important commercial sponsors of the zones, who had put in more than £160 million towards the cost. In 1851, those people and institutions that responded to the appeal for funds had done so from altruistic motives, with no prospect of reward. A century and a half on, they wanted a return on their investment, and a say in how it would be deployed. Some critics resented the sponsors' influence. Jonathan Glancey, architecture and design editor of *The Guardian*, summed up the Dome as

> less a vision of the future as we might dream it and much more a powerful symbol of how our lives at the end of the twentieth century have been shaped by capitalism, corporate energy, political spin and a new-found love for Seventies design and colour schemes.

Demonisation of the large corporation was a late twentieth-century phenomenon, widespread among the young and on the political left. The Victorians would scarcely have understood it. The Great Exhibition, funded by donations from industrialists and their workers, was to a much greater degree a celebration of capitalism than the Dome was. Names of the manufacturers of exhibits were meticulously noted in the 1851 catalogue, even if it was not permitted to attach price tags to the goods. It is true that globalisation and the multinational corporation had yet to be invented (although the East India Company in some ways came quite close to the modern concept of a multinational), but against that it was undoubtedly the case that the large manufacturing and mining companies of the time treated their employees much worse, and committed more serious offences against the environment, than their present-day counterparts.

The build-up to the two national showcases was similar in several regards. Both were housed in state-of-the-art structures that had to be put up unusually fast to meet the advertised opening dates. Some exhibits were late in arriving, so that when the doors opened to the public not everything was quite in place; though that was less of a factor in the Dome than at the Crystal Palace, still garnering new items only a month before it closed. Both events were opened by the Queen; but at least the Great Exhibition did not have to endure the Dome's disastrous opening ceremony, whose fallout blighted the attraction throughout its year-long existence.

The late twentieth-century obsession with security meant that the list of ten thousand guests at the Dome's opening had to be vetted carefully before admission tickets were issued, even though the majority of those invited were well-known public figures – including, crucially, the editors of national newspapers and executives of broadcasting organisations. The vetting process took longer than had been allowed for, and it became too late for all the tickets to be entrusted to the mail. This meant that a large number of invitees had to collect them in person from nearby railway and Underground stations. Long queues built up and hundreds of influential men and women in evening dress were kept waiting for two hours and more, some missing the start of the celebratory programme and, worse still, arriving after the bars were closed.

Such symptoms of abysmal organisation were also evident on the first day of public admissions on 1 January, with more long queues inside the Dome, at the entrance to the Body Zone and to other attractions. Those editors who had been kept waiting in such an undignified manner on New Year's Eve took delight in publishing critical reports about this and the Dome's other shortcomings, until the perception grew that it was a dismal failure, despite the generally positive public reaction. *The Times* called it 'a collection of educational toys and politically correct propaganda'.

Bad publicity as it opened was not the only reason for the Dome's inability to attract the daily average of 35,000 visitors – or around twelve million for the whole year – that it would need to break even. It was an ambitious total, seeing that the Alton Towers theme park, the most popular visitor attraction in Britain, attracted only 2,800,000 in 1999. Advance Dome tickets had been available since September, but no days were sold out, and during January the daily average was only just above ten thousand, with the highest attendance 23,304 and the lowest just 5,084.

Although the Government continued to insist that the Dome was a success, they dismissed the chief executive, Jennie Page, a month after the opening and replaced her with a Frenchman, Pierre-Yves Gerbeau, an executive with Disneyland in Paris. He revised the target attendance for the year first to ten million and then, when sales still did not pick up, to seven million. Gerbeau introduced some new attractions, plus cheaper tickets and longer opening hours, but still the crowds refused to come in the required numbers, and the final total, when the doors closed for the last time on 31 December, was six and a half million – only slightly more than attended the Great Exhibition at a time when the British population was less than half its level in 2000 – and the Crystal Palace was open for only five and a half months compared with the Dome's whole year – including Sundays.

Along the way the Millennium Commission had been forced to pump in an extra £29 million to keep the project afloat, despite protests from Members of Parliament and others who regarded it as a terrible waste of public money. The Commission chairman, the former British Airways chief Bob Ayling, was forced to resign. Halfway through the year, agreement was reached in principle to sell the Dome for £105 million – about an eighth of its final cost – to Nomura, a Japanese consortium that planned to keep it as a visitor attraction after the Millennium exhibition closed in December. But a few weeks after the deal was agreed, the Commission had to commit another £47 million, arguing that it would be more expensive to close the Dome down – a course that more and more people were recommending – than to keep it open for the whole year. At that point Nomura decided not to go ahead with the purchase, and a new buyer had to be sought. Addressing the Labour Party conference in September 2000, Tony Blair, the Prime Minister, admitted that the project had been a failure. 'If I had my time again,' he declared, 'I would have listened to those who said governments shouldn't try to run big visitor attractions.'

The Dome's publicists had maintained that it would change the lives and perceptions of all who visited it. That is a lot to ask of an exhibition. If it happened at all, it was more likely to have been at the Crystal Palace than on the banks of the Thames at Greenwich – a point made by several who commented on the Dome's perceived failure. The actor Tony Robinson, one of the stars of its *Blackadder* film and also a member of the National Executive Committee of the Labour

Party, said on BBC Radio 5 that the Great Exhibition was making a statement about Britain as a leading manufacturing national and imperial power. 'Those days are over,' he observed. 'We don't make those big national statements any more.'

The Guardian concurred, observing in a leading article:

> With the Great Exhibition of 1851 and the Festival of Britain 100 years later, there was no doubt at all what we were celebrating. In 1851, the politicians kept out of things. In 1951, they were in the thick of it. This time they were half-in, half-out. That may prove to have been one of the main ingredients of disaster.

Where the Great Exhibition inspired popular songs and verses celebrating its wonders and patriotically praising its creators, the Dome provided material only for a string of sour jokes from stand-up comedians and cartoons in the press. It failed to inspire that sense of awe for which it strove so hard – almost certainly too hard and too blatantly to be successful.

Of course it was much easier to inspire awe in 1851, when optimism about the benefits of seemingly limitless progress had yet to be overwhelmed by a century and a half of conflict and growing cynicism. Queen Victoria was expressing perhaps more than she intended when she confided to her journal on the day the Exhibition closed: 'This great and bright time is past.'

SELECT BIBLIOGRAPHY

Auerbach, Jeffrey, *The Great Exhibition of 1851: A Nation on Display*, Yale, 1999.

Babbage, Charles, *The Exposition of 1851; or Views of the Industry, the Science and the Government of England*, John Murray, 1851.

Beaver, Patrick, *The Crystal Palace*, Hugh Evelyn, 1970.

Benson, Arthur C., and Viscount Esher (eds), *The Letters of Queen Victoria, 1837–61*, John Murray, 1907.

Berlyn, Peter, and Fowler, Charles Jr, *The Crystal Palace: Its Architectural History and Constructive Marvels*, James Gilbert (London), 1851.

Brendon, Piers, *Thomas Cook*, Secker & Warburg, 1991.

Briggs, Asa, *Victorian People*, Odhams Press, 1954.

Briggs, Asa, *Victorian Things*, Batsford, 1988.

Callery, Sean, *Harrods: The Story of Society's Favourite Store*, Ebury Press, 1991.

Cole, Sir Henry, *Fifty Years of Public Work*, George Bell and Sons, 1884.

Davis, John, *The Great Exhibition*, Sutton, 1999.

Dodd, E. E., *Bingley: A Yorkshire Town through Nine Centuries*, T. Harrison, 1958.

Fay, C. R., *Palace of Industry, 1851: A Study of the Great Exhibition and its Fruits*, Cambridge University Press, 1951.

Ffrench, Yvonne, *The Great Exhibition 1851*, The Harvill Press, 1950.

Fieldhouse, Joseph, *Bradford*, Longmans, 1972 (2nd revised edition 1981).

Gibbs-Smith, C. H., *The Great Exhibition of 1851: a Commemorative Album*, HMSO, 1950.

Golby, J. M. (ed.), *Culture and Society in Britain, 1850–1890*, Oxford University Press, 1986.

Hardy, Thomas, *Life's Little Ironies*, Harper and Brothers, 1898.

Hibbert, Christopher, *Wellington: A Personal History*, HarperCollins, 1997.

Hobhouse, Christopher, *1851 and the Crystal Palace*, John Murray, 1950.

Hobhouse, Hermione, *Prince Albert: His Life and Work*, Hamish Hamilton, 1983.

Hunt, Robert (ed.), *Hunt's Handbook to the Official Catalogues*, Spicer Bros. and Wm. Clowes and Sons, 1851.

Inwood, Stephen, *A History of London*, Macmillan, 1998.

James, Robert Rhodes, *Albert, Prince Consort*, Hamish Hamilton, 1983.

Lardner, D., *The Great Exhibition and London in 1851*, Longman, Brown, Green and Longmans, 1852.

Mayhew, Henry, and Cruikshank, George, *1851; or the Adventures of Mr and Mrs Cursty Sandboys . . .*, David Bogue, 1851.

Olalquiaga, Celeste, *The Artificial Kingdom: a Treasury of the Kitsch Experience*, Bloomsbury, 1999.

Pevsner, Nikolaus, *High Victorian Design: A Study of the Exhibits of 1851*, Architectural Press, 1951.

Porter, Roy, *London: A Social History*, Hamish Hamilton, 1994.

Rae, W. Fraser, *The Business of Travel*, Thomas Cook and Co., 1891.

Reeves, Graham, *Palace of the People*, London Borough of Bromley Library Service, 1986.

Reynolds, Jack, *The Great Paternalist: Titus Salt and the Growth of 19th-Century Bradford*, Temple Smith, 1983.

Suddards, R. W., *Titus of Salts*, Watmoughs Ltd. (Bradford), 1976.

Trevelyan, Sir G. O. (ed.), *The Life and Letters of Lord Macaulay*, 1978 edition, Oxford University Press.

Weinreb, Ben, and Hibbert, Christopher, *The London Encyclopaedia*, Macmillan, 1983.

Winter, James, *London's Teeming Streets, 1813–1914*, Routledge, 1993.

Wright, Lawrence, *Clean and Decent: The Fascinating History of the Bathroom and the Water Closet*, Routledge & Kegan Paul, 1960.

INDEX

Numbers in **bold** type refer to illustrations. Those in the unnumbered plate section are indicated by **pl**.

Abbreviations: CP – Crystal Palace; GE – Great Exhibition

More Non-fiction from Headline

PICKLED, POTTED AND CANNED
The Story of Food Preserving

SUE SHEPHARD

The history of food preserving is the story of civilisation itself. The development of portable, preserved food enabled explorers to map unknown territories; facilitated the conquering of new lands and created routes for the expansion of trade and the exchange of knowledge and culture which opened up our world.

Pickled, Potted & Canned weaves together fascinating stories of inventors with the important developments in food preservation, creating a tale that spans centuries and continents. Rich in extraordinary characters, old legends and new revelations, it describes how cooks became chemists and chemists became cooks, how men made or lost fortunes and some even lost their lives. From this lively and richly detailed narrative we gain a unique insight into the histories, cultures and ingenuity of people struggling to invent new ways to 'cheat the seasons'.

'A fascinating and well-researched book, seething with anecdotes and information' *Sunday Telegraph*

'One of the very few books I would have loved to have written myself' Clarissa Dickson Wright, *Mail on Sunday*

NON-FICTION / HISTORY / FOOD 0 7472 6207 1

Now you can buy any of these other bestselling non-fiction titles from your bookshop or *direct from the publisher*.

FREE P&P AND UK DELIVERY
(Overseas and Ireland £3.50 per book)

Geisha *Lesley Downer* £7.99
An award-winning writer for the first time fully and brilliantly explores the *real* secret history of the geisha.

Alpha Beta *John Man* £6.99
How 26 letters shaped the Western world: the epic story of the evolution of the alphabet, from man's earliest scratches on bone to the digital age and beyond.

The Second *Ian Wilmut, Keith Campbell,* £7.99
 Creation *Colin Tudge*
The scientists who cloned Dolly give the definitive account of their achievement, explain the history of cloning and discuss the ethical issues it raises – and where *they* believe this technology will lead.

The Ingenious *Michael Leapman* £7.99
 Mr Fairchild
The biography of Thomas Fairchild, whose discovery of the secret of plant hybridisation revolutionised horticultural understanding.

TO ORDER SIMPLY CALL THIS NUMBER AND QUOTE REF *50 NF*

01235 400 414

or e-mail orders@bookpoint.co.uk

Prices and availability subject to change without notice.

P9-CQS-942

THE MYSTERY OF THE
NERVOUS
LION

A bird squawked in alarm. The Three Investigators froze in their tracks. They listened tensely to the swish of the tall jungle grass. Then they heard footfalls, soft and stealthy.

Holding their breath, the boys edged closer to a large tree. Then, almost directly behind them, they heard a blood-chilling sound—the roar of an angry lion!

Alfred Hitchcock and The Three Investigators in

THE MYSTERY OF THE NERVOUS LION

Text by Nick West

Based on characters created by Robert Arthur

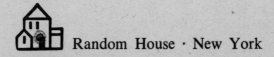

Random House · New York

The Mystery of the Nervous Lion

Originally published by Random House in 1971
First Random House paperback edition, 1981

Copyright © 1971 by Random House, Inc.
All rights reserved under International and Pan-American Copyright
Conventions. Published in the United States by Random House, Inc.,
New York, and simultaneously in Canada by Random House of Canada
Limited, Toronto.

Library of Congress Cataloging in Publication Data
West, Nick.
  Alfred Hitchcock and the three investigators in
The mystery of the nervous lion.
  (Alfred Hitchcock mystery series ;   16)
  SUMMARY: Hired to discover why a wild-animal farm's tame lion has
become unpredictably nervous, three young detectives begin an investigation
that uncovers a smuggling operation.
  [1. Mystery and detective stories]   I. Arthur, Robert.   II. Title.
III. Title: The mystery of the nervous lion.   IV. Series.
[PZ7.W5187Ao 1981]   [Fic]   80-18981
ISBN 0-394-84665-6 (pbk.)

Also available in Gibraltar Library Binding

Manufactured in the United States of America
   2 3 4 5 6 7 8 9 0

Contents

A Few Words from Mr. Hitchcock

Greetings and salutations! It is a pleasure to have you join me for another adventure with that remarkable trio of lads who call themselves The Three Investigators. This time a nervous lion leads them into a tangled web of mystery and excitement.

I imagine that you have already met The Three Investigators and know that they are Jupiter Jones, Bob Andrews, and Pete Crenshaw, all of Rocky Beach, California, a small community on the shores of the Pacific not far from Hollywood. But just in case this is your first meeting with the three, let me add that they make their Headquarters in a mobile home trailer cleverly hidden from sight in The Jones Salvage Yard. This fabulous junkyard is owned by Jupiter's aunt and uncle, for whom the trio works to earn spending money when they are not busy with their investigations.

Enough of introductions. On with the case! Our lion is growing nervous!

ALFRED HITCHCOCK

THE MYSTERY OF THE NERVOUS LION

Empty Cages

1

Jupiter Jones turned his head at the sound of a horn and groaned. "Oh, no! Here comes my uncle Titus with a truckload for the yard. You know what that means—work!"

Pete Crenshaw and Bob Andrews followed Jupiter's despairing look. Coming through the big iron gates of The Jones Salvage Yard was a small pickup truck. Konrad, one of the two Bavarian yard helpers, was driving. Titus Jones, a small man with an enormous mustache, sat beside him.

As the truck stopped, Mr. Jones hopped off. Jupiter and his friends could see that the truck was filled with a lot of rusty pipes and other odds and ends. Some of the junk appeared to be broken cages.

Jupiter's Aunt Mathilda, who had been sitting in her wrought-iron garden chair outside the office cabin, leaped to her feet.

"Titus Jones!" she yelled. "Have you gone out of your senses? How do you expect to sell a truckload of pipes and iron bars?"

"No problem, my dear," Titus Jones said, unruffled. He knew from past experience that almost everything that interested him eventually sold to a buyer. And usually at a tidy profit. "Some of these bars come with cages."

"Cages?" his wife repeated. She came closer, squinting into the truck. "You'd need some especially large canaries for those cages, Titus Jones."

"These are animal cages, woman," her spouse declared. "Or rather, they used to be. I'll leave it to Jupiter and his friends here. Take a look, Jupiter. Could we put them to some use?"

Jupiter looked over the lot. "Well," he answered slowly, "they could be repaired, I suppose. New bars added, roofs put on, the cage floors mended, everything painted. We could do it, all right, but then what?"

"Then what?" his uncle roared. "Why then we'd have animal cages ready for them when they need them, wouldn't we?"

"When who needs them, Uncle Titus?" asked Jupiter.

"Why, the circus, my boy," his uncle replied. "Circus comes to town every year, don't it? Well, then, next time they come, we'll be ready in case they need some good solid cages for their brutes."

Jupe shrugged. "I guess so," he said doubtfully.

"You guess so!" his uncle roared. "Don't forget I spent my early years traveling with a circus. I guess I ought to know what they'd be looking for, wouldn't you say?"

Jupiter smiled. "Yes, Uncle Titus." He had forgotten how proud his uncle was of his past association with the big top.

"Fine!" Titus said. "Hans! Konrad! Get this stuff off the truck. Stack the cages separate so we can get to work on them soon."

Konrad's brother, Hans, appeared from the back of the yard, and the Bavarian helpers began unloading the truck. Uncle Titus got his pipe out, searched his pockets for a match, and slowly began puffing.

"Those cages," he began. "Got 'em for a song out in

the valley. Found them with a lot of old junked cars. Feller didn't see much need for cages and such, so I bought the lot cheap. I'll be heading back in a while to try again. Just might be another load there."

He walked away puffing contentedly on his briar. Jupiter and his friends idly watched him go. Mrs. Jones had a better idea of how the boys should pass their time.

"Jupiter!" she called. "Those iron bars and railings on the truck should be stacked together. Perhaps we can sell them at a bargain price for the lot."

"Right, Aunt Mathilda," Jupe said. The stocky boy scrambled awkwardly up into the truck with Pete and Bob. "Okay, fellows," he said. "You heard the order."

Pete Crenshaw stared down at the pile of rusty rails and bars. "It sure beats me, Jupe, where your uncle ever finds this junk. But what puzzles me even more is how he ever manages to sell it."

Jupiter grinned. "Uncle Titus has always been lucky that way, Pete. He's brought in stuff you'd swear nobody in the world would ever want, and sells it the very next day. So if he says he can sell these pipes, I believe it."

Bob put in, "Well, anyway, we get paid for working. And we can use the money. We need some new equipment for Headquarters."

Headquarters was a damaged mobile home trailer that Mr. Jones had given to Jupiter to use as a meeting place for his friends. It was over at one side of the salvage yard, hidden by junk the boys had piled around it. Close by was Jupe's workshop section, fitted out with various tools and a printing press.

Inside Headquarters, the boys had equipped a tiny office with telephone, desk, tape recorder, and filing cabinets. There was also a small lab and a darkroom for

developing pictures. Most of the equipment had been
rebuilt by Jupe and his friends from junk that had come
into The Jones Salvage Yard.

Bob, Pete, and Jupiter had started a puzzle-solving
club originally, which they later turned into a junior detective firm called The Three Investigators. Although
they had started the club in fun, they had solved several
genuine mysteries that had come their way and had decided to pursue detective work more seriously.

Peter Crenshaw, the strongest member of the trio,
now looked unhappily at the large pile of pipes remaining after the two big Bavarian helpers had unloaded the
cages. "Okay," he said reluctantly, "might as well get
started." He dragged out several long bars and hoisted
them to his shoulder. "Where do you want them
stacked, Jupe?" he asked, staggering under the heavy
load.

Jupe pointed out an area near a shed. "We'll stack
them in a pile there, Pete."

Pete grunted and backed off with his load. Jupe and
Bob then took turns feeding the bars to Pete on return
trips. Work progressed rapidly and soon the pile in the
truck was down to one.

Rubbing his hands, Pete stepped up. "All right,
Jupe," he said, "I'll take that last little one now."

Jupe leaned forward to hand the bar over, and hesitated. He hefted the bar again. "We'd better set this
aside. It's just the size I've been looking for."

Bob looked puzzled. "For what? You starting your
own junkyard now?"

"It just happens to be shorter than the rest," said
Jupe. "We can use it for a slide bolt inside our headquarters door. For security reasons."

"Security?" Bob asked.

Jupe reddened. "I'm getting tired of crawling through our tunnel into Headquarters. There's got to be an easier way of doing things. I thought we might unlock the door."

Pete and Bob smiled at this roundabout explanation. The truth was that Jupiter was a little too fat to enjoy using their secret tunnel all the time.

Jumping off the truck, Jupe walked over to Headquarters and the junk surrounding the trailer. "Maybe Uncle Titus won't need it," he said. "Or we can work off the price."

Pete wiped sweat from his brow. "I think we already did that. If you ask me, we did a good day's work in an hour."

"Okay, Jupe," Bob said. "Now what—?"

At that moment the red light mounted over their printing press blinked!

"A phone call!" Pete cried. "Maybe it's somebody wanting a mystery solved."

"I hope so," Jupe said excitedly. "We haven't had any to investigate in a long time."

Quickly they pushed aside the iron grillwork beside the printing press. Crawling through the box behind it, they entered Tunnel Two. This was a large corrugated pipe leading to a trap door in the floor of the hidden trailer. The boys rushed through on their hands and knees and surfaced in the small office of Headquarters.

Jupiter snatched up the ringing telephone.

"Jupiter Jones speaking," he said.

"One moment, please." A woman's voice could be heard clearly through the loudspeaker attachment Jupe had rigged up. "Mr. Alfred Hitchcock is calling."

The three boys exchanged surprised and happy grins. As a rule, they found an exciting mystery waiting for them whenever Mr. Hitchcock called.

"Hello there!" the famous director boomed. "Is this young Jupiter?"

"Yes, Mr. Hitchcock," Jupe said.

"I hope you and your friends are not too busy just now. I have a friend who is in need of help, and I think you three lads are just the ones to solve his problem."

"We'd like to try, sir," Jupe said. "Can you give us an idea of your friend's problem?"

"Certainly," Mr. Hitchcock said. "If you boys can arrange to be at my office tomorrow morning, I shall be happy to tell you all about it."

A Case in Lion Territory

2

Some time ago, Jupiter and his friends had won the use of an antique Rolls-Royce, complete with chauffeur, in a contest. Their prize time eventually ran out, but then they helped a youthful client to gain an enormous inheritance. The grateful client arranged for the boys to have the use of the Rolls whenever needed. It had proved invaluable to them as investigators. Distances in southern California are vast, and it is difficult to cover them except by car.

Now Jupiter leaned forward and tapped the shoulder of the tall English chauffeur, Worthington. "This will be fine, Worthington," he said. "Wait here. We won't be too long with Mr. Hitchcock."

"Very good, Master Jones," Worthington replied. He guided the old, boxlike automobile to a careful stop. Then he got out and held the door open for the boys. "I trust Mr. Hitchcock has an interesting mission for you young gentlemen."

"We hope so, too, Worthington," Bob said. "Things have been kind of dull lately. We could use some excitement."

He quickly joined Jupe and Pete as they entered the Hollywood studio building where Mr. Hitchcock had his office.

Alfred Hitchcock motioned them to seats in front of his big desk. He pushed some business correspondence

9

aside and looked at the boys thoughtfully. Then casually he asked, "How comfortable are you lads with wild animals?"

Opposite him, The Three Investigators looked startled.

Jupiter cleared his throat. "It all depends on what kind of animals, sir, and the proximity involved. Given a reasonable distance between them and us and a measure of protection, I would say we are all quite at ease with them, and interested in their behavior and habits."

"Jupe means we like them," Pete said. "It just goes against his nature to say something simple."

"Why, Mr. Hitchcock?" asked Bob. "Is this about a mystery?"

"Perhaps," Mr. Hitchcock said slowly. "And if not indeed a mystery, certainly a case that merits investigation. The wild animals I mentioned are part of the background where certain mysterious happenings are taking place."

Alfred Hitchcock paused. "Have you lads heard of a place called Jungle Land?"

"That's over in the valley near Chatwick," Bob replied. "It's some kind of wild-animal farm with lions and other animals roaming around. It's supposed to be a tourist attraction, I think."

"Yes," Alfred Hitchcock said. "The owner, Jim Hall, is an old friend. Lately he's run into a problem and I thought at once of you boys and your investigative talents."

"What's Mr. Hall's problem exactly, sir?" asked Jupiter.

"It would appear he has a nervous lion," Mr. Hitchcock said.

The boys looked at each other wide-eyed.

"To continue," Mr. Hitchcock said. "Jungle Land is indeed open to the public. In addition, various movie companies at times rent the use of its premises. Its terrain and vegetation are suggestive of Western and African locales. Occasionally Jim Hall rents his animals. Some of them are wild, but several have been brought up gently and trained by Jim.

"Jim Hall's favorite lion is a remarkable example of his way with animals. This lion has been featured in many commercials for TV and has been used in films. It has always been a great attraction at Jungle Land and a good financial asset to Jim Hall."

"You mean, until now," Jupe said. "Your friend's lion is nervous and now he can't depend on it. That's his problem, isn't it?"

Alfred Hitchcock gave Jupiter a penetrating stare. "As usual, my astute young friend, your powers of deduction are equal to the task at hand. A film unit has rented the farm now to shoot sequences for a jungle film. Naturally Jim Hall cannot afford any accidents that might interfere with the film's speedy and successful completion. If anything were to go wrong, it would be ruinous to his entire operation."

"And we're supposed to go there and solve the mystery of the nervous lion," Jupe said. "Is that it?"

"Precisely," intoned Mr. Hitchcock. "Quickly and quietly. Without fuss or fanfare. And I need hardly add, without further disturbing the already unsettled lion."

Pete Crenshaw licked his lips. "How close do we have to get to this crazy cat?"

Alfred Hitchcock smiled affably. "Closeness is its own definition, young Peter. You will all be on the Jungle Land premises. Jim Hall's lion is there. And while ordinarily it might be considered reasonably safe to be in the lion's vicinity, I must warn you the situation has changed. A nervous lion—any nervous animal—can be dangerous."

The Three Investigators gulped.

"You can tell your friend Jim Hall not to worry," said Bob. "His lion won't be the only nervous one there anymore."

"That's right," Pete added. "I'm not even there yet and I'm nervous already."

Mr. Hitchcock turned to Jupiter. "Any further comment, young Jupiter, before I call my friend to say you lads are willing to undertake the assignment?"

Jupe shook his head. "No comment. But it might be a good idea to ask Mr. Hall to put in a word for us with his lion!"

Mr. Hitchcock smiled and picked up his phone. "I shall convey your message. And I shall expect a full report from you soon. Good-bye and good luck."

The Three Investigators waved and walked out wondering what kind of luck they could expect dealing with a nervous lion!

Welcome to Jungle Land

3

It was past noon when The Three Investigators careened down the last steep grade of a narrow back road. Rolling mountains encircled the valley, which was a scant thirty minutes from Rocky Beach. Jupiter's Uncle Titus had sent Konrad on a pickup job in nearby Chatwick and had allowed the boys to go along for their appointment in Jungle Land.

"Slow down, Konrad," Jupe ordered. "That's the place."

"Hokay, Jupe." The big Bavarian braked the small pickup truck to a jolting stop outside the main gate. The entrance sign read:

WELCOME TO JUNGLE LAND!
ADMISSION ONE DOLLAR, CHILDREN FIFTY CENTS

As the boys got out, they heard strange hooting and chattering cries. In the distance a loud trumpeting sound echoed in the hills. As if in answer to this challenge, there came a deep, rumbling roar that sent chills down their spines.

Konrad gestured to the gate. "You fellers going in there?" he asked. "You better watch it. I think I hear lions."

"There's nothing to worry about, Konrad," Bob said. "Mr. Hitchcock wouldn't have sent us on this job if he thought it was really dangerous."

"We just have to look into something for the owner," Jupe said. "This is a safe tourist attraction."

Konrad shrugged. "Hokay," he said. "If you say it's safe, hokay. But better take care all the same. I be back for you a little later."

He waved and wheeled the truck back to the main road. Soon the truck was out of sight.

Jupe looked at his friends. "Well, what are we waiting for?"

Pete pointed to a small sign posted at the gate:

CLOSED TODAY

"I wondered why there wasn't anyone around," he said.

"It might be because the movie company is inside shooting," said Jupe.

Bob peered inside. "Shouldn't Mr. Hall be here to meet us?"

Jupe nodded. "I expected him. But maybe he's busy with other things inside."

"Like his nervous lion," Pete said. "Maybe he's having a hard time convincing him we're not here for his dinner."

Jupe pressed on the gate. It opened to his touch.

"It's not locked," he said cheerfully. "That's either so the movie people can get in and out—or for us. Let's go."

The gate creaked shut behind them as they stepped inside. From beyond the trees, they heard chattering sounds punctuated by harsh screeches.

"Monkeys and birds," Jupe observed. "Harmless creatures."

"We'll find out soon enough," Bob said in a low voice.

The entrance road was narrow and twisting, bordered on either side by trees and thick foliage. Large curling vines looped down from trees.

"Looks like a jungle, all right," Pete observed.

The others nodded. As they advanced slowly, they cast suspicious eyes at the dense undergrowth on either side, wondering what strange creature might be crouching there waiting to spring. The odd sounds beyond continued, and again they heard the dull, reverberating roar.

They stopped at a signpost at a fork in the road.

" 'Western Village and Ghost Town,' " Bob read on the sign pointing left. "What's the other say?"

Jupe was looking up at it quizzically. "To the animals," he said.

They turned right at the fork. After a few hundred yards, Pete pointed ahead. "There's a house. Maybe Mr. Hall has his office there."

"It looks like a bunkhouse," Jupe said as they drew closer. "There's a corral behind it."

Suddenly there was a loud, ear-piercing scream. The boys froze, and then, as if with a single mind, dived into the shrubbery for cover.

Hidden behind the thick trunk of a barrel palm, Pete peered across the dirt road at the bunkhouse. Jupe and Bob, crouched behind a bush, also looked out anxiously. They waited for more sounds, their hearts beating fast. But now the thick jungle was silent.

"Jupe," Pete whispered. "What was that?"

Jupe shook his head. "I'm not sure. Maybe a cheetah."

"It could have been a monkey," Bob whispered.

They stayed in the shrubbery, waiting.

"Good grief!" Pete said hoarsely. "We came here to find out about a nervous lion. Nobody said anything about nervous monkeys or cheetahs!"

"We've got to expect the animals here will be making some kind of sounds," Jupe said. "It's only natural. Whatever that was, it's quiet now. Let's get to the house and find out what's happening."

The others hesitated as Jupe started forward, moving slowly and warily. Then they joined him.

"Anyway, that sound came from way up ahead," Pete muttered.

"Where the wild animals are locked up tight—I hope," Bob added.

"Come on," Jupe urged. "We're almost there."

The bunkhouse was old and needed paint. Pails and feedbins were scattered carelessly at the side. Tracks from many vehicles had carved deep ruts in the road. The corral fence sagged.

The old house stood silent, as if waiting for them.

"Now what?" Pete asked in a low voice.

Jupe stepped onto the low, slatted porch. There was a determined expression on his face. "We knock on the door," he said flatly, "and tell Mr. Hall we're here."

He rapped vigorously. There was no response. "Mr. Hall!" Jupiter called loudly.

Bob scratched his head. "Guess he's not home."

Pete held up his hand warningly. "Hold it!" he whispered. "I hear something."

They all heard it then. A low, muttering sound in an odd cadence. The sound came closer, approaching from the rear of the house. They could hear the crunching of footsteps on gravel. They drew back, eyes wide.

Suddenly it came at them, darting forward in an erratic line, head bobbing angrily. Yellow legs dug fiercely into the ground.

The Three Investigators stared.

Stalking a Lion

4

Jupiter Jones was the first to recover his voice. "Careful now!" he cautioned. "We don't want to be scared off by a mad rooster!"

"Gleeps!" Pete said sheepishly. "Is that all it is?"

Bob let out a relieved sigh. "I never would have believed it!"

He looked down at the clucking black fowl that had sounded so ominous only a moment before, and laughed.

"Shoo, bird!" he yelled, waving his arms.

Startled, the cock lifted its black wings. Making angry sounds, it scuttled across the road, its high red comb bobbing.

The boys all laughed.

"There's proof of how the mind can deceive you," Jupe said. "We were intimidated by the jungle growth and the sounds of wild animals. We all expected something dangerous to be coming at us. We were conditioned for it."

He started for the door again.

"Hey, look over there, Jupe," Bob said.

The other boys followed Bob's pointing finger. In the shadows of the thick jungle, they caught a sudden movement. A figure in khaki stepped from behind a tree.

"Mr. Hall!" Jupe yelled.

The man waited as the boys ran toward him.

"Hi," Pete said. "We've been looking for you."

The man looked at the boys questioningly. He was stocky and deep-chested, his faded safari shirt open at the throat. His light blue eyes contrasted vividly with the deep tan of his face. His nose was long and dented to one side. On his head was an old Aussie campaign hat, its wide brim folded over one ear.

As the boys came closer, he made an impatient movement with his hand. Something glinted.

Jupe and his friends stared down at the long, broad-bladed machete the man held carelessly at his side.

Jupiter spoke quickly. "We're The Three Investigators, Mr. Hall. Didn't Mr. Hitchcock tell you we were coming?"

The man blinked and looked surprised. "Oh, yes. Hitchcock. You say you're the three investigators?"

"That's right, Mr. Hall," Jupe said. He reached into his pocket and produced a business card on which was printed:

THE THREE INVESTIGATORS

"We Investigate Anything"

? ? ?

First Investigator .... Jupiter Jones
Second Investigator .... Peter Crenshaw
Records and Research .... Bob Andrews

"I'm Jupiter Jones. These are my partners, Pete Crenshaw and Bob Andrews."

"Nice to meet you, boys." He took the card and studied it. "What are the question marks for?"

"The question marks stand for things unknown," Jupiter explained. "For questions unanswered, riddles, enigmas. It's our business to answer those questions, unravel the riddles, and find solutions for the enigmas. That's why we're here. Mr. Hitchcock told us about the trouble you're having with your nervous lion."

"Oh, he did?"

"Actually, he merely mentioned your lion was nervous. I imagine he expected you to fill in the details."

The stocky man nodded, and slipped the card into his shirt pocket. He frowned and squinted into the distance. There was a trumpeting sound, almost immediately followed by an answering roar.

"Well," he said smiling. "If you're feeling up to it, we can go out and have a look at him."

"That's what we're here for," said Jupe.

"Fine. Let's get moving then."

Turning abruptly, he skirted the bunkhouse and followed a faint trail through the jungle. The boys fell into step behind him.

"Perhaps you can fill us in on the way, Mr. Hall," Jupe said, dodging a thick vine.

The long machete flashed in the air. The vine parted as if it were paper. "What d'ya want to know?" the man asked, resuming his rapid pace.

Jupe struggled to stay close behind. "Well, for example, all we know is that your lion is nervous. That's—well—rather unusual for a lion, isn't it?"

The man nodded, walking fast and slashing at the undergrowth looming in their path. "Not usual, at all. Know anything about lions?"

Jupiter gulped. "No, sir. That's why we'd like to know. It's curious, isn't it? I mean, this is a new development, isn't it?"

"Yep," the man said shortly. He held up his hand for silence. There were faint chattering sounds. Then came a booming roar. The man smiled. "Just up ahead," he said. "That's him out there." He cocked his head at Jupiter. "I'll leave it to you. Does he sound nervous?"

"I—I don't know. It sounds like—well, a normal lion roar." Jupe was determined to let Mr. Hall know he wasn't the least bit nervous himself.

"That's right," the man said. He stopped for a moment, swishing his machete at the tall grass surrounding them. "Y'see, the lion is not a nervous animal, at all."

"But—" Jupe started, perplexed.

The man nodded. "Unless," he said, "unless somebody or something is making him that way. How does that strike you?"

The boys, together now, nodded.

"Sure, but what?" Bob asked.

The man shifted his position suddenly. "Don't move," he whispered. "Something out there."

Before they realized it, he had disappeared into the tall grass. They heard his footsteps, the swish of grass, and then suddenly nothing at all.

Somewhere overhead a bird screeched and they jumped nervously.

"Relax, fellows," Pete said. "That was only a bird."

"Only a bird!" Bob repeated. "Some bird! It sounded like a vulture."

The boys waited for several minutes. Jupe glanced at his watch. "I've a funny feeling that vulture is trying to tell us something," he said.

"Oh, come on, Jupe," Bob protested. "Tell us what?"

Jupe's face was pale. He licked his lips. "I have the feeling that Mr. Hall isn't coming back. I think he's arranged some kind of test for us—to see how we react to the danger of the jungle."

"But why, Jupe?" asked Pete. "What would his reason be? We're here to help him, aren't we? He knows that."

Jupe listened for a moment before answering. Strange calls came from high in the trees. Then once again they heard a deep, menacing roar.

Jupiter inclined his head in the direction of the last frightening sound. "I don't know what Mr. Hall's reason can be. But I know that lion out there sounds a lot closer than before. He seems to be coming this way. I think that's what the vulture is telling us—that we're the prey! They usually circle a dead or soon-to-be-dead animal. In this case, us!"

Pete and Bob stared at Jupe. They knew he wasn't apt to joke in serious circumstances. Instinctively the three boys moved closer together.

They listened tensely.

They heard the swish of grass. Then footfalls, soft and stealthy.

Holding their breath, they edged closer to a large tree.

Then, almost directly behind them, they heard a blood-chilling sound—*the roar of the lion!*

Dangerous Game

5

"Quick!" Jupe whispered tightly. "Up this tree! It's our only chance!"

In an instant the three had scrambled up a smooth-boled gum tree. They huddled breathlessly in its fork barely ten feet from the ground, looking intently at the waist-high grass beyond.

Pete pointed toward a thick cluster of growth. "I—I just saw some grass bend there. You hear it? Something is moving—"

He blinked at a soft call, a whistle from the high grass. Then to the amazement of all three, a young boy stepped out of the brush, peering cautiously about.

"Hey!" Bob called. "Up here!"

The boy whirled. In the same motion, he swung a rifle upward. "Who are you?" he demanded.

"F-friends," Bob gasped weakly. "Put down that gun."

"We've been invited here," Pete added. "We're The Three Investigators."

"We're waiting for Mr. Hall to come back," Jupe put in. "He left us waiting while he went out there to investigate something."

The boy swung the rifle down. "Come down out of there," he said.

Cautiously the three slid down the trunk. Jupe pointed into the grass. "We heard a lion out there a little while ago. We thought we'd be safer up in the tree."

The boy smiled. He appeared to be about their age. "That was George," he said.

Pete gulped. "George? The lion's name is George?"

The boy nodded. "You don't have to be afraid of George. He's friendly."

A deep roar came from the high grass. It sounded terrifyingly close.

The Three Investigators stiffened.

"Y-you call that roar friendly?" Pete asked.

"I suppose you've got to get used to it first. But that's George—and he wouldn't harm anybody."

A twig snapped sharply. Bob paled. "What makes you so sure?"

"I work here," the boy answered, smiling. "I see George every day. By the way, my name's Mike Hall."

"We're glad to meet you, Mike," said Jupe. He introduced himself and his companions. Then, "I'm not sure we appreciate your father's sense of humor."

Mike Hall looked surprised.

"Bringing us out here and then deserting us with a lion close by," Pete burst in heatedly. "That's no joke."

"That's probably why he's in trouble here," Bob added. "You can lose a lot of people trying to help you if you play games like that."

The youth looked at the three angry investigators, puzzled. "I don't understand. First, I'm Jim Hall's nephew, not his son. Second, Jim wouldn't have left you here with the lion. We've all been looking for him— George got out somehow, and we forgot you were coming, in the excitement. I've heard George roaring and been trying to catch up with him."

Jupe listened to this explanation calmly. "I'm sorry, Mike. We're telling the truth. Mr. Hall led us out here and then abandoned us. The lion roared out there, and he told us to wait. He disappeared into the grass—and

—well, we've had a long wait—and a worried one!"

Mike shook his head stubbornly. "There must be some mistake. That couldn't have been Jim. I've been with him all day and I just left him. You must have met somebody else. What did he look like?"

Bob described the stocky man with the Aussie campaign hat. "We called him Mr. Hall and he never denied it," he added.

"He carried a long machete," Pete said, "and knew how to use it. He also knew his way around. He cut his way right to this spot to show us the lion."

Jupe added, "I suppose we can't blame you for sticking up for your uncle, Mike, but—"

"I'm not," Mike interrupted angrily. "That man you described was Hank Morton. He used to work here as an animal trainer and handler."

He stared out at the high grass, listening intently. "What I don't understand is how he got here. My uncle Jim fired him."

"Fired him?" Jupe asked. "What for?"

"He was cruel to the animals, for one thing," Mike said. "My uncle Jim won't stand for that. For another, he's mean—a troublemaker. He drinks a lot. When he's in that condition, he doesn't know what he's doing."

"Perhaps," Jupe said thoughtfully. "But if that was Hank Morton who brought us out here, he wasn't the least bit drunk. He was cold sober—and knew exactly what he was doing."

"But why?" Bob asked. "Why did he do it? What was his idea—marooning us out here?"

"I don't know," Mike Hall said. "Perhaps—" His eyes gleamed. "Did you tell him anything—about why you're here?"

Jupe clapped his head ruefully. "That's it! We told

him Alfred Hitchcock sent us to see him about his nervous lion. I recall now that he looked surprised at first."

"I can think of a reason," Pete said. "He was trying to get even with Jim Hall for firing him. We just happened along conveniently."

"But why us?" asked Bob. "We've got nothing to do with Jim Hall and his getting fired."

"The nervous lion," Jupe reminded. "The case we're on and the reason we're here. Perhaps he didn't want us to find out why that lion is nervous."

"That could be it," young Mike Hall said. "And Hank Morton probably let George get loose, too. George couldn't have got out by himself."

"Well," said Jupe. "When we see your uncle, he might have a better explanation. I suggest we start back now, Mike, and have a talk with him."

"I don't think we can do that right now," Bob said quietly.

Jupe looked at Bob, surprised. "Why not? What's wrong with that idea?"

Bob's voice was low and shaking. "It's—right behind you, fellows. A great big lion just came out of the brush. Maybe it's George—but he sure doesn't look friendly!"

Mike turned around. "It's George, all right. But he knows me. Just don't make any sudden movements, fellows. I'll handle him."

The boys watched uneasily as Mike took a step forward. He lifted one hand, carefully extending it palm up. "All right, George. Easy now, fellow. Nice boy, George."

His reassuring voice was answered by a snarl. Slowly and menacingly a massive, thick-maned lion advanced. Its head was down and its huge yellow eyes were narrowed. It turned its big head to one side and snarled again. Less than ten feet away it halted. The huge jaws opened, exposing long, frightening fangs.

Then, with a deep roar rumbling in its throat, the lion came forward again.

The Three Investigators stared at it helplessly, unable to move, their throats tight with fear.

Mike was speaking again. "Easy, George," he said quietly. "Easy, boy. You know me, fellow. Easy now. Nice and easy."

The huge tawny beast flicked its tail. A low rumble came rolling like thunder. It came forward another step.

Young Mike shook his head. "Something's wrong, fellows. George knows me. But he isn't acting his usual friendly way."

Slowly, the boy backed away.

The lion came on.

A Narrow Escape

6

The Three Investigators stood rooted to the ground as inch by inch young Mike Hall retreated before the advancing lion. His voice was still low and friendly but the lion ignored it.

Jupiter Jones was as paralyzed with fear as his companions. But his brain was still active. He was puzzled by the lion's behavior toward somebody it knew. It gave no sign that it recognized young Mike Hall.

Suddenly Jupe discovered what was wrong. He tried to keep his voice low and not attract the lion's attention.

"Look at his left foreleg, Mike," he said. "He's wounded!"

Mike looked quickly at the lion's leg. It was covered by a thick film of blood.

"No wonder George isn't obeying," said Mike softly. "I'm afraid I've got bad news for you guys. A hurt animal is dangerous. I don't know if I can handle him."

"You've got a rifle," Bob whispered. "Maybe you ought to shoot."

"This is only a .22 caliber. It wouldn't do more than tickle George. It might make him even madder. I just carry it for emergencies, for firing a warning shot."

The lion took another step forward. The huge beast winced as the bloody leg took its weight. Its mouth opened in a twisting snarl.

The Three Investigators inched backward to the gum tree. Mike saw their movement and shook his head.

"Don't try it, fellows," he cautioned. "He'd be on you before you got one leg up."

"Okay, Mike," said Jupe. "But why not fire a warning shot? Wouldn't that scare George off?"

Mike smiled grimly. "Not a chance. He's got his head down. That means his mind is made up and nothing is going to change it." He bit his lip. "I just wish my uncle Jim was here."

A soft whistle trilled from the high grass. Abruptly a tall, bronzed man stepped out.

"You've got your wish, Mike," he said dryly. "Now nobody moves, nobody talks except me, understand?"

The man stepped lithely forward. "Now, Georgie, what's going on here?" he asked pleasantly.

The words were spoken in a light, conversational tone. They had their effect. The lion turned its head toward the man. Its long tail flicked. Then, cocking its head, it opened its jaws and roared.

The tall man nodded. "I see," he said softly. "You're hurt. Is that it?"

Then to the amazement of the boys, he strode up to the lion and took its huge head in his hands.

"Come on, George," he said. "Let's have a look at it."

The lion opened its jaws again. The expected roar became a moaning sound instead. Slowly it extended its bleeding leg.

"Oh, it's your leg, is it?" asked Jim Hall. "Okay, old fellow, take it easy. I'll take care of it for you."

He removed a handkerchief from his pocket and bent to one knee. Deftly, he bandaged the wound, his face dangerously close to the lion's jaws.

The lion stood patiently as Jim Hall knotted the handkerchief. The man rose. He rubbed the lion's ears and twisted his mane. Then, affectionately, he pounded the beast's shoulders.

"There you are, George—almost as good as new."

Smiling, he turned away. The lion's voice rumbled in its thick throat. Its muscles quivered. Then suddenly there was a quick, blurring yellow movement. Instantly Jim Hall was down, the lion upon him.

"Look out!" Pete cried.

The Three Investigators looked on in horror as the man writhed under the weight of the big jungle cat.

Jupe turned to Mike Hall. The boy was watching calmly, a slight smile on his lips. Jupe couldn't understand. "Do something!" he shouted.

"Use your gun, Mike!" Bob yelled.

Mike Hall lifted his hand. "It's nothing to worry about, fellows. They're only playing. George was brought up by Jim and loves him."

"But—" Jupe started to say. His eyes bugged out as he saw the huge lion thrown aside by Jim Hall. With a ferocious snarling sound, it lashed back, wrapping its forelegs around the man's shoulders. It opened its jaws wide, its large teeth inches from the man's face.

Unbelievably, Jim Hall laughed!

He braced to confront the snarling lion, and as he was knocked aside, pounded its ribs and yanked at the long mane. The animal moaned and flicked its long tail. Then to the utter bewilderment of the boys, it rolled over on its back, a strange sound coming from its throat.

"He's purring!" Bob exclaimed.

Jim Hall sat up and dusted himself off. "Whew!" he said in mock dismay. "That cat's a lot heavier than he thinks! It was easier when George was a cub."

Jupiter sighed his relief. He turned to Mike. "That just about scared me out of my wits. Do they always play that rough?"

"It scared me too when I first saw them at it," Mike admitted. "But I'm used to it now. George is so well-trained, he acts like a big overgrown puppy. You can see how good-natured he really is, now."

Jupe narrowed his eyes. "But Mr. Hitchcock said—" He turned to the tall man stroking the lion's chest. "Mr. Hall, we're The Three Investigators. Alfred Hitchcock told us you were having trouble, that your lion was nervous for some reason."

"That's right, son," Jim Hall said. "Take what happened here. Ol' George never acted that way before. He knows Mike and never should have come on that mean and ornery. I've brought him up, so naturally he listens to me, but lately he hasn't been dependable, at all."

"Maybe we can find out why," Jupe offered. "That wound on his leg, for example. Does that strike you as an accident?"

"What do you mean?"

"It looked like a slashing cut," Jupe said. "Something that could have been made by a long, sharp instrument —a machete, for instance."

The man nodded. "Yes. But—"

"When we arrived, we mistook another man for you, sir. He led us out here and he was wielding a machete—"

"It was Hank Morton," Mike interrupted. "Jupe described him to me. He must have let George loose."

Jim Hall's jaw set grimly. "Hank Morton was here? When I fired him, I warned him not to come back." He looked at his lion, puzzled. "*Somebody* let George out. It might have been Hank. You say he brought you out here?"

"Yes," Bob put in. "Then he left us and went off into the high grass, telling us to wait."

"If he used to handle your lion, maybe he was able to get close enough to wound him with that machete, and make him mad enough to go for *us,*" Pete said.

"If he did," Jim Hall said angrily, "that will be Hank Morton's last trick. Because if I don't catch up with him for that, *George will!*"

He tugged at the lion's ears affectionately. "Come on, boy. We're going to have Doc Dawson take a look at you."

Mike answered Jupe's inquiring look. "Doc Dawson is our veterinarian. An animal doctor. He takes care of George and all our other animals here."

Jim Hall led his lion off through the jungle. "Come along, boys. I'll fill you in on what's been happening when we get back to the house. Alfred Hitchcock said you fellows were pretty good at unraveling mysteries. Maybe you can spot what's wrong. Because sure as shooting, something is going on around here that I can't figure out."

The Trouble with George

"Here we are."

Jim Hall stopped at a small covered van parked on a side road. He dropped the tailgate, urged George up, then fastened it in place.

"Come on," Mike said to Jupe and his friends. "We'll sit up front with Jim."

The Jungle Land owner got behind the wheel and started the vehicle. As he backed up and turned around, Jupe leaned forward.

"How did George get out, Mr. Hall? Where do you usually keep him—in his own compound?"

Jim Hall shook his head. "He stays in our house— with Mike and me. I don't know how he got out unless Hank Morton saw me leave. He could have let him out then. George was used to him being around so that would have been no problem. Once George was out, he could have wandered anywhere. That's what had me worried," he added, his lips tightening.

He followed the narrow, winding road up a hill and swung up a gravel drive leading to a large white clapboard house.

"Here we are," he announced. "Run inside and call Doc Dawson, will you, Mike?"

As Mike jumped off, Jupiter looked around in surprise. "Is this where you live? We thought that first one we came to—the bunkhouse—"

"That's for show," Jim Hall answered, smiling. "People come to Jungle Land for a lot of reasons. It's an animal farm and ranch, and we throw in a bit of the old Wild West for them, too. Sometimes we use the place for filming movies. One is being shot right now, matter of fact—a jungle picture."

"So Mr. Hitchcock told us," Jupe said. "He led us to believe that was your concern at the moment, your lion not being trustworthy while a movie was being made here."

"Correct," Hall said. "George happens to be rented out, too, for the production. If he forgets he's supposed to be gentle and doesn't respond to my commands, Jay Eastland might lose a valuable leading man."

"Who's Jay Eastland?" Bob asked.

"That name sounds familiar," Pete said. "My dad does special effects for film companies. I'm sure I've heard him mention Jay Eastland's name."

Jim Hall said, "Eastland is a very important film producer and director—at least, he thinks he is."

He turned to unfasten the tailgate of the van. Mike Hall, who had just come out of the house, whistled and pointed off at an approaching cloud of dust.

"Here comes trouble, Uncle Jim," he called.

Jim Hall looked up, his brow darkening. "Trouble is right—here it comes in the person of Mr. Eastland himself."

The cloud of dust cleared to reveal a station wagon. In a few seconds it pulled up and stopped. A short, beefy, bald-headed man hopped out of the back seat. He advanced with jerky steps, his face flushed and angry.

"Hall," he shouted, "I'm holding you to the terms of our contract."

Jim Hall looked down at the perspiring director. "I don't know what you're talking about, Eastland. What's up?"

Eastland shook his fist at the animal owner. "That contract states no danger to myself or my people, remember? I guess you have a good explanation for what's happened?"

Jim Hall's eyebrows flew up. "My contract and agreement stands," he said coldly. "What happened?"

"Rock Randall's been hurt," Eastland yelled. "One of your animals got loose and attacked him—that's what happened!"

"That's impossible!" Hall said firmly.

The angry visitor pointed accusingly at the big lion in the rear of the van.

"There's all the proof I need, right there! Your pet lion! I happen to know he was loose and roaming around an hour ago. I'd like to hear you deny it!"

"You're right, Eastland. George was loose awhile ago. But that's no proof he attacked Randall. I can't believe it."

"You'll believe it when you see him," Eastland sneered.

"Is he hurt bad?" asked Hall quickly.

Eastland shrugged. "Let's say that being attacked by a bad-tempered lion doesn't do anybody any good."

Jim Hall's lips tightened. "Now, hold on there. We still don't know for certain George did it."

"Who else could do a job like that? Wait till you see—"

"I'm going to do that right now," Jim Hall snapped. "Just as soon as I lock George in the house."

As he lowered the tailgate, a horn sounded. A small, old panel truck came bouncing around the turn.

"It's Doc Dawson," Mike Hall whispered to the boys.

The driver braked to a skidding stop and jumped out. He was tall and thin. Under his grizzled mustache jutted the stub of an unlit stogy. He hurried toward the group with long strides, carrying a black leather medical bag.

The visitor stopped as he saw the lion in the van. Ignoring Eastland, he addressed Jim Hall in a gruff voice. "Got here as fast as I could, Jim, after Mike's call. What's that about George being hurt?"

"Flesh wound on his leg, Doc," Jim answered. "Somebody let George out while Mike and I were away. We rounded him up north of the bunkhouse."

"It looks like somebody cut him with a knife or machete, Doc," Mike Hall put in.

The angular vet turned to Mike, frowning. "Who could have done that to old George? I'd better have a look. Hold him steady for me, will you, Jim?"

The vet leaned forward as Jim Hall held the lion's mane. "Let's have a look, Georgie, boy," the vet said softly.

He slipped off the handkerchief bandage and lifted the lion's leg. The animal whimpered.

"Come on, George," the vet said. "I won't hurt you. Been taking care of you since you were a baby."

After a cursory glance, Dawson dropped the leg. "Superficial cut, Jim, but nasty. I'd better take him back to the dispensary for a better look. We don't want to risk an infection."

"Right," Jim Hall said. "You're going with Doc Dawson, George," he informed the lion, guiding him down the slanted tailgate.

As the vet started for his truck, the irate film producer stepped in his way. "What's going on?" he bellowed. "Where you taking that lion? We hired him for the movie. He starts work tomorrow morning at eight sharp."

Doc Dawson stopped to light his stub of cigar and blew smoke in Eastland's face. "That lion will be ready to work when I say he is. His leg may be better by to-morrow morning, and then again it may not. My job is to keep George healthy. I don't care two cents for your crummy movie. Now get out of my way, mister, or I'll walk right over you!"

Jupe and his companions quietly watched the drama. At the sudden vehemence in the vet's voice, Eastland paled and backed off. Dawson opened the rear door of his truck. Jim Hall brought George forward, patted the lion's flank, and raised his hand.

"Up you go, Georgie."

Obediently, the lion leaped into the truck. Hall closed the door and Dawson drove off. The lion pressed against the open-mesh sides of the truck, looking sad, a whimpering sound in its throat.

Eastland stepped forward again. "I'm telling you now, Hall, that lion better be ready," he threatened. "Now do you want to see what he did to Rock Randall, or not?"

Without a word, Jim Hall followed the film producer into his station wagon. He waved to Mike as the driver spun the long car around, calling as he caught Jupe's eye, "Sorry, fellows—I'll see you later."

Jupe watched thoughtfully until the station wagon disappeared into the jungle. "That sounds like a bad scene, if it's true," he said.

"If what's true?" Mike Hall snapped. "My uncle Jim's story or Mr. Eastland's?"

Jupe shrugged. "I'm not disputing your uncle's word, Mike. But you have to admit he looked worried."

"I'm sorry, Jupe," Mike said, his voice breaking. "I didn't mean to flare up at you. But anything that concerns my uncle, concerns me, too. I—well, I'm living with him because my parents were killed in a freeway accident. He's my father's brother, and my only family now—except for Cal."

"Cal?" asked Bob.

"Who's he?" Pete put in.

"Cal Hall is my other uncle. He's a big game hunter and explorer in Africa," Mike explained. "He sends Jim animals for Jungle Land. If Jim gets them young enough, like with George, he can train them easily. He puts the others on exhibit here and hopes to train them all some day. But it's a lot harder to do once they're full grown."

"How come Jay Eastland acts so nasty?" Pete asked. "What's he got against your uncle Jim?"

"Nothing I know of," Mike said. "He's worried about his movie getting done on schedule. And before he leased Jungle Land, he wanted an agreement it would be safe working here, with the animals around. Jim guaranteed it would."

"What happens if your uncle guessed wrong—and there's an accident?" Bob asked.

"Jim would lose a lot of money. He had to put up a bond of fifty thousand dollars as a guarantee. He signed over Jungle Land as security for the bond. So he could lose everything. He's losing money already because tourists aren't allowed in when we rent out for a movie. They might disrupt things."

Jupiter listened carefully. "I assume, though, that your uncle will make a considerable amount of money if the movie goes through on schedule, without any accidents. Correct?"

"Yes," Mike admitted. "I don't know the exact amount but it's so much a day. And George gets paid five hundred dollars when he works. Trained animals are rented for a lot of money—just like movie stars."

"Has George had any accidents before?" asked Jupe. "Has he ever attacked anybody?"

"No," Mike said. "Never. He's a very gentle animal and well-trained. That is—" he bit his lip "—until lately, anyway. Recently he's been acting up."

Bob, in charge of Records and Research, had his little memo book open. "We still have no information about that," he said. "How has George been acting? What's he doing now that he didn't do before? Maybe that might give us a hint, Mike, about what's making him nervous."

"Well, he's not himself. He's on edge. He stays in the house with us but lately he hasn't slept well. Almost every night, he's up and growling, walking around, trying to get out. Jim can't get him to go back to sleep, and he doesn't take orders as he used to. He's getting so hard to handle now I'm afraid he's not the good-natured, well-trained animal he used to be."

"It could be something outside is exciting him," Jupe said. "Are any animals here allowed to roam loose at night?"

Mike shook his head. "We have deer in a compound but they can't get out. We have horses that are used in a lot of Westerns. They're kept in a corral. We've got two elephants down by the lake but they're in their own compound, too, and stay there. We've got raccoons, monkeys, birds, dogs, chickens, and a lot of other animals—but they're all penned up at night and accounted for."

"Nevertheless," Jupe said, "something or somebody is making George nervous."

"Nervous enough, maybe, to attack that actor, Rock Randall," said Pete. "Though maybe he asked for it. I remember hearing he's a pretty nasty guy."

"He'd have to be pretty stupid as well as nasty to start up with George," Bob said. "George didn't look too friendly and gentle when we ran into him. Maybe it was because he got that cut on his leg. Maybe not."

"We can't say anything for sure yet, fellows," Jupe said. "We can't blame George for Randall's accident until Jim comes back and tells us what happened. Maybe it was another kind of accident. One that none of the animals here were—"

Mike clapped his hands suddenly. "The gorilla!" he cried.

"What gorilla?" Pete asked.

"Do you have a gorilla here, too?" Bob said.

"Not yet—but we're expecting one. Part of a new shipment from my uncle Cal. Maybe it got here already, and got loose—and attacked Rock Randall!"

Jupe held his hand up. "Assuming it already got here, how could it escape? Wouldn't it be in a locked cage?"

Mike nodded. "You're right. I'm acting as nervous as George, myself. Jim didn't say anything about the gorilla arriving, and he'd know. Besides, if it was here, there's no way it could get out of its cage unless—unless—"

"Unless what, Mike?" asked Bob.

The young boy licked his lips. "Unless somebody who didn't like my uncle Jim opened its cage and let it out!"

A Tough Customer

8

It was still early afternoon and The Three Investigators were on their way back to The Jones Salvage Yard with Konrad. Their time to visit had run out before Jim Hall returned. The boys left Mike with the promise that they would return at the earliest opportunity.

Konrad, already waiting for them outside the Jungle Land gate, looked relieved when they came out. "You look hokay," he said. "I guess maybe you get along all right with that lion inside."

"He sounds a lot tougher than he is, Konrad," Jupe said. "We'll see what happens next time."

The big Bavarian shook his head dubiously. "You coming back here again? You push your luck too much maybe, Jupe."

Jupe smiled. "I don't think so, Konrad. At least, I hope not. Anyway, we're involved in a mystery and we'll have to keep coming back until it's solved."

Konrad only shook his head again and started the truck, remaining gloomily silent on the trip home.

The boys resumed their conversation.

"We have one possible suspect anyway," Bob said. "Hank Morton. He has a motive for letting George out —to get even for being fired. I'd suspect Jay Eastland, too, but what could his motive be? I don't see that he gains anything by delaying his movie. Usually they try to get them done on time, don't they, Pete?"

"Sure," Pete replied. "I've heard it from my dad often. Film companies have a limited budget and a tight schedule, as a rule. Especially so when they're working on location, like Mr. Eastland is now at Jungle Land. What do you think, Jupe?"

"I'm not certain yet what to think," their stocky leader said slowly. "It could be an act of revenge on Hank Morton's part. Or something to do with Jim Hall's putting up his whole operation as security for his animals' good behavior while the movie is being shot. He stands to lose an awful lot if anything goes wrong. Too much, if you ask me."

"Anyway, that's not what we came out for," Pete said. "It was because of a nervous lion, remember? Nothing anybody's said so far deals with that. We still don't know what's making George nervous."

"That's true," Jupe admitted. "And for all we know, the lion's getting out of the house and then getting himself wounded could be purely accidental. He could have jumped out a window, or the wind might have blown a door open. He could have cut his leg any number of ways. His nervousness is something else."

"Maybe what they need there is a good animal psychologist instead of a vet," said Bob.

Konrad interrupted their speculations by announcing their arrival at the salvage yard with a warning blast of his horn.

Jupe looked up surprised. "Thanks, Konrad. You made good time."

"I go back that way again for more pickup stuff tomorrow," Konrad said. "In case you fellows still got business with that lion."

"Swell, Konrad," said Jupe. "I'll let you know if we're going."

The boys jumped out of the cab as Konrad continued to the far end of the junkyard. Jupe started toward Headquarters, then stopped abruptly, an astonished look on his face.

"They're gone!" he cried.

"What's gone?" Pete asked.

"The bars!" Jupe exclaimed. "That whole stack we unloaded from the truck yesterday morning. All gone! Uncle Titus must have made a fast deal."

Bob scratched his head, puzzled. "Who would want to buy a truckload of rusty iron bars?"

Jupe shrugged. "I don't know. But it's the kind of luck my uncle always has."

Bob looked over Jupe's shoulder and groaned. "Uh-oh! Here comes your aunt, Jupe. She's got that look in her eye that means work!"

Jupiter turned to face his aunt. "Were you looking for us, Aunt Mathilda?"

"Indeed I was," his aunt said. "Where were you boys? A customer came and bought up all those iron bars, and there wasn't a soul around to help him load them."

Jupiter explained that Uncle Titus had given them permission to ride with Konrad on his trip to Chatwick. "Wasn't Hans around?" he asked.

"Indeed he wasn't," his aunt replied. "He was off again with your uncle to pick up some more of those bars. Apparently he's found a place that has plenty of them cheap."

Jupe smiled. "All right, Aunt Mathilda. We'll try to be around if that customer returns for more of the same."

"I wouldn't be at all surprised if he did," his aunt said. "So mind you are here tomorrow." As she turned to go, she added over her shoulder, "And by the way,

I've fixed up a stack of sandwiches. They're in the office. You and your friends might be hungry."

As the boys started happily off toward the office cabin, Mathilda Jones added, "And when you're done, Jupiter, you'll have to mind the office. I have to go downtown to do some shopping now. Titus should be back soon."

"All right, Aunt Mathilda," Jupe said.

"Konrad is driving me in the small truck," Mrs. Jones said. "Now mind you don't leave, and don't miss any sales, Jupiter."

"I won't. Don't worry."

Mrs. Jones nodded and walked away.

Inside the small office, the boys found piles of sandwiches wrapped in wax paper and several bottles of root beer and orange pop.

"Too bad, Jupe, about having to work tomorrow," Pete said, wolfing down a thick sandwich. "I was ready to go back to Jungle Land and have Mike show us around."

"We'd have some news then," Bob said, "about what happened to Rock Randall. If George really did it, they're in big trouble."

Jupe looked glum. "We still have a lot of work ahead of us at Jungle Land. We don't know the terrain at all yet. And there are far too many possibilities of what might be going on at night. Mike stated that George became nervous and restless at that time. So we'll have to check that out." He scowled. "Animals tend to become restless before an approaching storm. But Mike didn't mention the weather. Far as I can recall, it's been pretty good the past month. If not that, then who or what could be getting the lion nervous? It's still a complete mystery."

"Why did Hank Morton pretend to be Jim Hall and bring us out to where George was?" asked Bob. "If you ask me, that's a mystery, too. What did he have against us?"

"I don't know," answered Jupe. "But notice another curious thing. George was roaring before we got to him. It's possible that Hank Morton did not inflict that wound. No," he concluded, shaking his head, "I'm afraid next time we go back we'll have to keep our eyes and ears open. We have to learn a lot more than we know."

Pete noticed a movement out the window. "Uh-oh, Jupe—I think you have a customer. Somebody just came in. Didn't your aunt tell you not to miss any sales?"

A dark sedan had pulled into the salvage yard. A light-haired man was looking around the neatly arranged junk. He walked quickly around the piles, lifting objects off the top to peer behind and below. Seeming unsatisfied, he wiped dust from his hands and turned to the door of the office.

Jupe was standing there waiting. Bob and Pete were behind him, ready to help.

The customer was thin and broad-shouldered, wearing a business suit and a bow tie. His eyes were a very pale blue and his face had a curious hatchet-like shape, wide at the cheekbones and tapering abruptly to a narrow, pointed chin. When he spoke, his voice had the toughness of a man used to giving orders.

"I'm looking for some iron bars," he said. He looked at Jupe questioningly. "Is the owner around?"

"No, sir," Jupe replied. "But I work here. I'm sorry, but we don't have any more iron bars. We just sold the whole stack of them."

"What? When was this—who bought them?"

"Earlier today, I guess. I don't know who purchased them, sir."

"Why not?" the man demanded. "Don't you people keep records of your sales here?"

"Only of money received," Jupiter said. "Whoever bought those iron bars loaded and transported them himself. So we have no record of delivery. In a junkyard business like this, people generally just come in, pick what they want, and take it home with them."

"I see," the man said. He looked around again, disappointed.

"My uncle Titus, the owner, is out now," Jupe said. "He might be hauling back some more iron bars. If you care to leave your name and address, he could get in touch with you."

"That's a thought," the man said. His eyes kept darting about the junk piled in the yard. "But so far as you know, there's not a single bar available now, big or small. Is that right?"

"Yes, sir," Jupe said. "I'm sorry. Maybe if you told me what you wanted them for, I might be able to find something else here you could use as a substitute."

The man shook his head. "I'm not interested in any substitutes." He suddenly pointed, his voice loud and triumphant. "What's that over there? What are you trying to do, kid—hold out on me?"

Jupe looked toward where the man was pointing. "Those are animal cages," he said.

"I know they are," the man said nastily. "But they have bars, don't they?"

Jupe shrugged. "Some do and some don't. We have to repair those cages, replace the missing bars, rebuild and repaint the tops and bottoms, you see, and—"

"Never mind all that," the man said impatiently. "I'm just interested in buying the iron bars. As many as I can get. How much?"

He took a thick billfold out and started to leaf through a lot of bills.

Jupiter blinked. "You want the bars? Not the cages?"

"That's right, genius. How much?"

Jupe frowned. He remembered his uncle's plans to fix up the cages for the circus. Jupiter never questioned what his uncle wanted, nor his reasons.

"I'm sorry," he said. "Those bars aren't for sale. We need them to complete the cages so they can be sold to the circus."

The man grinned. "Okay," he said. "That's fine. That's just what I want—circus cages. I'll take them as is, and fix them up myself. How much?"

Again he riffled the thick pile of bills impatiently.

"Do you work for a circus?" Jupe asked.

"What's the difference?" the man snapped. "I want circus cages, and you got them. How much, kid? C'mon. I'm in a hurry."

Jupe looked speculatively at the cages. There were four of them, all in extremely poor condition.

"That would be one thousand dollars," he said sleepily.

The man's fingers tightened on his billfold. "A thousand dollars for that junk? Are you kidding? Take a look at them—they're falling apart!"

Jupe heard Bob and Pete clear their throats nervously behind him. He looked again at the cages, then very deliberately at the man. "That would be one thousand dollars apiece," he said distinctly. "Four thousand dollars for all four."

The hatchet-faced man stared at Jupiter and slowly

replaced his billfold in his pocket. "Maybe you shouldn't be left alone to run a business, kid. I can get new cages for that kind of money."

Jupe shrugged. Having been a child actor when he was very young, he appreciated the scene he was playing now. "Perhaps you can, sir. I've no idea what the current market price is for new circus cages. If you should care to drop back when my uncle is here, perhaps he might give you a more satisfactory price."

The visitor shook his head impatiently. "I don't have time for that, kid." He brought a bill out of his pocket and offered it. "Here's twenty bucks for the lot. Take it or leave it. My guess is your uncle bought the whole lot for five bucks. That's all junk, kid." He waved the twenty-dollar bill under Jupe's nose. "Well, what do you say? Twenty bucks?"

Jupiter sucked in his breath, hesitating. He knew the man was right. The bars as well as the cages were practically worthless. But he had learned to trust his instincts.

"Sorry," he said, turning away. "No deal."

He saw the man's hand dart to his pocket. For a long moment, Jupe held his breath, wondering if he had made a mistake.

More Trouble

9

The hatched-faced man's voice was cold and threatening. "All right, kid—have it your way. I'll be back!"

The man quickly got into his car, gunned his engine, and roared out of the salvage yard.

Jupe slumped, blowing out his cheeks in a long, relieved sigh.

"Whiskers!" Bob exclaimed. "What was that all about?"

"A thousand dollars for each of those crummy cages?" Pete asked sarcastically. "I bet that man was right—that your uncle didn't pay more than five bucks for the lot—including the loose bars and pipes that we stacked."

Jupe nodded, feeling deflated. "I know," he said. "Uncle Titus hardly ever pays more than five dollars for anything."

"Then why did you ask so much?" Bob demanded. "That was a tough-looking customer. He wasn't happy when he left."

"I know." Jupe started to explain. "I—I had a hunch something was wrong, that's all. I'm not sure why. I felt he wanted those bars too much. So I just stepped up the price to find out how much they really were worth to him."

"Well, you found out," Pete said. "Twenty dollars. And when your uncle finds out you turned down that much money, I'll bet he blows his stack."

Jupe looked up and sighed. "We'll find out soon enough. Here comes Uncle Titus now!"

The large pickup truck rolled into the yard with Hans behind the wheel. As Titus Jones got down from the cab, Jupe noticed that the truck was empty.

"What happened, Uncle Titus?"

His uncle tugged at his long walrus mustache. "Seems as if there's been a run on iron bars lately. Guess I got to the place too late. Every last one of them was gone."

Jupe cleared his throat. "Aunt Mathilda already sold that batch you bought yesterday. And we just had another customer looking for some, too."

"That so?" his uncle asked. He dug out his pipe and lit it. "Well, no mind. We'll get some more in some day."

Jupe moved his feet uneasily. "This customer wanted to buy those last few bars, the ones for the cages. He was willing to buy them with or without the cages."

His uncle looked at him. "Buy the bars without the cages? How much did he offer?"

"Twenty dollars," Jupe replied, swallowing hard.

"Twenty dollars?" Titus thought about it. "What did you tell him?"

"I said it wasn't enough. That we didn't want to sell the bars alone. That we were planning to fix up the cages to sell to the circus."

Titus Jones rocked back and forth, blowing smoke. "How much did you ask him for the cages?"

Jupe took another deep breath. "A thousand dollars," he said, waiting for the explosion. The only response was more smoke as Titus Jones puffed silently away. "A thousand dollars apiece," Jupe added slowly. "Four thousand for the lot."

His uncle removed the pipe from his mouth. As Jupe

waited for the expected tongue-lashing, a car swung into the yard. It came to a quick, bucking stop near them. A man stepped out.

"That's him," Jupe said.

The hatchet-faced man walked up. "You the owner of this junkyard?" he demanded.

"I am," Mr. Jones said.

"My name's Olsen." The visitor jabbed his finger in Jupe's direction. "Fine help you leave when you're away. I tried to buy some of your old junk bars and this kid tried to scalp me."

"That so?" Mr. Jones asked in a matter-of-fact voice. "Sorry to hear about it, mister."

The man grinned. "I thought you would be." He took out his billfold and extracted a twenty-dollar bill. "I offered him twenty bucks for those bars over on that pile and he turned me down flat."

Titus Jones inclined his head toward the pile the man indicated. "Ain't no bars there, mister. Just some old animal cages."

"I know," Mr. Olsen said impatiently. "But I don't need the cages. Just the bars." He extended the money to Titus Jones. "Here you are—twenty bucks. Is it a deal?"

Titus Jones relit his pipe and puffed hard to get it going properly. Jupe waited. The man stirred restlessly.

"Sorry, mister," Titus said at last. "But my nephew here told you the truth. Those bars you're talking about there are for animal cages. When we get 'em fixed up nice and proper, I figure on selling them to the circus for their animals."

Jupe stared at his uncle. Pete and Bob stood openmouthed.

Mr. Olsen scowled. "Okay—animal cages. Do you

know what he wanted for the four of them? Four thousand dollars! He asked a thousand bucks apiece!"

"Well," Titus said, "the boy's young, and he did make a mistake quoting the price."

"I thought so," the man said, smiling with satisfaction.

"The price is six thousand dollars," Titus Jones said. "That would come to fifteen hundred dollars apiece."

The visitor stared. Titus Jones put his pipe in his mouth, puffed, and rocked on his heels. Once more Jupe held his breath, waiting for Mr. Olsen to explode.

At that moment Hans walked up. "Anything else I can do, boss?" he asked Mr. Jones. "I still got time to do some cleaning up."

Mr. Olsen looked at the hulking figure of the yard helper. His cold eyes flickered. Then he snarled, "Forget it, mister. I've got better use for my money."

Jupiter watched the sedan roar out of the yard. He felt like hugging his uncle.

A few minutes later, The Three Investigators were crawling through the big pipe leading to Headquarters. As soon as they were inside, Jupe squinted into the See-All periscope, which let him see over the piles of junk outside the trailer.

"All clear," he reported. "Mr. Olsen hasn't returned."

"Whiskers!" Bob exclaimed. "You could have knocked me over with a feather when your uncle Titus backed you up."

"Six thousand dollars!" Pete said. "And I thought that *you* were off your rocker!"

Jupiter nodded. "I don't blame you, Second. But Uncle Titus has an affection for the circus that goes far beyond his usual desire to do business and make a reasonable profit."

"What beats me," Bob said, "is why everyone wants to buy bars all of a sudden?"

"You should have asked your aunt Mathilda who the other buyer was—the one who bought up the whole lot," Pete said to Jupe.

Jupe was about to reply when the telephone rang.

"Hello, Jupiter Jones speaking."

They could all hear the incoming voice through the loudspeaker attachment. "Hi, Jupe. This is Mike Hall. How would you fellows like to come back to our place again tonight?"

"I don't know if we can get away, Mike," Jupe said. "Why—is anything wrong at Jungle Land?"

"Not exactly," Mike said. "I just thought you'd like to see the gorilla. He just arrived."

"Swell," Jupe said. "Is he a big one?"

Mike laughed. "Big enough. Of course, he'll keep, but our big problem is still with George. And I hope you remember that he gets nervous after dark."

"We haven't forgotten, Mike. As a matter of fact, we were discussing that same point—that we don't know yet what goes on there after dark."

"Well, here's your chance to find out," Mike said cheerfully.

"All right, Mike. We'll try to get permission, and then it'll be just the matter of securing transportation."

"Great," Mike said. "I can meet you at the gate. You coming by pickup truck again?"

"I don't think so," Jupe replied. "This time I believe we'll be using the Rolls."

There was a gasp. "You have a Rolls-Royce?" Mike asked. Then he began to laugh.

"Ask him what's so funny," Bob said.

"I heard that," Mike said. "It's funny because Mr. Jay Eastland acts like such a big shot, you know. And that's the car he drives to impress people."

Jupe consulted his watch. "We'll be there about nine, Mike, after dinner. As soon as I call Worthington."

"Worthington? Who's he?"

"Our chauffeur."

There was loud laughter from the other end. "Wow!" Mike managed to say finally. "Okay, see you later."

Jupiter replaced the phone. "I guess I should have explained to Mike we don't actually own the Rolls and Worthington."

"It's better this way," Bob put in. "At least we cheered him up. The way things are going at Jungle Land, he needs a laugh."

Promptly at nine o'clock that evening, the gleaming old Rolls-Royce rolled up to the main gate at Jungle Land.

Jupe peered out the window. "I thought Mike said he would meet us here."

There was an overhead light illuminating the gate area. Beyond that Jungle Land was dark. Palm leaves rustled in the night breeze. From the distance came strange chattering sounds.

Pete jumped out and opened the gate. As the Rolls passed through, he closed it again and got back into the car. "I'm glad Worthington is driving us in," he said. "This place is kind of scary at night."

Following Pete's unerring sense of direction, Worthington threaded his way through several junctions and side roads. As he was about to turn up the road leading to the big white house on the hill, Pete touched the dignified chauffeur's shoulder. "Hold it a second, Worthington."

Jupe raised his eyebrows. "What's up, Pete?"

"I thought I heard shouting up ahead—and some other noises."

They sat waiting, concentrating on listening. Soon they all heard sounds in the undergrowth. Then they heard the faraway wail of a siren.

Bob pointed into the dark. "Look! Searchlights!"

As their eyes watched the blue arcs of light sweeping the skies, they became aware of crashing sounds directly ahead of them. They heard the rasp of heavy breathing. In the next instant, a figure broke out of the jungle. The headlights of the Rolls picked him out clearly as he ran across the road.

His eyes were wide and staring. Sweat glistened on the dirt-streaked face under the old Aussie campaign hat. There was no mistaking the man caught for a brief moment in the bright headlights.

"Hank Morton!" Bob exclaimed.

"Running wild through the woods—and looking mighty scared," added Pete. "I wonder what he's been up to now."

The panting man plunged into the thick jungle on the other side and disappeared. The crashing sounds of his flight gradually diminished.

They heard angry cries up ahead, and saw the beams of bobbing flashlights.

"It looks like some kind of trouble," Bob said, peering out.

"Let's see what's going on," Jupe cried.

In a moment the boys were scrambling out and running. A voice called out.

"Jupiter! Bob! Pete!"

Jupe turned, peering uncertainly into the darkness. A flashlight signaled. "Over here. It's me—Mike."

He directed them with the flashlight until they were together. Jupe noticed Mike was breathing hard. Behind him, dim figures were walking slowly through the jungle, swinging flashlights from side to side, and then up toward the trees. A few men were holding rifles.

Jupe caught his breath as he took in the eerie scene. "What's going on?" he asked. "Did George break out again?"

"It's not George this time," Mike said breathlessly. "It's a lot more trouble than that."

"What happened?" asked Bob. "Some of those men have rifles. Are they looking for Hank Morton?"

"Who?"

"Hank Morton," Pete said. "We just saw him running scared. He broke out of the jungle below the hill and ran across the road."

"So that's it!" Mike Hall said grimly. "I knew it!"

"Knew what, Mike?" Bob demanded. "What's going on here?"

"The gorilla I told you about," Mike began. "He broke out of his cage and escaped!"

"When?" Pete demanded. "You mean there's a wild gorilla running loose here?"

"It happened a little while ago, right after Doc Dawson brought George home this evening."

"A wild gorilla and a lion," Jupiter said thoughtfully. "I don't know much about how those two species get along, Mike. Would a gorilla be that frightened at the presence of a lion that he would break out of his cage?"

Mike shrugged. "Jim knows more about that than I

do. But after what you told me, I'm not at all sure he did break out of his cage."

"What do you mean, Mike?" asked Pete.

"I mean somebody could have let him out. Somebody who hated my uncle Jim bad enough to pull a stunt like that. You said yourselves you saw him running through the woods.

"Unless I'm dead wrong, it was Hank Morton who let him out!" he said bitterly.

In the Dark

10

Jupe shook his head. "Hank Morton could have been running through the woods for any number of reasons. That's not proof that he let your gorilla escape. Perhaps if we could see its cage, we might find some clues."

"Okay, you fellows are the investigators," said Mike. "Maybe you'll discover something." He led them up the hill. "Say, where's that Rolls-Royce you said you were coming in?"

"Down at the foot of the hill," said Bob. "Worthington is used to us. He'll just wait until we show up again."

Mike chuckled and brought the boys to a clearing at the side of the house. Lights blazed in every room, lighting up the nearby area. Mike pointed and The Three Investigators found themselves staring at a large, empty cage.

"The shipment arrived not long after you left this afternoon. There were two cages this time and—"

"Two cages?" Jupe asked.

A snarling, spitting sound behind him made him whirl in fright. Bob and Pete flinched.

"Whiskers!" Bob gasped. "What was that?"

Mike directed his flashlight to the far end of the house. "I guess I should have warned you first. Take a look! Isn't that a beauty?"

The boys looked in awe at the sinister creature caged

barely twenty feet from them. As they slowly approached, it snarled again.

"It's a black panther," Mike said. "How do you like it?"

Gleaming yellow eyes stared unwinkingly at them from behind thick iron bars. As they took another cautious step forward, the panther hissed. Its mouth opened, showing long, white pointed fangs. Hastily, the boys stepped backward.

Bob gulped. "I like him fine. Just so long as he stays locked up in that cage."

"Wow!" Pete exclaimed. "Look at those muscles! If you ask me, that panther looks a lot tougher than old George."

As if acting in support of Pete's observation, the beast snarled and lunged at the bars with a frightening thud. The boys retreated another step, watching the black animal warily.

"It would be a pretty good fight, at that, Pete—lion against panther," Mike said. "Panthers, this kind, are really leopards. They strike like lightning. They've got terrible raking claws as well as sharp teeth. But don't let George fool you with his dumb, gentle act. He's still a lion—a good-sized one at that—over four hundred pounds—and he's simply too big and powerful for the panther. No panther ever beat a lion yet, that I ever heard of. It would take a tiger to do it."

The boys stared in silence at the animal pacing restlessly in its cage. "I kind of agree with Pete," Bob said finally. "This baby looks real mean and tough. What do you think, Jupe?" He looked around. "Jupe?"

The First Investigator was spotted by the cage the gorilla had escaped from. He motioned them over.

"What's up, Jupe?" asked Bob.

"This cage has been tampered with, fellows," Jupe announced. "While I'm not certain that Hank Morton was responsible for the gorilla getting out, somebody was!"

"How can you tell?" asked Pete.

Jupe pointed dramatically to the side of the cage. "See there? One bar has been removed. The adjoining two are bent. The bars are set approximately six inches apart. I think whoever removed the bar gave the gorilla his chance. He bent the other two far enough apart to slip out. You said he was a big one? How big?"

"He wasn't full size, but big enough," Mike said. "About our size." He shook his head as they appraised each other. "Don't let the size fool you. He's twice as powerful as a grown man."

"Where did he come from?" Jupe asked.

"Rwanda, in Central Africa. We were expecting a young gorilla from there. We've been waiting a long time. Uncle Cal went through all the mountain gorilla habitat—Rwanda, the Congo, and Uganda. He finally wrote us from Rwanda that he had a gorilla, but he was having trouble getting it out of the country. Gorillas are on the endangered species list—there aren't very many of them left—and only zoos and scientists can get export permits for them. It took Uncle Cal awhile to convince the authorities that Jungle Land was a kind of zoo."

"Gee," said Pete. "Wouldn't it have been easier to just get another kind of gorilla?"

"Well, there are lowland gorillas, but there's an embargo on them, too. I'm not even sure which species Uncle Cal finally sent us."

"It was a young male mountain gorilla," said a voice

from the darkness. Jim Hall stepped out of the shadows and nodded to the boys.

"Did you find him yet?" Mike asked.

Jim Hall shook his head. His face was tired and dust-stained. "I just heard he's been seen up by the canyon. I wanted to check back here again before heading out."

"What happened with Mr. Eastland?" Jupe asked. "Did George really attack Rock Randall?"

Jim Hall laughed harshly. "That was hogwash. It seems Randall got into a fight with somebody and got thrown around on some rocks on the movie set. He was beat up and bloody, and it did look as if George might have mauled him. But a doctor looked him over and said no animal could have made those marks. So we're clear of that mess, and now we have another. I'm glad you're back tonight, boys. You can see for yourselves Alfred Hitchcock wasn't exaggerating when he told you something's wrong at Jungle Land."

There were shouts in the distance, and Jim Hall made an impatient gesture. "Sorry, boys, but I've got to get moving and trap that gorilla before something happens."

"I guess he'd be pretty dangerous to run up against," Pete ventured.

"He might be frightened now by all the racket out there. But if you happen to run into him, don't worry. Just get out of his way."

Bob blinked. "What? Meet a gorilla face to face and not worry? How do you manage that?"

Hall laughed. "I'll tell you something about gorillas. It applies to a lot of wild animals generally. Gorillas almost never behave aggressively. Oh, they bluff a lot, and scream and charge—that's how they frighten away any animal that seems threatening. But mostly gorillas are peaceful animals that mind their own business. They graze in the same area as elephants, for example, and although they eat the same food, there's no problem."

"What happens?" asked Bob.

The tall man shrugged. "Mutual disregard," he said. He glanced at his watch. A horn sounded. "That'll be Doc." He waved and walked away.

A moment later he passed, driving an open jeep. The thin, mustached man sitting next to him was holding a rifle.

Mike smiled. "It figures good old Doc Dawson would be around to help. He's crazy about animals."

Pete turned to look at the jeep carrying the two men off. They looked prepared for action.

"If he likes animals all that much, why is he holding a rifle?"

"That's a stun gun," Mike said. "It shoots a tranquilizer dart—not bullets. Whatever gets hit is only knocked out temporarily, Pete—not really hurt."

"Jim Hall and the search party should be able to find the gorilla," said Jupiter. "I suggest we look around now while we have the opportunity. Perhaps we can learn what's behind these animal escapes. First there was George, and now the gorilla."

"Well, George seems okay now," Mike said. "He's in the house sleeping off the tetanus and tranquilizer shots Doc Dawson gave him. Doc cleaned up the wound and George will be able to face the camera tomorrow and earn a day's pay for us."

Jupiter was looking around. "Does George have a cage, too?"

"No, we got rid of George's cage over a month ago," said Mike. "He sleeps in the house with Jim and me. He has his own room but he prefers to share Jim's."

Jupe glanced up at the lighted house. "You said somebody must have let him out before. Couldn't it happen again?"

Mike put his hand in his pocket and produced a key. "This time the house is locked. Only Jim and I have keys."

Jupe pondered. "You've told us, Mike, that George becomes nervous and restless at night. I suggest we walk around to see if we can't uncover some reason for his nervousness. We should explore the area closest to the house to begin with."

"Swell," Mike said. "As you can see, the house is set in a clearing on this knoll. Over there's a shed for tools and firewood. It could be a garage but Jim parks outside here. The road at the foot of the drive leads north and runs into other roads."

He led the boys around the area. The night was quiet after the earlier excitement. The moon was now up, and the sky was cloudless.

Jupe nodded as if satisfied when they completed their circuit of the house. They returned to the cage area. The gorilla cage remained empty. The panther in the other lay quietly, switching its long tail and watching them balefully.

The Three Investigators followed Mike down the hill into the jungle. "I'll explain Jungle Land as we go along. Then the next time you come, you'll know your way around here without me."

"How big is Jungle Land?" asked Bob. "It seems with so much land to cover, you'd never know what's going on."

"It's about a hundred acres, and diamond-shaped. That's a lot maybe, but we never had any trouble keeping track of things before."

"Where is the Jay Eastland movie being shot?" Pete asked.

"North of here, about a five-minute ride," Mike said. "We're heading due east now, toward our closest border fence."

The trail descended steeply through brush, rocks, and fissures. Faint patches of moonlight showed between trees.

"Where's the canyon your uncle said the gorilla was seen at?" asked Bob. "He seemed to be heading north, too."

"He was, but he'll cut left on another road. The canyon is northwest, about fifteen minutes away. Just below it, we have several acres that look like the African veldt, grassy and flat. We have the elephants there, contained by a moat. So they can't get out. But you can hear them trumpeting." He grinned. "I like that sound."

"I like it better myself now," said Pete, "knowing they can't get out."

Mike continued to describe Jungle Land as they went on downhill. "At the far west end opposite us is the built-up tourist section. Our main attraction used to be the jungle and animals, but a lot of folks seem to prefer the Wild West. So we have a frontier town, a mock graveyard, a ghost town, and a stagecoach ride for the kids. We keep the horses pretty near that area.

"In the southern part is the entrance where you come in, and lots of jungle. In the central part is the lake and then above that, where Eastland is, more jungle. At the northern end are mountains, with one high precipice. It's been used for a lot of movies where the hero has to dive off a cliff. Doc Dawson has his dispensary up that way."

There was an outburst of chattering cries and hoots. The boys stopped and looked at their guide.

"Those are monkeys and owls," Mike explained. "We've also got a snakehouse in the northeast section but the snakes don't make any noise. We keep them farthest away because they're the hardest to find in case they ever get away. We've a good collection of sidewinders—they're rattlesnakes—and a water moccasin and a good-sized king snake."

Jupe was peering intently back through the trees. "How far are we from your house now, Mike?"

"About five hundred yards. There's a fence down the end of this slope here—"

"Wait!" Pete whispered. "What's that?"

They all heard it then. A slow, dull, crunching sound echoing with a measured beat. The Three Investigators looked at each other. The crunching sound became louder, seeming to come closer. Prickly chills ran down their spines. Then they heard a new sound. It started as a low whine and began to rise on a shrill, insistent note.

"I don't like that," Pete said hoarsely. "Maybe we ought to be getting back—"

Jupiter's eyes were wide with fear, too, but they were also puzzled. "That sound—" he started to say. "It—it's—"

As he groped for words, the shrill, whining noise ascended to a full-noted shriek. The screeching seemed to be all around, engulfing them.

EEEE—ooo—EEEEE! EEE—ooo—EEEEE!

Bob yelled, "I'm getting out of here!"

With one mind, The Three Investigators wheeled and ran.

"Wait!" Mike called.

They turned to stare in utter amazement.

Mike Hall was laughing.

"It's nothing to worry about," he called. "That's only the *metal shredder!*"

Steps into Terror

11

The shrill, wailing sound slowly fell until it became a low, whistling note.

"Metal shredder?" Jupiter repeated dumbly.

Mike was pointing ahead through some trees. "Yes, Jupe. Over the fence, the other side of our property. There's a salvage yard—steel and scrap iron. It's full of scrapped cars and other junk."

"What does the metal shredder do—besides scare people?" Bob asked.

"It's a new recycling process to salvage precious metal," Mike said. "Part of the new ecology drive. The cars used to be just pounded down and sold as scrap iron and steel. But now they have this new device— some kind of claw with a computer-selector-processing operation. It shreds the cars into little bits. The metal is separated from the other material, and then the more precious metals, like copper, are separated from the iron and steel."

"Whew!" Pete exclaimed weakly. "Is that all? It sounded like all the gorillas in town were holding a convention!"

Jupe was plucking at his lower lip. He glanced at his wristwatch.

"It is now nine thirty," he stated. "Does George usually become nervous and restless about this time, Mike?"

Mike shrugged. "Sometimes sooner or later. I don't know exactly what time—except that it's always after it gets dark."

"Always at night? Never during the day?"

"Never," Mike said firmly. "But I'm not counting this afternoon. George wasn't nervous then—just acting mean. I'd say because he was hurt."

"What's your idea, Jupe?" Bob asked. "That the sound of the metal shredder made George nervous?"

"Animals are more sensitive to sounds than humans," Jupe said. "Perhaps George is reacting to that high whine of the metal shredder."

"But he'd hear it all the time then," Pete put in. "Not just at night."

"A good point, Second," said Jupe. "Does this metal-shredding process operate during the day, too, Mike?"

"Sometimes," Mike said. "Off and on again. I don't pay much attention to the sound anymore. It isn't nearly as loud up by our house."

"Hmmm," Jupe said. "How long has that machine been in operation?"

"It's kind of new, Jupe. The scrap yard has been here a long time, a number of years. And the wrecking part of it, also. But offhand my guess is they haven't been using this metal shredder more than a month."

"A month," Jupe repeated. "And how long has George been acting nervous and restless?"

"Since about two or three months ago," Mike said. "I remember it started just before the rainy season when Jim decided to bring George inside the house for good."

Jupiter scowled, puzzled.

"Don't forget, he didn't act up every night," Mike added. "He was restless at times, then seemed to be all right. But the last week or so, he's been getting much worse, and it's been regular since."

"So he was nervous before the metal shredder came in," Bob said.

Jupe looked thoughtful. "It would seem that George isn't used to being cooped up indoors at night. That might account for his actions. The metal shredder could be a factor, or perhaps not. There could be different reasons."

"Maybe it's working in the movie that's making him nervous," Pete suggested, grinning. "A lot of actors get nervous at night trying to memorize their lines for the next day's shooting."

Jupiter snapped his fingers. "A humorous suggestion but nevertheless a possibility, Pete." He turned to Mike. "How long have Jay Eastland and his crew been working at Jungle Land?"

"They've been around here about two months," Mike said. "But a lot of that time was spent checking the locations, getting the setups planned for the shooting scenes, the right backgrounds, and so forth. They didn't move in completely and start shooting until two weeks ago."

"Do they shoot at night, too?" Jupe asked.

"Sometimes."

Jupe frowned. "You said their set is about five minutes away from your house. Would their mikes pick up the sounds of the metal shredder?"

"It's possible," Mike admitted. "I don't know. Mr. Eastland hasn't complained."

"He might not have to do his sound work at Jungle Land," said Pete, drawing on information he'd picked up from his father. "Sometimes the sound is dubbed in later—even the actors' voices."

Jupe nodded. "What about the actors and work crew? Do they live here, too?"

"Most of them go home at night," Mike said. "The freeway is near here and most of them don't live too far away—Westwood, Hollywood, West Los Angeles—it's only a half-hour ride."

"What about Mr. Eastland?" Jupe asked. "Does he stay here?"

"He can. He has his own trailer out there, and one apiece for the two stars, Rock Randall and Sue Stone. Uncle Jim rented them all of Jungle Land so they can stay if they want to. The gate is open and they come and go as they please. I don't check and neither does Jim."

"But they could be here," Jupe said stubbornly. "They could be snooping around your house at night and making George nervous."

"Why would they be doing that, Jupe?" asked Bob.

"I can't think of any sensible reason, Bob," he said. "All I say is the possibility exists."

"Let's get on with the tour, fellows," said Mike. "Come on down to the fence and then we'll circle around to the other side of the house."

As the boys approached the fence, the strange sounds from the scrap yard began again. The rhythmical crunching, grinding noises ebbed and then the wailing sound started. This time the boys were expecting the almost human shriek of the mechanism and remained calm.

"Happy metal shredding!" Bob said, holding his ears. "I'm surprised *all* your animals aren't a nervous wreck!"

Jupe looked at the fence gleaming in the moonlight. Metal stakes were pegged into the ground several yards apart, supporting a netting of wire links.

"Does this fence run all the way along your property line, Mike?" he asked.

"Yes," Mike said. "It continues north past the salvage yard. Then there's a big drainage ditch behind it which runs parallel the rest of the way. The fence is six feet high all the way, like it is here, and is strong enough to keep practically all our animals from escaping if they should happen to get loose."

The boys continued north along the fence and then began to cut back up the hill through trees and tall grass. Suddenly Pete stopped.

"What's up, Pete?" Bob said.

The tall boy pointed unsteadily ahead.

"Did you hear that?" Pete whispered.

The sounds from the salvage yard had ceased for the moment, and the boys all stood still, listening hard.

"Where, Pete?" asked Jupe. "What is it?"

Pete pointed again. "There."

They heard a rustling sound in the tall grass and then heavy breathing.

"*There!*" Pete whispered hoarsely again.

The others followed the line of his keen sight. As they stared into the jungle darkness, they saw a shadowy movement.

They froze, scarcely daring to breathe.

Something moved from behind a tree.

It came forward, moving in a peculiar way. Then they saw the dark head, swaying between hunched, shaggy shoulders.

Jim Hall had told them they would be in no particular danger. Somehow they could not believe it as the panting gorilla came closer!

Noises in the Night

12

Jupiter recovered his senses first.

"Run!" the stocky leader of The Three Investigators shouted. "Ramble and scramble!"

The three turned and ran. Mike hesitated, torn between flight and duty. He stared a moment longer at the oncoming gorilla. Red-rimmed eyes glowered at him from beneath the shaggy, beetling brows.

Jupe, glancing back, saw the situation. "Run, Mike! He might be dangerous now!"

The creature raised its long arms and bared yellow teeth. Mike, with a sharp intake of breath, wavered, then broke and ran to join the others.

The gorilla pounded its chest, veered, and disappeared into the high grass.

"Where'd he go?" Bob called.

"He's in the grass. I think we scared him off," cried Mike. "Come on—I think we'd better head for the house."

Warily they circled the area, their hearts pounding. They were nearly at the crest of the incline when suddenly the grass parted in front of them. Too late, they saw the shaggy creature step out.

The boys stood frozen with fear. The hulking creature raised its heavy arms and opened its mouth. A strange sound issued from its throat.

"Hit the ground!" a voice called sharply.

As the boys dived to the side, they heard a dull, thudding sound. They looked up to see Jim Hall and the vet with his stun gun raised.

The gorilla swayed, a puzzled look on its dark face. Then it moaned and toppled heavily to the ground.

"You boys all right?" Hall asked. They nodded dumbly, still shaken. "Nice shooting, Doc," he said.

The vet nodded without changing expression. He walked up quickly and stood over the fallen gorilla as it feebly moved its limbs.

"He's not hurt," he told the boys as they crowded around. "It just takes a few seconds for the tranquilizing drug to take effect. Then he'll have a nice long sleep and we'll be able to get him back to his cage."

"Looks like we circled back in time," Jim Hall said, frowning. "Somebody sent us off on a wild goose chase to the canyon for nothing. He could have been hiding in the trees here all the time."

"Who told you the gorilla was in the canyon?" Jupe asked.

"Jay Eastland," Hall said tersely.

Doc Dawson leaned over the inert simian. "He's out already, Jim. Give me a hand and we can lug him to the car."

Hall stooped and deftly roped the gorilla. He and Doc dragged the unconscious animal off. The boys followed as the two men hoisted it into the rear of the open jeep.

"Where are you taking him now, Mr. Hall?" Jupe asked.

"Back to his cage. Let's hope he stays put this time."

"Uncle Jim," Mike put in, "Jupe noticed that one of the cage bars was missing. The ones next to it were bent, so that's how he got out."

Hall glanced keenly at Jupiter. "That's how it happened, all right. Sure looks like somebody is trying to sabotage us, doesn't it?"

"It would appear so, sir. But now I'm wondering how you can put the gorilla back into that cage and expect him to stay there."

"That's easy," Hall said. "There's a man at work now replacing the missing bar and straightening the bent ones."

The jeep nosed out along the trail and Jupiter and the others followed at a dogtrot. Workmen were busy at the gorilla's cage when they arrived at the house.

A large man with close-cropped hair turned to face them. His arms were thick and muscular, one of them heavily tattooed. He held a long hammer in one hamlike hand.

"She's all set now," he said to Jim Hall. He glanced at Doc Dawson. "Got him already? That was fast work, Doc."

Jim Hall strode forward to the cage and the burly helper stepped aside. Hall put his weight against the cage bars, gripping them tightly and jerking his body from side to side.

"Okay. That ought to hold him, Bo. Thanks." He turned to the jeep. "Better give us a hand here with Kong."

"Sure thing," the man said, tossing down his hammer.

"Hold it a second!" Doc Dawson said. "I want to check out that cage myself. I've got enough to do without running around day and night looking for lost animals."

The helper shrugged and grinned. "Sure, Doc. You want us to lock you up inside and then see if you can get out?"

"Very funny, Jenkins," Dawson snapped.

He came forward and picked up the heavy hammer. He slowly tapped each bar on the empty cage. He bent forward attentively as if he were listening for a flaw in the metal. Then he grabbed the bars in his strong, weatherbeaten hands, tugging and twisting, applying pressure from all sides.

"Satisfied?" Bo Jenkins asked.

"Seems okay," Doc Dawson growled. "Those bars stand up to me all right, but then I don't have the strength of a gorilla." He looked at Bo Jenkins coldly. "Reckon you don't either, Bo. But if you're taking Hank Morton's place here, you can't afford to make any mistakes!"

Jim Hall turned to Doc Dawson. "Bo is working out fine, Doc. You're the one who told me he could take Hank Morton's place and do a good job, and I'm satisfied so far. Why needle him?"

"Just want him to be on his toes, that's all," Dawson said gruffly. "We don't want any more accidents around here." He stepped back to look at the empty gorilla cage again, and shook his head. "Derned if I can figure out how that bar got removed. I'd better check the panther's cage too."

Carrying the hammer, he walked abruptly to the cage opposite. The black cat leaped to its feet, hissing and snarling. The vet walked around the cage striking each of the bars in turn.

"He appears to be checking for a metal fault," Jupe said to his friends. "I've heard of something called metal fatigue. Airplane parts are checked for that periodically."

"With a hammer?" Bob asked.

Jupe shrugged. "Maybe Doc Dawson has his own

method of detection. After all, he spends a lot of time with caged animals."

After several ringing blows, Doc Dawson stepped back and nodded as if satisfied. "Okay, Jim," he said. "Far as I can tell, the bars check out with equal resistance. No cracks or fissures, and they're all securely in place. I guess you can put the gorilla back in now."

Jim Hall signaled the work crew, who lifted the still slumbering gorilla into its cage. Hall slipped the ropes off, swung the cage door shut, and padlocked it.

Doc Dawson stepped into his jeep. "Looks like you're all set now, Jim. I've got a sick horse to look after at the corral. If you need me again, just holler."

"Let's hope I don't, for a while, Doc. Thanks again for your help."

"Put it on the bill!" Dawson yelled. He waved and drove off.

Bob nudged Jupiter. "More fun coming," he whispered. "Here comes Jay Eastland."

The long station wagon roared up and the fat, bald-headed producer jumped out. Hall's lips tightened.

Eastland strode up quickly and peered into the gorilla cage. "So you got him finally, eh? Sure took you long enough, Hall. You had my crew scared out of their wits!"

"Yes, we got him," Jim Hall said slowly. "We might have caught up with him sooner, but somebody gave us a wrong tip. It turned out he wasn't in the canyon area at all but right around here, down by the fence."

The producer shrugged. "So what? I heard he was seen near the canyon and passed the word on to you." His voice rose. "How do you expect me to shoot a movie if you can't keep your wild animals under lock and key? My actors are worried sick that any moment they're going to be attacked by another one you let get away!"

"I'm sorry, Eastland," Hall said quietly. "We've had a few accidents, but nothing serious has happened. Everything's fine now and under control. You can tell your actors not to worry. Go on back and shoot your movie and leave us alone. You're only getting my animals stirred up and excited."

Eastland's face turned a mottled red. He backed up a few steps and shook his fist. "Don't tell me what to do, Hall. I've rented this place and—"

Suddenly there was an ear-splitting snarl from behind him. Eastland turned in alarm. The black panther leaped forward, and Eastland screamed in terror as the big cat crashed against its cage bars and fell back snarling.

The producer looked ill. His face was white and his eyes rolled. Then he noticed Jupiter and his friends watching.

"What are these kids doing here?" he barked. "What are you running—a sideshow?"

"They're here at my invitation, Eastland," said Jim Hall. "They've a job to do for me here. Now, is anything else bothering you?"

Eastland glowered. His chest rose and fell quickly. "Just make sure your animals don't get loose again, or you'll be sorry!"

Head down, he stomped away.

As the station wagon roared off, Jupe looked after it, puzzled. "That man certainly doesn't act like a movie producer, Pete. He acts—well—very unstable!"

Pete smiled. "He's what they call a 'quickie' producer in the trade, Jupe. They're hustlers, only interested in grinding out something fast and getting their money back even faster. If you ask me, Mr. Eastland has money problems. So what he does is holler and bully and bluster."

"Speaking of noise," said Jupe, "we haven't heard the metal shredder for a while. Let's go back to the fence. I want to have another look around down there before we leave."

"I'd go with you, Jupe, but I've a lot of chores to do around here yet," Mike said. "I'll have to say goodnight."

Jupe glanced at his watch. "We'll have a quick look. And we'll try to come back tomorrow to continue our investigation."

With that, the stocky boy headed away from the house into the darkness. Pete and Bob shrugged and slowly followed.

"Here goes," Bob said. "We're off to test the sound barrier again. Remind me next time to bring along ear-muffs."

"Remind me next time to stay home," Pete said. "I've had enough excitement tonight with that gorilla chasing us."

They walked down the slope and soon overhauled Jupiter. He was crouching behind a tree near the bottom.

"What—" began Pete, stopping when Jupe held up his hand.

Putting his finger to his lips, Jupe motioned them toward him. Quietly they stooped and scuttled over.

The metal shredder was quiet, but something else wasn't. They heard a dull thud, then a clanking noise. Then a crackling sound.

"In the salvage yard," Jupe whispered. "There's a man there. Tell me if he looks familiar."

Pete and Bob peered intently through the fence into

the moonlit yard. Suddenly there was a flare as a man struck a match and held it to a cigarette. His sharp features were clearly seen.

"Hatchet-Face!" Pete whispered. "The man who came to the junkyard!"

"That's him, all right," Bob whispered. "He said his name was Olsen, didn't he? What's he doing here?"

"Listen," Jupe said.

They heard a crackling, sputtering sound.

The hatchet-faced man hunched over. Something dark glittered in his hand. His lips moved.

Again there was the sputtering sound.

"Walkie-talkie," Jupe said. "Hatchet-face is transmitting!"

Pursued!

13

"Come on," said Jupiter, "I want to hear this."

He pointed diagonally ahead to a clump of eucalyptus trees right by the fence. Their low-hanging branches would give good cover if the boys could get under them unobserved. Cautiously Jupiter wriggled forward, practically on his stomach. Pete and Bob slithered after him. Soon they were safely under the trees, enveloped by darkness and the oily, medicinal smell of the eucalyptus leaves. The boys peered out and found themselves staring at Olsen barely twenty feet away.

A metallic sputter came from Olsen's walkie-talkie. He bent to speak into it, and this time the boys could hear him clearly.

"Come on over this way," Hatchet-Face ordered.

His walkie-talkie crackled. "Okay," came the answer.

A dark figure was making his way slowly across the huge, disorderly pile of scrap. He held a walkie-talkie, too, with its long antenna extended.

The hatchet-faced man spoke. "Any luck yet, Dobbsie?"

The other shook his head as he slowly advanced, peering closely at the scrap metal under his feet. "Not a thing," he said, his voice filtering through Olsen's walkie-talkie.

"Stay with it," Hatchet-Face said. "It could be buried."

Olsen stooped and tossed an old fender aside. It fell with a dull clank. He repeated the action with a bumper and a radiator grill, scrutinized the area closely, and shook his head.

The other man drew closer, also lifting and discarding objects in his path. At last he came close enough to join Olsen. He was dressed like Olsen, in a dark business suit.

Both men pushed down their walkie-talkie antennas. "It's like looking for a needle in a haystack," the other man complained wearily.

"I know," Hatchet-Face said. "But we can't take the risk of losing it now. It's too big a haul to let get away."

"What about the other place?"

"The junkyard? Probably clean, but we'll have to keep an eye on it. The fat kid may be wise to something. We'll get back to him later."

Jupe and his companions exchanged glances. He was the only fat kid they knew of connected with a junkyard. Jupe swallowed. He didn't like being called fat. And he liked even less the threat in Olsen's last words.

The other grinned. His face was square and pale, centered by a flat, mashed nose under little beady eyes. "What about the two new ones Hall just got in? Shouldn't we go for those?"

Olsen shook his head. He reached into his pocket for a scrap of paper and looked closely at it. "Not yet. It would be too risky and our birds might fly away." He tapped the paper. "The information we got from Dora's alarm spells it out for us. DOX ROX NOX EX REX BOX. Six X's. It could be the cable code or else they're talking about six hundred K's. That's about half a million bucks, Dobbsie—not bad, at all. That's a lot of rocks."

The beady-eyed man shrugged. "Sure it is, and we might blow the whole deal by waiting. Why don't we just move in on him?"

Hatchet-Face replaced the paper in his pocket. "We wait," he said firmly. "He'll give us an opening. Somebody got careless tonight. If we can find the rocks first, we'll wrap them both up."

"Okay. You're running the show."

"You bet. I'm going up now to find out if Eastland has his finger in this. He's hurting for money and maybe he let the gorilla out for his own reasons. Remember, he'd have Hall on the hook for fifty grand if anything were to happen."

The other grinned and smacked his fists together. "I'd like a crack at Eastland. He ran me off the set."

Hatchet-Face laughed. "He won't bother me. Okay, Dobbsie, we check tomorrow same time."

Olsen waved abruptly and turned away. The other moved off in the opposite direction, across the salvage yard.

Pete nudged Jupe and pointed along the wire fence. The section toward which Olsen was heading had been tampered with. Where earlier it had been erect, it now sagged nearly to the ground.

As they watched, the hatchet-faced man carefully stepped over the lowered wire. He found a metal post and pulled it up straight, raising the wire along with it. That done, he wheeled, dusted his hands, and headed up the slope in the direction of the Hall house. Darkness covered him as he moved into the jungle. His footsteps could be heard for a while longer, and then they faded into silence.

The Three Investigators waited and then slowly got to their feet. The salvage yard was quiet, as if closed down for the night. The beady-eyed man had disappeared from view, too. The boys started back up the hill.

Pete suddenly hissed a warning and they froze.

They heard a stealthy movement in the grass and, as their pulses quickened, the sound of soft footsteps. Peering into the darkness of the jungle, they backed off uncertainly.

A thick, shadowy shape detached itself from a tree and stepped toward them. With hearts leaping, the boys turned and ran. A hidden root caught Jupe's foot and he fell heavily to the ground. His hand struck something hard and cold. He heard a growl behind him and grasped the hard object as he jumped to his feet. It was a length of metal pipe.

Pete grabbed Jupiter's arm and started to pull him along. There was an angry bellow from the darkness, and they were suddenly caught in the gleam of a flashlight.

Heavy footsteps crashed through the undergrowth. Still holding on to his weapon, Jupe fled, propelled by Pete. Bob was just ahead of them, his feet flying across the slope. He lost his footing and as he fell, Jupe and Pete charged into him, carrying him up and along.

The flash beam stabbed at them again, and they heard a harsh voice yelling for them to stop. Instead, they ran faster.

Panting noisily, following Pete's unerring sense of direction, the boys cut across the hillside. They burst out of the jungle onto the road to the Hall house. Just ahead was the gleaming Rolls-Royce. As they ran for it, its headlights flicked on.

Jupiter flung the door open and threw himself inside. "Quick! Step on it, Worthington!"

Bob and Pete tumbled in beside him as the tall

chauffeur calmly answered, "Very good, Master Jones." The motor was already purring smoothly, and deftly he wheeled the big car around.

As they headed back for the exit gate, a man broke out of the jungle and leaped for the car. Worthington swerved instantly, and they had a brief glance at the contorted face of the man. He raised his fist and ran after them.

"Wow!" breathed Pete. "That's Bo Jenkins, the new animal helper."

Looking rearward through the glass, they saw Jenkins stop and shake his huge fist in a threatening gesture. It carried so much menace that they instinctively slumped low in the back seat of the car, although they were already safely away from their pursuer.

Pete jumped out as Worthington slowed for the gate. He opened it, and after the car glided through, swung it closed again. Then Pete leaped back in and sat back, slowly shaking his head.

"What was that all about?" he asked.

Jupe had no reply. He could only scowl, puzzled, as he gripped the weapon he had not used.

Pete, Bob, and Jupiter stood by the gates to The Jones Salvage Yard. Worthington had brought them back safely and had been thanked and dismissed.

"It's late," Jupiter said, "but I suggest we have a quick meeting. We have to put down what happened this evening between that man Olsen and the other, Dobbsie. It might contain clues we will need for solving this mystery."

He led the way swiftly into Headquarters, tossing the metal bar he had found at Jungle Land onto his workbench before stooping to enter Tunnel Two. Inside the boys clustered around the office desk, and Bob drew out his notebook.

"I take it we can skip the last part with that big guy Jenkins chasing us," said Bob. "There wasn't any mystery about that—he was just plain mad."

"We'll omit Bo Jenkins for the time being," Jupe agreed. "I imagine he was merely patrolling the property. Perhaps he was within his rights to chase off trespassers who might disturb the animals."

"I don't know about that," Pete protested. "We weren't exactly strangers there. He saw us earlier at the cage when Mr. Hall and Doc Dawson brought the escaped gorilla back. He could have acted a lot nicer about it, if you want my opinion."

"True," Jupe said, "but it was dark. Perhaps he didn't see us clearly, and thought we were just some kids who had broken in. I'm inclined to give Bo Jenkins the benefit of the doubt. I suggest we ignore him and get to the discussion between Mr. Olsen and Mr. Dobbsie."

While Bob scribbled furiously, the boys reconstructed the conversation they had overheard and discussed what it might mean.

"What could be right under their feet?" asked Bob.

"It must be small," Pete said. "Because he also said it was like looking for a needle in a haystack."

"Not necessarily small," Jupe said. "It would be difficult to find something that looked like all the other junk in that heap."

"Like what?" asked Bob.

"I don't know," Jupe said. "But we have clues. Read back that part about rocks and X's, Bob."

"Okay," Bob said. "It went something like this: 'The

information from Dora's alarm tells us. DOX ROX NOX EX REX BOX.' I assume all those words end in X because of the next bit. 'Six X's. Could be the code or six hundred K's. That's half a million bucks, Dobbsie. That's a lot of rocks.' "

"More or less correct, I believe," said Jupe. "Olsen also used the word 'cable.' We don't know who Dora is or what her alarm is, but Dora's message sounds like a cable. It's typical of what is called cablese—all the words are short and only important words are included. And, like many cables, this one seems to be in code. As a rule, parties who want to keep their business transactions secret establish a private code or cipher. Usually there's a key letter or word that lets them decipher each other's messages easily."

"Well, we don't have the key to the code," said Pete.

"I don't think we need one," said Jupe. "All those words probably end in X, as Bob said. But most of those words translate easily into plain English. The message can be read DOCKS ROCKS KNOCKS EX WRECKS BOX." He printed the decoded message for them on Bob's pad.

"Great," said Pete. "What's that supposed to mean?"

"I'm not sure," said Jupe, "but I'm getting an idea." He straightened up excitedly. "I think ROCKS is the important word. Olsen said something was half a million bucks, and then he said that was a lot of rocks. Does that suggest anything to you?"

"Half a million bucks worth of rocks?" asked Pete. "Rocks out of the ground? How's that possible? I mean, who'd want it?"

" 'Rocks' has another meaning, Pete," Jupe said. "It's also slang for 'money.' Olsen and Dobbsie are looking for money! Half a million dollars! My guess is that

Olsen and Dobbsie are involved in some crooked scheme. They sound like gangsters, and that much money sounds like somebody's loot!"

"That's quite a guess," said Bob dubiously. "But even if that's true, what's the rest of the message supposed to mean?"

Jupe frowned. "I don't know, Bob. Apparently it tells where to find the money. Maybe the rest of the conversation will give us some clues."

"What about that part about wrapping them both up?" Pete asked. "Who's he talking about?"

Bob read from his notes. " 'If we can find the rocks first, we'll wrap them both up.' "

Jupe shook his head. "They spoke about one man first. They said, 'Why don't we move in on him?' Then later Hatchet-Face said, 'He'll give us an opening. Somebody got careless tonight.' "

"Who?" asked Pete.

Bob looked over his notes. "If being careless refers to letting the gorilla out, they think Eastland might have done it."

Jupe scowled. "I don't see why he would take such a risk. It's true that according to the agreement Jim Hall would have to pay Eastland fifty thousand dollars as forfeit for an accident. But I don't think Eastland would be foolish enough to take such a chance. That gorilla was dangerous! I'd sooner believe that Hank Morton was being spiteful again."

"Fine, but that has nothing to do with rocks," said Bob. "We're not getting anywhere."

Jupe tapped his fingers on the desk and thought awhile. "We're forgetting the first thing we ever learned about Olsen," he said finally. "He came here to the junkyard and wanted to buy cages. Then tonight he seemed to refer to me and the cages." Jupe winced as he remembered Olsen's calling him "the fat kid."

"Maybe he thinks he'll find his rocks in cages," said Pete sarcastically.

"Don't laugh," said Jupe. "Look! BOX in the cable might mean cage! WRECKS BOX means pull apart the cage and you'll find the money!"

"Your cages are already wrecked," objected Pete, "and Olsen didn't seem to think they were very valuable. He only offered you twenty dollars."

"True, true," said Jupe. "I can't explain that. But perhaps Olsen's really looking for another cage."

"Sure. In the scrap yard. Blending right in with the cars," said Pete. "I think we're all tired and just going around in circles."

Jupe stood up and stretched. "You're probably right, Pete. I suggest we quit for tonight. We haven't come to any definite conclusions—but at least we're sure of one thing."

"What's that?" asked Bob.

"We've got a mystery to solve," said Jupe with satisfaction.

Bob Makes a Discovery

14

The next morning Bob came downstairs to breakfast more puzzled than ever. So much had happened the day before, and so little of it made any sense. He wondered if Jupiter wasn't grasping at straws in deducing the meaning of that crazy code.

Bob said good morning to his father, who grunted a reply from behind the morning newspaper. He was still on his first cup of coffee and obviously wasn't ready to talk to anyone yet. Bob looked around for something to read himself. He had read all the cereal boxes, so he turned to the stack of out-of-town newspapers lying on a nearby bookcase. His father, a newspaperman, frequently brought home papers from other parts of the country. He had explained to Bob that no one newspaper could carry all the news, and that he liked to see what stories other papers considered newsworthy.

Bob leafed idly through a paper, reading the comics and checking the headlines. He picked up another, and an article caught his eye. It was a UPI dispatch from Koster, South Africa. It read:

79-YEAR-OLD OPENS
AFRICA DIAMOND RUSH

With a whoop belying his 79 years, Pieter

Bester leaped into the air, snatched his claim certificate, and took off running.

While 3,000 spectators cheered, he opened what could be the last official South African diamond rush, as 165 prospectors were turned loose Wednesday on the Swartrand alluvial diamond field.

Veteran prospector Hendrik Swanpoel, 72, who discovered the diamond field, had his usual luck. While staking out the first of his claims on the site, he unearthed a 48.12-carat diamond which he sold later for $42,000.

"I don't want to discourage anybody," Swanpoel said with a grin, "but I've already got most of the good stuff."

The article went on to detail the government-sponsored diamond rush. The region was 75 miles northwest of Johannesburg, once known as the "Land of the Diamonds." In the uproarious boom days of 1927 and 1928, the article continued, 150,000 diggers scooped $28 million worth of high-quality gems from the Grasfontein and Bakerville diggings 50 miles west. The rules were, hopeful prospectors had their names put into a hat, and only the lucky ones whose names were drawn were permitted to the starting line. Each one was allowed three 45-square-yard claims. Veterans of earlier rushes hired local athletes for the sprint, or after careful coaching, had their sons run for them.

"Whiskers!" breathed Bob. "Forty-two thousand dollars for one diamond! That's a lot of money!"

He turned the page and another news item caught his eye.

MAN INDICTED IN GEM CASE

Porto Ferraro, a former assistant to the Minister of Mines in Koster, South Africa, was indicted by a federal grand jury Tuesday on charges of smuggling diamonds into the United States last year. He was arrested at Los Angeles International Airport.

Customs agents found on his person five packages of cut and polished diamonds weighing a total of 659.14 carats, with a retail value of about $750,000. The two-count indictment charges Ferraro with smuggling and with failing to pay duty. Each count carries a possible sentence of two years in jail and a fine of $5000.

"Wow!" said Bob. He'd never known diamonds were worth that much money.

"What's that?" said his father, putting down his newspaper and taking a sip of coffee.

"I was just reading about diamonds," explained Bob. "It says here that a 48-carat diamond sold for $42,000. That's a lot of money! What is a carat, anyway?"

"Well, it's a unit of weight used for gem stones. It's divided into 100 points, just the way a dollar is divided into 100 cents. A one-point diamond is very small. A 100-point, or one carat, diamond is a pretty good size."

"How big would that 48-carat diamond be, then?"

"Very large, for a diamond. Let's see, there was a famous Indian diamond called The Sancy. It was about the size and shape of a peach pit and weighed 55 carats. Your 48-carat diamond would be slightly smaller."

"How much would that weigh in pounds and ounces?"

"Here"—Mr. Andrews pulled a reference book out of the bookcase and handed it to Bob—"look up the table of weights and measures in this and see if you can figure it out."

Bob read that a carat was equal to 3.17 grains troy or .2 of a gram. A gram, the basic unit of weight in the metric system, equalled one twenty-eighth ounce. He scribbled some figures in his notebook and looked up in astonishment. "Forty-eight carats are only about one-third of an ounce."

His father nodded. "Yes, a carat is a very small unit of weight. You need a system with units that small when you're measuring such valuable things."

"Okay, how much is a carat worth?"

"No fixed amount. But for a diamond, you can figure roughly about a thousand dollars to a carat, depending upon the quality and brilliance of the stone. That 48-carat diamond sold for $42,000, you said. The gem was therefore not quite perfect, or a lot was lost in cutting."

"Cutting?"

Mr. Andrews nodded. "Size and quality are important, but you can't evaluate a diamond until it's been cut into its usual 58 facets, and polished. Sometimes a lot is lost in the cutting process. You see, Bob, those found in diamond fields or mines are very rough stones, looking like ordinary rocks or pebbles—"

"Whiskers!" Bob cried. "Excuse me, Dad! Thanks a lot—but I've got to make a phone call!"

Mr. Andrews smiled as his son dashed off for the phone. He was used to these abrupt endings to their conversations.

Bob quickly called Jupiter. "Hey, Jupe, did you know

that uncut diamonds look like ordinary little rocks?" He went on to report what he'd learned from the newspaper and his father. "So maybe Olsen really is after rocks— diamonds!"

"Of course, of course!" said Jupiter. " 'Rocks' is also slang for 'jewels.' " Jupiter was silent for a moment. "Good work, Records. Your information fits in very nicely with some further deductions I made this morning.

"Now, can you come right over here? Mike Hall called. George is acting a scene for Jay Eastland today and he'd like us to be there."

"Sure," said Bob, "but I thought you had to work today."

"Uncle Titus decided to stay home and work in the yard, so I'm not needed. Which is just as well. I have a strong feeling that things will continue to go wrong at Jungle Land until we solve its mystery. Meet me in Headquarters as soon as you can. Pete is already on his way."

"Konrad has offered to take us to Jungle Land today," Jupe was saying. "We've only a few minutes to discuss a serious problem that has come up. If my conclusions are correct, it may direct our actions when we get there."

Bob looked at Pete, mystified, "What's going on?"

Pete shrugged.

Jupiter announced importantly, "On the basis of Bob's new information and my own deductions, I believe that the Hall brothers are involved in a smuggling racket!"

"What?" Bob protested.

Jupiter continued, "Cal Hall is shipping animals to

his brother here. I think that under cover of those ship-ments he's also smuggling diamonds out of Africa."

Bob turned to Jupe. "But diamonds come from South Africa, and Cal Hall is operating in Central Africa. Aren't those two places a long way apart?"

"Mike told us that Cal Hall was in Rwanda for the mountain gorilla," Jupe said. "But for his kind of work, he would travel all over Africa. And there are a lot of other countries in Africa besides South Africa that pro-duce diamonds. The Congo, Ghana, the Ivory Coast, Liberia, Sierra Leone, the Republic of Central Africa—all export diamonds."

He picked an atlas off a shelf and turned to a page showing Africa. "Here's a country in East Africa, not far from Rwanda. It used to be Tanganyika. See it? Right near Uganda and Kenya. It's called Tanzania now. It has diamond mines, too. Also, according to this atlas, the most abundant wild life is in East Africa. Cal has to get to the east coast to ship his animals, and he would naturally pass through Tanzania. If you note, there's a big coastal city. That's the capital, Dar es Sa-laam."

Pete whistled. "That sounds familiar. Get out your notes, Bob."

Bob whipped out his notebook and flipped to the page of the night before. " 'The information from Dora's alarm tells us,' " he read. He whistled. "Dora's alarm—Dar es Salaam—they sound pretty much the same."

"We don't yet know why Olsen should have that cable message," Jupe said. "But obviously Cal Hall sent it to his brother from the point of shipment, to let him know the diamonds were coming."

His eyes gleamed. "The first word of the cable makes sense now. DOX, spelled d-o-c-k-s, refers to a landing pier for ships. The diamonds and the animals are being shipped from the docks."

Bob printed out the two forms of the cable message on a clean piece of paper.

DOX ROX NOX EX REX BOX
DOCKS ROCKS KNOCKS EX WRECKS BOX

"We now think ROCKS means diamonds, and you think WRECKS BOX means to pull apart the cage," Bob said. "What about the other words?"

"I haven't figured out the third and fourth words yet," Jupe admitted. "But I think I was also incorrect about WRECKS. We should have left it as R-E-X, because that way everything falls into place!"

He paused significantly.

"C'mon, Jupe!" said Pete. "Out with it!"

"Rex is the Latin word for king. The lion is the king of beasts. REX BOX could mean, in this instance, George's cage! And George was shipped from Africa. I would say the message conclusively refers to smuggling diamonds into this country along with George and his cage. And, furthermore, I think the diamonds have become lost somehow, and whoever is looking for them is coming around too often—and making George nervous!"

Pete nodded. "Even an ordinary watchdog would be acting up if strangers were walking around at night near his house."

"But Jim Hall is no stranger," Bob protested. "And according to Jupe, he's part of the smuggling team."

"No, Jim Hall wouldn't make George nervous. It would have to be somebody else."

"Jay Eastland?" said Pete. "He'd get anybody upset."

"Well, I suppose he's a possibility," said Jupe. "But I can't see any connection at this point."

Pete snapped his fingers. "Hank Morton! I bet he's involved! Remember, he might have let George out the other day. He could have done it so that he could get a look at George's cage."

"You're forgetting George doesn't have his cage any more," said Jupe. "Remember Mike told us they got rid of it, and Jim allowed George to live in their house."

"What about Olsen and Dobbsie?" Bob asked. "Where do they fit in? They seem to know what they're looking for, and even where to look for it."

"Olsen and Dobbsie are definite suspects," Jupe said firmly. "They could be part of Jim's gang."

"Why are they looking in the scrap yard then?" Pete demanded.

"The diamonds could be lost there," Jupe said. "Remember what the man said—it was like looking for a needle in a haystack."

Bob flipped through his notes again and read, " 'They lost it and we'll wrap them up when we find it.' How do you explain that last part, Jupe? It doesn't sound like they're working with the Halls."

Jupe pondered. "I'd forgotten that part. According to that, Olsen and Dobbsie are against Cal Hall and Jim. The term 'wrap them up' suggests a threat, to me. Maybe Olsen and Dobbsie broke with the Hall brothers and are now trying to hijack the diamonds. Or perhaps they're a rival gang with no connection to the Halls."

"Whiskers!" Bob said. "It all sounds complicated. I

wonder if Mike knows anything about this."

"I doubt it," said Jupe. "And we must be careful not to accuse his uncle Jim, whom he idolizes, or his uncle Cal, until we've made absolutely sure. Agreed?"

Bob and Pete nodded. Jupe got up and stretched.

"All right then. Konrad is waiting for us outside. Perhaps this trip will be the one in which we unravel the mystery at Jungle Land."

They walked to the exit glumly. They enjoyed solving mysteries, but solving this one seemed to entail making several people unhappy. Jupe bit his lip. He wondered how he would ever break the news to young Mike Hall.

Black Death

15

Mike was waiting for The Three Investigators at his house when Konrad dropped them off. He guided them along a trail that served as a short cut to the location of the Jay Eastland movie set. It was a natural jungle setting, a flat clearing bordered by giant trees and thick undergrowth. Large rocks were scattered on the north side at the foot of a short but steep cliff. A ledge jutted out of the cliff a little way above the ground.

The movie set hummed with activity. The work crew was busy setting up cables and tall reflectors for the lights, which were set in huge iron tripods. Eastland was to one side, talking to a group of actors and checking their various positions while a few men pushed the camera into range.

Bob took in the bustling workers. "Have they started yet?"

Mike shook his head. "It's been overcast all morning. But the sun's coming out now and they'll start shooting any minute. George is in the first scene."

"Did he have a peaceful night?" Jupe asked. "Or was he nervous again?"

"He slept fine," Mike said. "He conked right out after Doc Dawson gave him the tranquilizer. A good thing, too, because that panther made a ruckus half the night."

"Oh, no," groaned Pete. "Don't tell me we have another mystery—a nervous panther!"

"I don't think so, Pete. He just needs to calm down from his trip and adjust to life here."

"How's George's wound, Mike?" asked Bob.

"Just about healed. You can barely even notice where he was cut."

Mike pointed to the edge of the set. Jim Hall stood alone with the big lion at his side. He saw them and waved them over. The Three Investigators walked up, cautiously watching George. The tawny beast sat quietly, its yellow eyes staring into the distance. Its long tail flicked as Hall rubbed its ears.

"Glad you could make it, boys," Jim Hall said. "As you can see, George is in great shape today. We've rehearsed his scene several times already, and he knows exactly what he's supposed to do." He glanced toward the busy producer-director. "I hope Eastland gets going soon while George is still nice and relaxed."

The big lion yawned, exposing long ivory teeth. A dull rumbling sound came from its throat.

As The Three Investigators looked up apprehensively, Jim Hall smiled. "He's purring, boys. That's a good sign. It means George is in a happy mood." He looked impatiently toward Eastland. "Come on, let's go," he muttered.

The fat producer moved across the set toward the cliff, giving instructions in a loud, fretting voice. "Over here with the camera," he ordered.

Eastland looked at a sheaf of notes. "We'll need to be on our toes for this scene. It's a quickie but we want to get it right the first time, understand?"

"No retakes makes it cheaper," Pete whispered in Jupe's ear.

Eastland waved an actress and an actor over. "Miss

Stone, you and Rock Randall stand here." He pointed below the overhanging ledge. "The lion will be up on the ledge, looking down. You two will have a scuffle. When Randall has his back to the ledge, the lion jumps on him. Is that clear? Any questions, Sue? No? You, Rock? All right, then."

Eastland turned to the cameraman. "You hold on the scene as George jumps. Randall will try to fight him off, and they'll wrestle a few feet. Then Randall slumps to the ground, the lion paws him, and it's all over.

"We cut then to the next scene, which gives Hall a chance to come in and get his lion calmed down while we prepare the next setup with Sue. Hopefully, there won't be any trouble."

Jim Hall flushed. "George understands what he's to do, Eastland. Just make sure Randall slumps to the ground and doesn't try to get up. If he does, George will knock him down again. There won't be any accidents."

The producer nodded with a smirk. "We all hope not." He turned to the actor. "I hope you've kept up your insurance policies, Rock."

The actor looked pale and frightened. "Come on, Jay. Cut the comedy."

He moved nervously away and lit a cigarette.

"Rock Randall looks awfully anxious," Jupe whispered to his friends. "And Eastland isn't helping him any by suggesting he can't trust George."

Pete looked at the big lion sitting placidly near its owner. "I don't blame Randall for looking nervous," he said. "How can you expect to be jumped by a big lion and not be nervous?"

"But he's trained," Mike said. "George won't hurt anybody. He'll only be pretending."

"I thought Rock Randall was in a fight yesterday," said Bob. "He doesn't look it."

"Make-up," said Pete knowledgeably.

Eastland walked across to the actress. "We'll shoot your scene with George right after that one, Sue. You'll be asleep in your tent. George pokes his head in the opening and goes in. He's just curious but you see him and wake up and scream. He opens his mouth and roars. That's it. Okay? You don't do anything silly like jumping out and hitting him. You just sit up, pull the covers up, and scream. You got it?"

The actress put her hand to her throat. "I've never worked with a lion before, Mr. Eastland. Are you sure he's safe?"

Eastland smiled. He took a folded paper from his pocket and waved it. "That's what Jim Hall, his owner and trainer, says. I've got the guarantee down here in black and white."

The actress turned away, visibly upset.

Pete touched Jupe's shoulder and glanced away. Following his gaze, Jupe saw the hatchet-faced man looking on from the edge of the set. He leaned forward to Mike. "That man over there, Mike—do you know him?"

"The thin-faced man—yeah—his name is Dunlop. He does some kind of work for Mr. Eastland."

"Dunlop? Are you sure? Not Olsen?"

"It's Dunlop, all right. I've heard Eastland calling him that. I think he's some kind of technical expert on firearms."

Jupe glanced at Pete and Bob to see if they had overheard. They nodded. The man now identified as Dunlop walked casually away without looking back. Jupe frowned. He remembered that the night before the hatchet-faced man had threatened to return to The Jones Salvage Yard. Learning he was an expert on firearms made Jupe even less happy about it.

"How about Hank Morton?" Jupe asked. "Have you seen him around again?"

Mike grimaced. "He wouldn't dare to show his face around here again. We're just lucky Doc Dawson got George in shape so fast for today's shooting."

"Say, Mike," said Jupiter, "what ever happened to George's cage? Where did you get rid of it?"

"I don't know. I suppose it was thrown over the fence into the scrap yard. That's where we throw most of our junk, and that cage was pretty old. Why?"

"Just curious," said Jupe.

Eastland suddenly snapped his fingers at Jim Hall. "Okay, Hall. We're all set. Get your lion up there and ready for action."

Jim Hall nodded and tugged gently at George's ear. "Come on, boy," he said softly. "We're putting you to work."

With George at his heels, he walked to the big rock formation. He stopped, leaned down, whispered, snapped his fingers, and pointed up to the ledge. George obeyed instantly and bounded lithely to the top. The lion stood there a moment, looking down majestically. It looked every bit its role of lord of the jungle, and Jupe and his friends gazed up at the animal admiringly.

Jim Hall whistled softly and gestured with his hand. The lion made a purring sound, then looked off into the distance, its long tail flicking restlessly.

Rock Randall and Sue Stone took their positions beneath the ledge. Eastland nodded. A man leaped forward. "Ready for action," he shouted. "Quiet on the set."

As all eyes focused on the impending action, Jupe caught his companions' attention and jerked his head to the side. He moved off quietly. Bob and Pete hesitated a moment, and then reluctantly followed.

"You picked a fine time to leave the set," Pete muttered when they were out of sight of the movie company. "Just when we finally had a chance to watch George act."

Jupe shrugged. "George's act is what I am depending on. I hope he has everybody's attention. That gives us a chance to do some investigating on our own."

"Where?" asked Bob.

Jupe pointed ahead in the direction of Jim Hall's house. "Diamond country," he said.

Cautiously, the boys approached the white house. "The new cages are around the other side," Jupe whispered. "I want to look them over first. It's quite likely that other cages besides George's are used for smuggling. We'll have to move quietly and make certain that we're not observed."

Bob looked surprised. "Observed by whom, Jupe? Everybody was around the movie set."

"Not everybody," Jupe said mysteriously.

Following Jupiter's example, Bob and Pete waited at the corner of the Hall house, listening. Then, they quickly moved around to the side, crouching low under the windows.

The two cages were separated by the length of the house. They approached the first one and peered in. "We're in luck," Bob said. "The gorilla's asleep."

The dark, shaggy form was huddled in a corner.

"What's so great about it?" Pete asked. "Are we going into its cage to look for smuggled diamonds?"

Jupiter moved slowly around the cage, examining it closely. "If diamonds are being smuggled in with these cages from Africa, how would it be done? Creating a false top or bottom seems a logical way, doesn't it?"

"Well, yes—" Bob agreed. "But can you tell just by looking?"

"No, it wouldn't be that obvious. The outside of this cage looks normal, the usual wood-frame roofing over the bars. But that seems too easy to get at. I've an idea the inside would be the more likely place. But for us to examine that thoroughly, the gorilla would have to be out of its cage."

Pete sighed with relief. "Thank goodness! I was afraid you'd want us to get in there with him."

Jupiter had already turned away. "Let's check the panther's cage," the stocky boy murmured. "Possibly we can detect someth—" He stopped suddenly and caught his breath.

Bob turned, puzzled. "What's wrong, Jupe?"

"Stay still!" Jupe hissed. "Don't make any sudden moves, and don't run!"

"What's going on?" asked Pete.

"Look straight ahead," Jupe said shakily. "The black panther's cage is open—and he's not in it!"

The boys stared at the empty cage. Prickly chills went down their spines and turned their legs to jelly. Then, horrified, they heard the sound they were dreading. A savage, spitting snarl behind them!

Jupiter gulped. He stood at a slight angle from Bob and Pete, and his quick sideways glance was enough to shake him further.

"H-he's up in the tree about twenty-feet behind us," he whispered. "We may have to take a chance and separate. Now when I count three—"

Jupe's voice faltered as he saw the tall grass ahead of him ripple. He gasped as it parted and he caught the glint of a rifle barrel. Incredibly, he saw the rifle slowly rise.

A harsh voice directed, "Don't anybody move!"

The boys held their breath as a man stepped slowly out. They recognized the grizzled vet, Doc Dawson.

The gray eyes of the vet squinted. He took a slow step forward, his finger tightening on the trigger.

Suddenly there was an unearthly, ear-splitting scream behind them. In the same instant, the gun went off.

The boys ducked as a great, soaring shape smacked to the ground with a sickening thud a few feet past them. The black body twitched once and was still.

Doc Dawson stepped forward, looking both angry and discouraged. His dusty boot kicked at the long, outstretched claws of the panther.

"Lucky for all concerned I'm a pretty good shot," he said.

Pete let his breath out. "Is he—is he—?"

"Yep, he's dead as nails, sonny. That was a real bullet. Never thought I'd have to kill one of Jim's animals." The vet shook his head ruefully.

Jupe tried to take his eyes off the spreading red stain. "Thanks, Dr. Dawson," he said, swallowing hard. Then, "How did he get out?"

The vet shook his head. "It's my fault, I reckon. I needed to check him over, so I gave him a tranquilizing shot. I stepped away for a few minutes while I was waiting for the drug to take effect. Next thing I knew he was on his feet and out of his cage. For some reason, the

drug didn't work. I ran back to the jeep to get my gun—
the one I use for killer hawks."

"Do you think somebody let the panther out?" asked
Jupe.

"Who'd do a crazy fool thing like that?" countered
the vet. "Anybody who tried that'd likely get mauled.
No, I expect the cage door just wasn't locked properly."

"Might that drug you used have been tampered with?
Weakened somehow by somebody?"

The vet looked shrewdly at Jupiter. "It could have
happened that way, son. I leave my medical kit around
a lot. Never saw no reason to distrust anybody here."
He shook his head. "It sure beats me. Appears as if
somebody sure has it in for Jim Hall. The shame of it is
he's such a real nice fellow."

Pete leaned over the panther. "I guess you had to
shoot to kill then, didn't you?"

"That's right, son. That baby might look like an overgrown pussy cat to you boys, but take it from me he was
a real mean killer. If he'd got away, there's no telling
what might have happened." He cocked his head and
addressed the boys in a sharper tone. "What are you
boys doing up this way, anyhow? Jim told me you'd be
over at the movie set today watching George acting in
the movie."

"We were there," Jupe started lamely, "but then—we
thought we'd look around."

Dawson eyed Jupe and Bob and Pete in turn. "Jim
told me you fellers were investigators." He smiled
thinly. "Find out anything yet?"

Jupe shook his head. "No, sir. We're still confused."

"Can't say I blame you," the vet said. "Lots of confusing things happening around here lately. Things that

don't make no sense at all. Want to hear one of the most confusing things about it?"

The boys looked at him questioningly.

Doc Dawson put a small stogy in his mouth, spat, put a match to it, inhaled smoke, and spat again. Then he leveled the thin cigar at them. "I'll tell you, then," he said. "Every time you kids show up here, another animal breaks loose. Think it over. Am I right?"

The boys looked at one another.

Dawson broke the spell by laughing sourly. "I'm right," he said.

He kicked at the body of the black panther. "I'll be right back for this baby," he said. "In the meantime, boys, I got some good advice for you—"

"What's that, sir?" asked Bob.

"Watch yourselves at all times," the vet said curtly.

He turned on his heels and walked away. In a moment he had disappeared into the tall, waving grass.

Iron Bars

16

As soon as Doc Dawson walked away from the dead panther, Jupiter led the other investigators down the hill to the fence by the salvage yard. The boys looked over at the huge spread of scrap iron, covering several acres. Workmen could be seen here and there.

"What are we doing here?" Pete asked.

"We're looking for the smuggled diamonds," Jupe replied. "And we're looking for George's old cage."

"You think those diamonds are still in George's cage?" asked Bob.

"I doubt it," said Jupe. "That cage has been around a long time. But we might get some ideas if we could find it."

"But, Jupe," complained Pete, "if the diamonds aren't in the cage, what are they in? What do we look for? A little paper bag?"

Jupe scowled. "Frankly, Pete, I don't know what the diamonds would be in. I don't think Olsen or Dobbsie know either, or they would have found them by now."

"Olsen and Dobbsie looked all over this place last night and didn't find anything," said Bob. "What makes you think we'll have better luck?"

"It's daylight," said Jupe. "That should give us an advantage."

"Craziest thing I ever heard of," muttered Pete.

A workman who had been near the fence moved away, leaving the area clear. "Let's go," said Jupe.

The boys found the section of fence that had been pulled out of line the night before. It was an easy matter to loosen the metal upright again, and the wire netting with it. Seconds later, they had crawled into the middle of a junk pile that seemed to contain all the abandoned automobiles in the state.

Heavy clanking noises began on the other side of the salvage yard, punctuated by shrill whining sounds.

"Let's see how that metal shredder works," Jupe said.

He pointed to a huge crane. It was several hundred yards away, operating at the opposite end of the yard. As they watched, they saw a tiny figure in the crane-house shift a gear. There was a complaining whine. A huge metal claw came up from behind a mound holding an old car.

The operator shifted a lever and the cranehouse swiveled to one side. Whining, the metal claw swung over the assorted debris of the yard. It stopped, causing the car to sway dangerously, and then lowered abruptly. The claw opened and the car dropped, landing with a heavy clank. Immediately there was a whup-whup-whup sound and the car jolted crazily forward.

"Conveyor belt," Pete said, standing on a pile of junk. "It's taking the car right into that shed."

The conveyor belt was a series of flat cars moving forward in steady jerks. When the old car disappeared into the mouth of the shed, the belt halted temporarily.

There was a shrill, screaming sound from the shed, a rising whine that blasted the air and threatened their eardrums with its intensity.

"Metal shredder at work," observed Jupe.

"Ugh!" said Pete. "It sounds as if the car is being eaten alive!"

The crane had swiveled again. Once more the huge

claw rose in the air, swaying until it had seemingly found its prey. Then, with a whine, it pounced on another derelict car. Once more it fed the car into the shed.

Jupe turned away. "Okay. Now we know how it works. Let's get back to our own mystery."

The boys poked around for a while, without any luck.

"Maybe I'd do a better job if I knew what to look for," said Pete, kicking a piece of junk.

"Hold it, Pete," Jupe cried. "What's that?"

He ran over and picked it up carefully.

"It looks like a cage," Bob said. "Or maybe something that once was a cage."

"How can you call it a cage?" Pete demanded. "It doesn't have any bars. It looks like a broken old box."

"Perhaps the metal shredder has already processed it," said Jupe. "If you recall, the shredder selects metal from objects and discards the rest."

"Uh-Unh," Pete said as he dived off the pile. He came up grinning, holding a long, black iron bar. "That metal shredder is a fake," he said. "It can't tell iron from anything. What do you call this?"

Jupe was so pleased, he almost shouted with joy. "Good work, Pete! That might be what we're looking for. Let me see it, please."

Pete handed the bar over and Jupe promptly dropped it.

"Butterfingers!" Pete scoffed.

"No, I didn't expect—" Jupe bent to pick up the bar again. "That's odd," he said. "It feels heavy."

"Of course it's heavy," Pete said. "Why do you think I was complaining the other day when we had to unload a ton of these from your uncle's truck?"

Jupe stared down at the bar, his eyes gleaming

thoughtfully. "I didn't notice. I'm certain the other one I had was—"

He stopped, his mouth open.

"What's wrong, Jupe?" asked Bob.

"N-nothing," Jupe said. He slung the bar across his shoulder. "Quick! We've got to get back to our junkyard at once!"

"But why!" Pete protested. "If you're so happy with one iron bar, how do you know I can't find more?"

"Because," Jupiter stated as he moved away, "there aren't too many that bear the specifications I have in mind."

"Such as what?" Pete demanded.

"Such as containing smuggled diamonds," Jupiter answered, heading rapidly for the wire fence.

They didn't have too long to wait for Konrad to pick them up on his return trip from nearby Chatwick. On the ride home, Jupiter refused to be drawn into conversation. Instead, pinching his lower lip, he stared out of the window, nodding to himself several times as if to confirm certain inner convictions. Bob and Pete were accustomed to their leader's temporary fits of silence and knew he wouldn't explain himself until he was ready.

Once at the yard, Jupe hurried to his workshop. He stopped at the workbench—and cried out in dismay.

"It's gone!"

"What's gone?" asked Bob.

"The iron bar I picked up last night when Bo Jenkins chased us." He ran over to the junk pile hiding Headquarters and returned, looking puzzled. "The first bar I had has disappeared, too."

"What's this all about?" asked Pete.

Jupe shook his head impatiently. "I'll tell you later. Come on, I have to find Uncle Titus. Maybe he knows something."

Uncle Titus was across the street at the Jones house, sitting and smoking his pipe. He nodded contentedly as the three boys approached.

"Howdy, boys," he said pleasantly. "Have a good time today?"

"Pretty good, Uncle Titus," Jupe began. "I wanted to ask—"

"We did pretty good here, too," interrupted his uncle. "Yes, sirree, had a good spell of business."

"What did you sell, Uncle Titus—some iron bars?"

His uncle rocked and nodded. "Right smart of you to guess, Jupe. Yes, sir, we did just that. Hans and your aunt scoured the yard for all we had. We needed them, you see," he added with a wink.

"What for, Mr. Jones?" asked Bob.

"What for? To make cages, of course. Told you the other day we were going to, didn't I, Jupiter? Well, today Hans and me started to work on them, and then this feller comes in. His problem is he needs some big animal cages—and he needs 'em bad. Some kind of an emergency, I figure, where you suddenly need a lot of cages.

"Well, sir, I had to think fast. Y'see, we meant to fix 'em all up but we were still a few bars shy."

Jupe felt sick inside. "Was it that man who was here the other day? The one called Olsen?"

"Not that feller. Another chap. Very likable sort of man. Truth is, Jupe, even though I had my mind made up to save those cages for a circus, this chap's work was close enough to help me change my mind."

"It was?" Jupe repeated dully.

Titus Jones nodded, drew deeply on his pipe, and blew smoke. He finally went on. "Well, on account of him being such a nice chap and worried so, needing 'em so bad, I decided to cooperate. We all worked like the dickens fixing the cages and hunting for bars. Now your aunt saw you drop a bar near your workshop—that was the other day—and she picked that one up."

"Oh, Aunt Mathilda did?" Jupiter groaned.

His uncle nodded. "A good thing, too. We were still shy a bar even with that, until Hans found another one on your workbench, Jupe. We figured you had no earthly use for it. Bars and junk like that come in here all the time, you know, and you're always welcome to what you want—providing we don't need it for a customer. Right?"

Jupe nodded dumbly.

His uncle smacked the dottle from his pipe. "Well, that feller couldn't believe his eyes when we showed him we had the four cages all ready to go. Paid me a hundred dollars apiece, without my even painting 'em up. Said his animals would feel at home in 'em just like they were."

"You got those cages over in the Chatwick Valley, didn't you, Uncle Titus."

"Yep. At a big scrap yard. They didn't care about cages. Their main business was in junked cars. Had a terrific machine to eat 'em up. Made a racket, it did."

Jupe gestured helplessly, his worst suspicions confirmed.

As Mr. Jones stretched and stood up to leave, Jupiter had only one more question. "This man with the animals, Uncle Titus—the one you sold the cages to—did you get his name?"

His uncle smiled benevolently. "Of course I did. Easy one to remember, too." He squinted into the distance to remember the easy name. "It was, lemme see—yep, Hall. That was his name, all right. Jim Hall."

Jupiter stared at his friends.

Jupiter Explains

17

A call to the Rent-'n-Ride Auto Agency found Worthington available soon for another trip to Jungle Land. While waiting for him to arrive, the boys gobbled some lunch in Aunt Mathilda's kitchen.

"All right, Jupe," said Bob as the boys settled into the back seat of the Rolls-Royce. "It's about time you explained what's going on."

"It's very simple," said Jupe. "The diamonds are being smuggled by the Hall brothers in iron bars."

"Are you feeling all right, Jupe?" Pete asked. "That iron bar I picked up at the scrap yard and handed you —are you talking about that kind of bar?"

Jupe nodded.

"But that bar was solid iron," Pete said. "How can you smuggle diamonds in something like that?"

"You can't," Jupe said. "But you can smuggle diamonds in a hollow bar. Remember I told you that your iron bar felt different? Well, it was. It was a lot heavier than the one I picked up last night when Bo Jenkins was after us. And it was a lot heavier than the bar I put aside when we were unloading Uncle Titus's truck. It was so much heavier that suddenly everything clicked.

"I knew that I had hollow cage bars, and that Uncle Titus must have bought his bars and cages at the scrap yard where Jim Hall had tossed George's cage and probably others, too."

"But how did you know that the two bars you had contained diamonds?" asked Bob.

"Well, I didn't know for sure," said Jupe, "until I heard that Jim Hall had bought the cages from Uncle Titus. He never would have returned for them if the smuggled diamonds weren't still in them. It's just my bad luck that I had the bars and then lost them. I still don't know why he waited so long."

Pete looked puzzled. "I don't get it. If he knew the diamonds were in the cages, why did he discard them in the first place?"

"Perhaps the heat was on," Jupe said. "He couldn't afford to have them traced to his property. My guess is he dumped them over the fence at the scrap yard as a temporary measure, thinking they'd be safe there and he could pick them apart later. But somehow they got mixed up with a lot of other junk there, and my Uncle Titus bought them from the yard owners, along with all the long bars and railings."

"That's possible," said Bob. "Mr. Hall could have then asked the yard owners who bought the junk and traced it to your uncle's junkyard. Olsen and Dobbsie must have known about the bars, too. Now that I think of it, Olsen first asked for bars when he came to your uncle's yard. Remember?"

Jupe nodded.

"I wonder if one of those men was the mystery buyer," added Bob.

"Mystery buyer?" asked Pete.

"Yes, the customer who bought the pile of bars and railings from Mrs. Jones when we were making our first visit to Jungle Land. Those bars might have had diamonds in them, too."

"Naw," said Pete. "Those bars were awfully heavy—don't forget I was the one who carried them. And they were much longer than all the cage bars we've ever seen."

"I'm inclined to agree with Pete," said Jupe. "I don't think it matters who bought those bars. It was probably an innocent customer. And, if it wasn't—well, Olsen and Jim Hall both showed up at our yard later, so they couldn't have found the diamonds earlier."

"Hey, Jupe," said Pete. "What about that bar you found last night? Where did that come from?"

"That one could have got loose and fallen out of a cage when Jim Hall was dumping it into the scrap yard. I wish I knew how many cages were involved here. We know what to look for now, but we don't know how much to look for."

"All those bars look alike," Bob put in. "How can anybody tell which is which? When the cages arrive, they're all in place. How would Jim Hall know which bars have the diamonds his brother Cal inserted?"

Jupe smiled mysteriously. "There's a way of knowing."

Bob and Pete looked at him sourly. They knew from past experience that Jupiter would never divulge the last remaining secret to a mystery until the last possible moment.

Bob frowned. "We still haven't solved the mystery we were called in to investigate," he said. "Who is making Jim Hall's lion nervous? And if Mr. Hall is tied in with the diamond smuggling, who's letting his wild animals escape from their cages? He might lose Jungle Land if there's an accident."

"We'll know the answer to that when we put all the loose ends together," Jupe said. "It's possible Jim Hall himself let George out when we got there the first time, as a diversion. He might have let the gorilla loose, too, and pretended to go off looking for him. If you recall, he came right back to where the gorilla really was pretty fast."

"Bringing Doc Dawson and his stun gun and saving our lives!" Pete said. "I won't hold that against him."

"What about this morning?" Bob asked. "Jim Hall was on the movie set with George. He couldn't have slipped away to let the black panther out, could he? And have Doc Dawson cover up for him and say it was his own fault?"

"It's possible," Jupe said thoughtfully. "Doc Dawson might have an idea of what Jim Hall is up to. He might be trying to cover up for him and maybe to protect Mike, as well. Doc Dawson always seems to turn up when he's needed. That suggests to me that he is aware of the situation, and able to anticipate just what is going to happen next."

Soon the Rolls-Royce was entering Jungle Land.

"Drop us at the foot of the hill leading to the Halls' house, Worthington," ordered Jupe. "I think that we should arrive discreetly."

The boys walked up to the quiet white house on the hill. As they came close, they stopped to listen.

"Not a sound," Pete whispered. "Maybe he's already found the diamonds and cleared out."

Jupe pushed his lower lip out. "We'll have to go in, anyway. We owe it to Mike to explain."

Bob and Pete nodded agreement. Jupe took a step forward and stopped.

"What's wrong?" whispered Bob.

"I thought I heard something," Jupe said. "Maybe we'd better check the cage area before we go in."

He turned and the others followed him into the shadows of the clearing.

"Seems quiet," Jupe said. "I don't see—"

He was interrupted as something heavy was thrown over his head. Bob and Pete were caught the same way. The boys were grasped by strong hands. Their cries were muffled, and although they struggled and kicked, they could not get away from their surprise attackers. Helpless, they were carried along in total darkness.

Trapped!

18

Covered by a heavy blanket, The Three Investigators were unable to make out the voices of their abductors. They were bouncing as if they were being carried over rough terrain. One of their carriers stumbled and complained loudly. Another voice curtly cut him off.

The caravan halted. Ropes were lashed around them. They felt themselves being lifted again and then heaved headlong onto a springy surface. A heavy door thunked shut.

"That oughta keep 'em out of the way," a voice said.

They heard receding footsteps and then silence. They struggled to straighten themselves, pausing as they heard another sound.

Whup-whup-whup---pp!

They felt themselves being jerked forward, then rocked back abruptly. There was a whining sound and a heavy crunch as if something had grabbed them from both sides. The whining sound became a groan. Suddenly they felt the odd sensation of being lifted.

"Whiskers!" Bob exclaimed. "Are we riding in something?"

"Apparently," Jupe said. "And I don't like the sound of it. We'd better work fast. Try to slip the blanket off first. That way we won't suffocate, and we may be able to see where we are—and be heard!"

Following Jupe's directions, they pushed and pulled

in turn. Gradually the heavy blanket over them was tugged down.

"Use your fingers," Jupe urged. "Keep pulling down and rolling the blanket under you."

They struggled to get free, their hearts thumping wildly as they heard the menacing sounds all around them. Something chattered and roared beneath them, while from above they heard groaning, creaking sounds that sent chills down their spines.

Suddenly they were rocking in a wide swinging arc.

"It's the claw!" Pete yelled.

In a last convulsive movement the boys jerked the blanket down from their heads.

They gasped.

Straight ahead they saw nothing but the sky.

Far below was the spread of junked cars in the scrap yard.

At either side were the huge metal talons of the giant claw, gripping the old car that they rode in. They were trapped in the air—and headed for the metal shredder! They began to yell for help, but the huge machine in the shed below started to chatter and scream, roaring out a series of deafening sounds.

Pete shook his head. "No chance! We can't compete with that monster. Not even if we yell our heads off!"

"Apparently the crane operator can't see us either," Jupe cried. "We've got to get out of these ropes so we can attract his attention!"

They struggled and rocked but the ropes held tight.

They heard a shrill whistle. Abruptly the giant claw dropped. Then, with a sickening lurch, they were falling to the ground.

They bounced as they hit. Almost immediately, they

were jerked forward. They stopped, rocked, and were jerked forward again.

"We're on the conveyor belt now!" Jupe said. "We don't have much time. Come on—the metal shredding process takes place right ahead!"

Again they struggled, but to no avail. Relentlessly the conveyor belt advanced.

They yelled again, but their voices sounded puny in the yard's roar. "Kick the doors!" Jupe yelled. "Maybe we can knock them open."

They tried to obey but their efforts were futile. The ropes lashed around them were too tight. Tied together as they were, they were unable to use their legs. They thrashed about uselessly, and fell back, exhausted.

"It's no use!" Pete gasped. "Our only hope is that somebody working the metal shredder inside sees us in time."

"I doubt that," Jupe said. "A processing machine like this is usually run by a computer. It's not a question of our not being metal. The car we're in *is!* The selective scanner couldn't possibly reject us until it was too late!"

"You're not kidding," a voice said.

They stared incredulously into the cold eyes of the hatchet-faced man!

"Get the door on the other side, Dobbsie," Hatchet-Face said.

Surprisingly, his touch was gentle, although they felt the strength in his hands as he lifted them out. As they rolled on the ground, the car they had been riding in jerked forward.

Staring wide-eyed, they saw it disappear into the shed, to be lost in a cloud of steam. Heavy clanking sounds reverberated and the machine inside screamed.

Jupe turned with a tremendous sigh of relief to the two men. His expression changed suddenly.

Dobbsie was holding a long-bladed knife!

"Be reasonable!" Hatchet-Face said cajolingly. "We have to cut those ropes off you kids, don't we?"

Jupe nodded dumbly. He looked at Bob and Pete. They returned his mystified glance.

The beady-eyed man bent and slashed deftly with his knife. In a moment they were free.

As they rubbed their arms and legs to regain circulation, the hatchet-faced man looked down coldly at them. "Looks as if we got here just in time," he rasped. "What happened?"

"Somebody threw a blanket over us, tied us up, and threw us in a car," said Jupe. "I don't know if we were intended for the metal shredder, or not. We're grateful to you for not having to find out."

"Any idea who did it?"

Jupe shook his head. "It happened too fast. We were rounding the corner of Jim Hall's house—" He stopped abruptly and glanced at the men. "How did you know we were trapped in the car?"

The hatchet-faced man sighed and looked over Jupe's head at the other man. "We happened to be in the yard. Dobbsie here thought he saw a moving kicking bundle being thrown into a car at the far end. That's a bit unusual, so we went to investigate. Whoever did it ran off before we could get over. Then the claw got you and dumped you on the conveyor track. We couldn't get the crane operator's attention or stop the belt moving. So we had to do it the hard way and drag you out ourselves."

Pete shivered. "I can't believe he would have done that to us. I just can't believe it!"

"Who, kid?" asked the hatchet-faced man. "And what do you kids know that's so dangerous somebody nearly had you killed because of it?"

Jupe lifted his head. "We're conducting an investigation," he said. "We have our suspicions but we're not at liberty yet to divulge any names."

The hatchet-faced man grinned. "Oh, you're not, eh? Maybe we should have kept out of it and let you continue your investigations—" he pointed to the throbbing shed "—in there!"

Jupe cocked his head. "As a matter of fact," he said, "both the actions of you and your friend have aroused our suspicions, too. But I don't suppose you have anything to do with the diamond smuggling, or else you wouldn't have rescued us."

Hatchet-Face looked at Dobbsie. "What'd I tell you? The kid is wise to the operation!" He looked down and laughed at Jupe. "I suppose you can tell us where they are, too."

"I suppose I can," Jupe said slowly. "But I won't."

Hatchet-Face jerked his head at the other man. "Come on, Dobbsie. We're wasting time. While we're here yakking, they could be getting away."

The beady-eyed man with the mashed nose came close to Jupe and raised a warning finger. "This is big time stuff, feller—not for kids. Watch yourselves!"

The menace in his powerful frame was unmistakable. He wheeled away to join his swift-moving companion, leaving The Three Investigators with a warning they could not afford to ignore!

In the Bag

19

Young Mike Hall looked surprised when he threw the door open. "Jupe! Hi, fellows! C'mon in. We didn't expect you back today."

"I know," Jupe said as he entered the house. "Have Mr. Olsen—the man you called Dunlop—and another man been here?"

Mike shook his head. "No, why?"

Jupe frowned. He wondered where they were. "I suppose your Uncle Jim is out, isn't he?"

Mike shook his head again. "What gave you that idea? He's in the back room with George, resting. Wait a second. I'll call him."

As he walked off, Jupe looked at Bob and Pete.

"It beats me, too," Pete said. "I was sure they were heading here."

"Maybe they're off looking for the cages," Bob said.

A cheery voice interrupted. "What cages?"

"Your old cages, Mr. Hall," Jupe said.

Jim Hall looked surprised. "What are you driving at?"

"You ought to know, Mr. Hall," Jupe said. "You're the one who bought back George's old cage, along with the other three, from my Uncle Titus."

Hall's face looked blank. "I—what?"

"You bought back the cages, and took them away," Bob put in. "The ones with the bars that hold the smuggled diamonds."

Jim Hall looked from one boy to the other with a dumbfounded expression. "Okay," he said. "Now you tell me. Maybe I'm not hearing so well today."

Pete shuffled his feet and looked uncomfortable. "But I guess you didn't have anything to do with shanghaiing us and dropping us off at the metal shredder?"

Hall shook his head dumbly and turned to Mike. "What are your friends talking about?"

"I don't know," Mike said.

"You told us you had a problem," Bob said. "It was a mystery and you wanted our help. Who was making George nervous? Or what? But it turns out the mystery is how your brother Cal ships you diamonds from Africa, along with some animals. Some of the cage bars with the diamonds in them got lost somehow and that's why you had to buy the cages back from Jupe's Uncle Titus earlier today."

"You're crazy!" Mike burst in. "I've been with Jim every minute since early this morning. He hasn't stepped out of Jungle Land once today!"

Jupe looked up at Jim Hall. "You didn't?"

Hall shook his head.

"My Uncle Titus said he sold the cages to a man named Jim Hall. I'm sorry I didn't ask him to describe the man. I think I can guess now who it was—"

"Dobbsie?" asked Bob.

"It's possible," Jupe said. "Uncle Titus said it wasn't Olsen-Dunlop. It could have been Dobbsie." He looked up at Jim Hall again. "You don't know anything about any diamonds?"

"I don't even know what you're talking about," said Hall.

"Why did you get rid of George's cage?"

Hall shrugged. "It seemed wrong to keep him locked

up in a cage when I was trying to train him with love and kindness. I felt we were losing touch every time I had to lock him inside again. Once Mike came to stay with us, I decided George had to be proven trustworthy. I got rid of the cage, had it thrown over the fence into the scrap yard, and that was the end of it. George became a regular member of the household, just like Mike and myself."

"But you kept the cage outside your house for a while after George moved in, didn't you?" Jupe persisted.

"Yes, until recently. I made up my mind to get rid of it completely when Jay Eastland came along and wanted to hire George for his movie. I didn't want him to get the idea George was still a wild animal. From that point on, Jay Eastland saw George only as a well-trained house pet."

Jupe looked rueful. "I owe you an apology, Mr. Hall. It appears all my deductions and assumptions have proven false."

"We all make mistakes, Jupe. Maybe it's time you told me what this is all about."

Jupe explained from the beginning, starting with the arrival of the cages in The Jones Salvage Yard, and then the man named Olsen. "Mike says he works for Mr. Eastland and is called Dunlop. But he told us his name was Olsen. A thin, hatchet-faced, light-haired man."

"I don't know him but I think I've seen him around the set," said Hall.

"He was looking over the scrap heap last night," Bob said. "Along with a man he called Dobbsie. They talked a lot about the smuggled diamonds. We couldn't figure out if they were part of a gang or what. They're the same two who rescued us awhile ago when we were on our way into the metal shredder!"

Jim Hall listened carefully. When they had finished telling all they knew, he shook his head. "I'm sorry, boys, but I don't understand a single part of what you've said. Maybe it's true that these goings on made George upset and nervous. Maybe it's true that somehow diamonds are being smuggled in here. But I'll tell you one thing you can bet on," he added, his eyes flashing. "My brother Cal wouldn't have a thing to do with anything crooked!"

Jupe nodded and thought a minute. "Can you tell us what other cages you've discarded over the past few months?" he asked.

"We threw out two or three old cages a year ago," Jim Hall said. "But the only one lately was George's."

"Apparently that was the start of it, then," Jupe said thoughtfully. Abruptly he asked, "How is George feeling today?"

Jim Hall smiled. "First rate. He did a good job on the movie set this morning and he's been fine ever since. He's inside snoozing now. Doc Dawson was here and gave him a tranquilizer."

Jupe motioned to his companions. "Well, we'd better be going. We still have some work to do, fellows."

Mike Hall opened the door. "Come on back again when you can," he said. "I'm sure Jim doesn't blame you—"

"He should," Jupe said severely. "I had no business making an accusation before I had sufficient evidence. I owe you both an apology, Mike."

As Jupe went out, his foot caught on the threshold of the door and he stumbled across the porch. He grabbed for the porch post, yelled, and yanked his hand away.

"Oww!" he cried. He looked down at the drop of

blood on his finger. "I just caught my finger on a splinter."

"Gosh, I'm sorry, Jupe," Mike said. "Come on inside. We'll find a Band-Aid for you."

"It's okay," Jupe said sheepishly as he went back in the door. He sucked on his finger. "Just a little cut."

Mike snapped his fingers suddenly and pointed. "I was about to say it's too bad Doc Dawson isn't around to fix you up. Look—he forgot his medical kit."

Jupe looked at the worn black leather bag sitting on a chair. "Would he mind if I helped myself to a bandage?"

"Are you kidding?" Mike said. "That's what it's for—emergencies. Help yourself."

Jupe opened the bag and reached inside for a roll of gauze wrapped neatly in blue paper. Holding it awkwardly, he fumbled with the protective cover. A small yellow piece of paper fluttered out.

Mike picked it up. "Looks like you dropped one of Doc's prescriptions, Jupe. Here, better put it back."

Jupe glanced at it automatically as it was handed to him. His lips moved wordlessly and he stared at it pop-eyed.

"What is it, Jupe?" asked Bob.

Jupe shook his head and looked at the scrap of paper again. "I can't believe it," he said slowly. Then, he sighed a long sigh. "But, of course. Now the whole thing begins to make sense."

"What can't you believe?" asked Pete. "What makes sense?"

Jupe held out the scrap of torn paper. "Read it yourself."

They stared at the paper in Jupe's hand. It read:

DOX ROX NOX EX REX BOX

Mike looked mystified. "What does it mean?"

"It means a man we never suspected is behind it all," Jupe said. He shook his head ruefully. "It's all perfectly clear now."

"What are you trying to tell us now, Jupe?" asked Jim Hall.

"You won't like it," Jupe said. "It's Doc Dawson."

Jim Hall smiled thinly. "I don't think you know what you're talking about, son. Doc's an old friend. Let me see that piece of paper."

As he held out his hand, the front door opened.

A burly figure stood there. Head close-shaven. Arm tattooed. "I came to pick up Doc's bag," he said. "He forgot it here."

His eyes narrowed as he saw the open medical bag, and then the small slip of yellow paper in Jupe's hand. His lips twisted angrily. "I'll take that, you snooping kid!" he roared.

Before Jupe could move, Bo Jenkins had snatched the paper from his hand. He crumpled it in his huge fist and reached for the leather bag.

Jim Hall spoke up mildly. "Hold it just a second, Bo. There's something going on here and—"

Jenkins made a sudden movement and pulled out a gun. "Stay out of it, Hall, if you know what's good for you. We got it all now and nothin's stopping us."

Jupe gulped. "You're the man who bought all the cages from my uncle—and gave Jim Hall's name!"

Jenkins grinned. "Wise apple, huh?"

Jim Hall whistled softly as the animal handler grabbed the black bag.

Heavy, padding steps sounded across the room. An ominous rumbling made Jenkins turn and stare. His jaw sagged and he paled.

A large, yellow-eyed lion stood there, head down and long tail twitching restlessly. The growling continued.

Instantly Jupe leaned against the door, closing it.

Jenkins whirled again at the sound, his gun jerking.

"Forget it, Jenkins," Jim Hall said calmly. "You're not going anyplace. One more step and George will have you for dinner." Hall turned to the lion. "Won't you, George?"

The lion slowly opened its cavernous mouth and moved forward.

There was a clattering sound as the gun fell from Bo Jenkins's fingers.

"That's better," Jim Hall said. He bent forward to retrieve the gun and waved the frightened man to a chair. The lion came forward and stopped at Bo's side, opening its mouth in a huge yawn.

"Now then, Bo," Jim Hall said pleasantly. "What can you tell us about some smuggled diamonds?"

End of the Puzzle

20

As they rounded a turn in the trail, Mike pointed ahead to a small house next to a barn. "That's Doc Dawson's place," he said. "The dispensary is in the back."

Sounds of hammering came from the barn.

Jupe smiled. "That's one thing he never figured on. When my uncle Titus has something fixed, he does a very thorough job."

"What do you mean, Jupe?" asked Mike.

"You'll see in a minute," Jupe said mysteriously.

A small pickup truck stood in the driveway by the barn. Alongside it four cages lay tumbled on the ground. The grizzled vet stood next to one with a hammer raised in one hand. In the other he held a long pair of pliers.

He paused as Jim Hall strode up, flanked by the boys. His eyes flicked past them and narrowed.

"Howdy, Jim," he said. "Anything wrong?"

Jim Hall shook his head. He tossed the black leather bag at the vet's feet. "Heard you were looking for your bag, Doc. You left it at the house."

"Thanks, Jim," Dawson said. He gazed beyond them and frowned. "I sent Bo Jenkins—I thought—" He looked at the cages, scowling. "I need him to help—"

Hall nodded. "Bo's all tied up at the moment, Doc. Maybe we can give you a hand. What's the trouble?"

The vet looked at the hammer in his hand. "No

trouble, Jim. Just wanted to make sure the bars are good and tight. Don't want any more accidents. That fellow Eastland will have every nickel of yours if one more animal gets away."

Hall smiled. "Thanks, Doc. I appreciate your concern." He looked at Jupe. "Can you tell which bars?"

"I think so, sir," Jupiter said. "But I'd need to borrow his hammer."

"No problem," Hall said. "Can you loan this young fellow your hammer for a moment, Doc?"

Dawson hesitated, then handed it to Jupe. "Guess so. What's up?"

"These young fellows are The Three Investigators. I hired them, you recall, to find out what's been making old George nervous. They've come up with some cockeyed notion that it's all because of some smuggled diamonds."

Dawson grinned. "No kidding? Cockeyed is right." He looked at Jupe. "Any idea where they might be?"

"Yes, sir," Jupe said. "If you would just step aside for a moment, please."

"Why, sure," Dawson said easily, moving away. "Only go easy with that hammer, son. I wouldn't want those bars loosened after all the trouble I've been to tightening them up."

"You didn't tighten them up," said Jupe. "Hans and Uncle Titus did, back at our junkyard."

Doc looked surprised.

"You'll notice," Jupe continued, "they didn't put back the bars the way they were. Uncle Titus is very fussy about giving a customer no reason for complaint. So he and Hans bolted and screwed the bars in this way so they wouldn't work loose as they did before."

"Very interesting," Dawson said.

"So you can't hammer them off," Jupe said. "All you can use the hammer for is this, really." He walked around the cage beating at the bars with the heavy hammer. He stopped at the fourth one from the end, then continued through the others, pausing once more. He returned to the fourth one again.

"There are two on this cage," he said.

Dawson glanced at Jim Hall. "Any idea what he's talking about?"

Hall frowned. "I'd rather wait and see, Doc."

"Most of these bars are rusted," Jupe said, "indicating they've been outside and exposed to the weather a long time. They could belong to any of the cages Mr. Hall discarded. But this rusty one gives off a different sound—it's hollow, you see. So my deduction is this one could have come from George's cage.

"This one here," Jupe continued, striding to the opposite end of the cage, "is hollow, too." He struck it with his hammer. "It's still in good condition because it just came in recently. It's from the gorilla's cage. Bo Jenkins took it off the night the gorilla arrived. The gorilla twisted the other bars apart and broke out. I believe the gorilla went after Bo and he became frightened and ran, tossing the bar away in his panic. I happened to come across it by accident."

"But how did Bo Jenkins know you had it?" Mike asked.

"He was out looking for it later that night," Jupe said. "He heard us and pointed his flashlight on us and saw me holding it. He'd seen us before and probably Doc Dawson told him who we were and where we came from. He came to the yard and found my uncle working on the cages. He must have been delighted when he heard they'd have to search the yard for extra bars. He couldn't be sure, but there was a good chance the gorilla bar would turn up. Of course, he had no idea that George's bar was around, too."

"How can you be sure you've found the right bars here?" asked Mike.

"I can't, until we take the bars off," said Jupe. "But I expect we'll find the diamonds in them, since I used the smugglers' own method of locating them."

"How do you know that?" asked Mike.

"The cable told me, and Doc Dawson confirmed it. The cable said, 'DOX ROX NOX EX REX BOX.' Which means, knock on the bars of the lion's cage and you'll find the diamonds inserted at the docks. EX, I would guess, stands for 'out of'—take the lion out first. A wise precaution, considering what happened with the gorilla.

"Now, do you recall what Doc did last night when the gorilla was brought back? Doc tested all the bars on its cage with the hammer. He did the same thing with the panther cage. At the time it merely seemed an odd way to test the strength of bars. But Doc was actually testing for diamonds—probably trying to make sure Jenkins had picked the right bar, or possibly making sure there were no others. Once they had the manner of smuggling arranged and the cable informing them how to look for the hollow bars—it was easy. Any bar that sounded hollow would contain diamonds."

Jupiter turned to Doc Dawson. "May I have the pliers, please?" Doc silently handed them over.

Jupe clamped the long pliers to the top bolt on the rusty bar he'd singled out. A few hard turns and the bolt came off. Jupe stooped and repeated the action with the bottom bolt. He took the hammer and knocked the bar through the drilled slots in the boards. As it came out, Hall and the boys crowded around.

Jupe knocked the top cap off the bar, then turned it over and struck it with the hammer. A thin trickle of greasy yellow stones came out.

"Those are diamonds?" Pete asked.

Jupe nodded. "Rough, uncut diamonds, Pete. They look like ordinary rocks and pebbles when they're found."

"Whiskers!" exclaimed Bob. "There's a ton of them there."

Jupe smiled, looking down at the pile of dull stones. "Well, not a ton exactly, Records. Mr. Olsen-Dunlop mentioned six hundred K's. He was talking about carats, I believe. A carat is worth approximately one thousand dollars. Allowing for some loss in cutting, we have a good half-million here. And with those in the gorilla bar, perhaps a million dollars' worth of diamonds altogether."

Jim Hall stared at the pile of stones and shook his head. "I'm sorry, Doc," he said. "I'm afraid you have some explaining to do."

There was no answer.

Jim Hall looked up, and twisted his head in surprise. Dawson was gone. They heard the sound of the truck engine starting up.

"He's getting away!" cried Pete.

The truck backed off with a roar as the boys started for it. Almost immediately two cars came from the trees and braked to a quick stop behind it, blocking the driveway. Two men leaped out.

"Hatchet-Face and Dobbsie!" cried Bob.

They grabbed Dawson as he jumped from the cab, and brought him forward to the barn.

"What's going on? Who are you two?" demanded Jim Hall.

Jupe pointed. "That one's Mr. Olsen—he's been after the bars from the beginning."

"No," said Mike. "His name is Dunlop. He works for Jay Eastland."

The hatchet-faced man shook his head. "Sorry, boys —but you're both wrong. Stevenson's the name."

He flipped open his wallet and held it out.

Jupe's face reddened. "His card says Stevenson, all right." He looked up at the grinning man. "We thought you were part of the gang."

"Customs agents have to act mysterious, son," the man explained. "Dobbs here is with the Treasury Department. We're both working for the same firm—the United States Government. And we've been trying to break up this smuggling ring for a long time."

Dobbs gestured to the pile of stones lying on the ground. "Looks like the kid saved us a lot of trouble. We knew Dawson was getting diamonds, but we couldn't move in until they actually showed up. We didn't know exactly where they were and that's the kind of evidence that's needed."

"You'll find some more in another bar," Jupe said.

The Treasury agent kicked at the pile of stones. "Now all we have to do is find the other man—Bo Jenkins. He seems to have taken a powder."

"You'll find him back at my house," said Jim Hall. "He'll be waiting for us."

The two men looked startled.

"He's not going anyplace," Jim Hall stated. "George is looking after him."

Dobbs looked at him wide-eyed. "George—the lion?"

Jim Hall nodded.

Stevenson grinned. He clapped Jupe on the shoulder. "Okay, Investigator—you already found half a million. Would you like to try for another?"

Jupe stepped forward to the cage. Pointing to the second bar he had selected, he said dramatically, "You will note, gentlemen, that this bar is not as rusted as the first one that was extracted from the lion's cage. The gorilla was a recent arrival and therefore—"

Bob and Pete exchanged grins. They knew how their leader loved to make the most out of a situation.

Doc Dawson laughed harshly. His shoulders sagged. He looked like a man who had bet a lot of money and lost.

"Hurry it up," he said. "I'd like to see how much I lost before I tell you everything."

Some Questions from
Mr. Hitchcock

21

A week later, The Three Investigators sat in Alfred Hitchcock's office, telling him of their latest adventures. The famous director smiled from behind his large desk.

"Well done, lads," he rumbled. "Your account of the affair of the nervous lion is most interesting, and I congratulate you upon bringing it to a successful conclusion."

"Thank you, sir!" chorused the boys.

"There are a few small points I should like to have cleared up," Mr. Hitchcock told them. "This barbarous device—the metal shredder—am I to assume that your nearly fatal engagement with it was accidental?"

"Yes, sir," Bob said. "Bo Jenkins and Doc Dawson tied us up and tossed us into an old junked car. They did it merely to get us out of the way. They never expected that the crane would drop the car on the conveyor belt."

Alfred Hitchcock nodded. "I would hope they would be more careful next time, if indeed there should ever be one, about the process they select for discouraging interlopers." He laced his fingers together. "This Hank Morton person—where does he fit in? Did he let George out deliberately and then wound him? And why was he running away the night the gorilla escaped? Was he involved in that, too?"

"No, sir," Bob said. "No to all of those questions. He

came back to Jungle Land after being fired because he was suspicious of Doc Dawson. According to Hank Morton, Dawson made it look as if he had mistreated the animals, and Jim Hall took his word for everything. Dawson, of course, was trying to replace him with Bo Jenkins. When Morton came back, Doc decided to fix him for good. He let George out himself, planning to blame it on Morton.

"George cut himself accidentally out in the jungle. I guess he didn't know how to take care of himself out there, since he grew up in captivity. When Morton led us out to him, he was only teasing us. He knew George and could handle him. But when he stepped away for a minute, Bo Jenkins found him, hit him over the head, and knocked him out. So Morton was blamed for getting us into that scrape, too.

"That night when the gorilla broke loose, Morton was trying to find Bo Jenkins. Instead he ran into the gorilla and was frightened away, just as Bo Jenkins was."

"What about the panther's escape?" asked Alfred Hitchcock. "Did Doc Dawson engineer that diversion, too?"

"No, sir," replied Pete. "At least, he said he didn't. We think it was a real accident. We're just grateful that Doc saved our lives. Mr. Stevenson said that might be a point in Doc's favor when his case comes to trial."

Alfred Hitchcock glanced down at the papers on which Bob had summarized the adventure. "Ah, yes, Mr. Stevenson, the government agent, also known as Olsen and Dunlop. You say he was planted with the Jay Eastland movie company by the authorities, to keep the suspected smugglers under surveillance?"

"Yes, sir," Jupe said. "He happens to be an expert on

firearms and was available to Jay Eastland in that capacity. Eastland was acting so violently against Jim Hall, however, that he aroused Stevenson's suspicions. As it turned out, Eastland had nothing to do with the smuggling itself. But he was trying to take advantage of the contract Jim Hall had agreed to. He could have used an extra fifty thousand dollars and was hoping to pin something on Hall. But he couldn't, and now that the filming is over, Jungle Land is safe."

"Now as to the smuggling itself," said Mr. Hitchcock. "Doc Dawson enlisted the aid of this Bo Jenkins to help retrieve the hollow bars. The diamond shipments originated in Africa, taking advantage of Cal Hall's deliveries of animals to his brother here. Was Dawson the ringleader? Did he plan the entire operation or was he merely an accessory? Exactly how did he fit in?"

"Doc Dawson planned it all," answered Jupe. "The diamonds were stolen from the surface portion of a deposit at Mwadui in the Shinyanga district of Tanzania. The smugglers followed Cal Hall to the port of Dar es Salaam and there switched the cage bars, first on George's cage, then on the gorilla's. When George left Africa, they alerted Doc Dawson with that coded cable."

"And why didn't Doc Dawson take the diamonds from the lion's cage as soon as it arrived?" Mr. Hitchcock asked Jupe.

"Because he was expecting a gorilla to arrive with more diamonds soon afterward. Only two shipments were planned. I guess he figured that the first lot were safe where they were, hidden in the cage bar, so he could wait till the second lot came and then clear out with a million dollars' worth of gems. But the gorilla didn't come for a long time. Meanwhile, Doc Dawson came down with the flu. While he was sick, Jim Hall threw out the lion's cage. It got broken up in the scrap yard and the bars misplaced. By the time Doc caught up with it, it was too late.

"It was also too late because by then the authorities were on to the smuggling operation. Stevenson wouldn't tell us how they learned about it—said he was sorry but he couldn't divulge his sources. As soon as he and Dobbs caught Dawson with the evidence, his confederates in Africa were rounded up. They'd been under surveillance too."

The director tapped Bob's report again. "You surmised that George was being made nervous by the various attempts to get at the bar with the diamonds. Were you correct in that assumption, young Jupiter?"

"Yes, sir. At first, I think, George was only restless because he was cooped up in the house at night. But then Stevenson and Dobbs started prowling around Jungle Land. They frequently came by the Halls' house after dark to check the cage area, and that upset George."

"I still do not understand," rumbled Alfred Hitchcock, "why Doc Dawson, a respectable veterinarian, would become a diamond smuggler."

"That's easy," offered Pete. "He was a smuggler *before* he came to Jungle Land. He'd been through Africa and pulled various small jobs there years before. When he found out about Cal and Jim Hall's operation, it seemed perfect for his plans. So he joined up with them, using his skill with animals to get by, while he planned the entire diamond operation in Tanzania. He really did love animals, but he also loved the excitement of getting rich quick and dangerously."

"Not to mention criminally," added Mr. Hitchcock.

"I believe we are well rid of the fellow. He failed in his biggest attempt, the always tempting million-dollar haul. And you boys thwarted him by dint of clever deductions and perseverance. I'm proud of you all. You solved the case and, I assume, received a generous reward for recovering the jewels."

"Yes, sir," Bob said. "Our savings accounts for college are now richer by—"

"No!" the director interrupted. "Don't tell me. I might find myself wondering the next time I have an important case whether you boys are too rich to bother with it!"

"Never!" said Jupiter Jones. "Mystery is our business!"

THE THREE INVESTIGATORS
MYSTERY SERIES